MW00788667

Karl Marx on Technology and A

Karl Marx on Technology and Alienation

Amy E. Wendling
Creighton University

First published 2009 by
PALGRAVE MACMILLAN

Palgrave Macmillan in the UK is an imprint of Macmillan Publishers Limited,
registered in England, company number 785998, of Houndmills, Basingstoke,
Hampshire RG21 6XS.

Palgrave Macmillan in the US is a division of St Martin's Press LLC,
175 Fifth Avenue, New York, NY 10010.

Palgrave Macmillan is the global academic imprint of the above companies
and has companies and representatives throughout the world.

Palgrave® and Macmillan® are registered trademarks in the United States,
the United Kingdom, Europe and other countries.

ISBN-13: 978–0–230–34848–6 paperback

A catalogue record for this book is available from the British Library.

Library of Congress Cataloging-in-Publication Data
Wendling, Amy E., 1976–
    Karl Marx on technology and alienation / Amy E Wendling.
       p.   cm.
    Includes bibliographical references and index.
    ISBN-13: 978–0–230–34848–6 (paperback)
    1. Marx, Karl, 1818–1883.   2. Technology—Philosophy
    3. Alienation (Philosophy)   I. Title.
    B3305.M74W45 2009
    335.4′1—dc22

                                                        2008046488

To the memory of my father, Neil Arthur Wendling

Contents

Acknowledgments

This book has been greatly enriched in scope and detail, thanks to the time I have spent, over a period of years, at the Karl Marx archives and research centers in Amsterdam and Berlin. I am grateful to the International Dissertation Field Research Fellowship Program—sponsored by the Social Science Research Council in partnership with the American Council of Learned Societies with funding from the Andrew W. Mellon Foundation—for their support of research in both European capitals in 2003 and 2004. I am also grateful to a J. William Fulbright Scholarship that allowed me to spend nine months in Amsterdam in 2003 and 2004. Finally, I am grateful for a Summer Faculty Fellowship from Creighton University that sent me to Berlin, in the summer of 2008, to give the finishing touches to the project. While abroad in Amsterdam, my research was aided by Fred Schrader and Goetz Lankau, and in Berlin, it was aided by Rolf Hecker.

I spent many years in State College, Pennsylvania, at The Pennsylvania State University, where my mentor Dan Conway read multiple drafts of this work from its inception. I also benefited from the generous readership of my dissertation committee, including Emily Grosholz, Shannon Sullivan, Mitchell Aboulafia, Nancy Tuana, and Susan Squier. The years would not have been as pleasant without the intellectual camaraderie of Al Lingis, Rick Lee, Claire Katz, Carl Mitcham, Vincent Colapietro, Will Roberts, Hasana Sharp, Sara Brill, Leigh Johnson, Michael Bray and Brian Armstrong.

While writing the book, I also spent a year in Austin, Texas, at Southwestern University, my alma mater, at the home of my first philosophy teacher, Shannon Winnubst. Shannon's quick mind and sharp wit make her the most precious of philosophical interlocutors.

All of my colleagues in the Philosophy Department at Creighton University have made it a warm and welcoming scholarly home. Patrick Murray and Jeanne Schuler share my love for Marx, and I treasure our scholarly exchanges. I am also grateful to Gene Selk, Elizabeth Cooke, William Stephens, Dick White, and Peggy Troy for their help on this project.

In addition, I wish to thank David J. Estrin for his editorial assistance in the final stages of the project.

The book would not have been possible without the loving partic-ipation of my family and personal friends. Nancy Wendling, Sarah Wendling Pittenger, Tiziana Aime, and The Wayne and Evelyn Smith Family have seen me through the book from beginning to end. My new friends in Omaha, Nebraska, helped me bring the project to completion and, what was even harder, let it go. Special thanks are due to Sharon Arnold, Marian Todd, Dana Bainbridge, Kristin Williams, Scott Eastman, and The River City Mixed Chorus.

Finally, I am grateful to the artist Jess Benjamin for our illuminat-ing conversations about materialism; for teaching me what she knows about jackstones, corn, water and ethanol molecules, and tetrahedrons; for making me laugh out loud; and for many, many other things.

All errors are, of course, my own.

Introduction

Traditionally regarded as a theme of Marx's early work, alienation remained a theme throughout his life, giving shape and form to his insights even when Marx does not name alienation as such. In Marx's later texts, alienation's operation must be discerned by the careful reader. As capitalism develops, so does alienation.

In this book, I offer a conceptual history of alienation as the concept developed in modern thought, was refined in Marx's work, and was handed on to the tradition that followed him. The concept of alienation—which had its modern origins in the texts of Hegel, Rousseau, Locke, Smith, and Feuerbach—was considerably developed by Marx. When Marx was finished transforming the concept, it had become a ringing indictment not only of the forms of life produced by the capitalist world, but also of the forms of thought characteristic of the alienated worlds of both nascent and developed capitalism. That is, Marx explained the philosophical concepts available to Hegel, Rousseau, Locke, Smith, and Feuerbach as products of the capitalist world. In *Capital*, Marx also showed how the scientific, technological, and philosophical ideas of his own world had been forged by capitalism's alienated norms.[1]

Marx believed that Hegel's political philosophy performed the contradictions of a nascent capitalist social world without resolving them, setting up an antinomy between the state and civil society. This antinomy perpetuates the illusion that civil society is the sphere of the natural human being, rather than always already being a political sphere. Through this illusion, the "natural" human being is an individualized homo economicus, whose ontology is labor and the self-interested exchange of this labor in the market. If the ontology of this natural human being is labor, it becomes impossible to imagine forms of subjectivity that are not produced through labor on the external world. This is demonstrated in Hegel's master–slave dialectic, where the master is stunted and undeveloped because of his failure to work on the world.

Rousseau, Locke, and Smith all participated in this illusion, drawing on this "natural" human being as the basis of their social compacts. In one of alienation's extreme conceptual forms, the social characteristics of the capitalist world are imputed to the "natural" world of civil society. Thus, human beings need not accept responsibility for their social and political life, because the characteristics of this are projected onto the natural world. And although Feuerbach exposed human alienation in the theological realm, he failed to contest the alienation that occurs in the worldly, economic realm, and especially failed to contest the displacement of human social and political characteristics onto both human nature and external nature.

Thus, it is unsurprising that Marx began to study science. Science takes as its primary task the description of the natural world, including human nature. In Marx's age, science had become a new way of contesting for the political power of who will give the definitive account of human nature. In our own age, this has only intensified.

In offering his own version of this account, Marx charted a clear separation between the "is" and "ought" of science. There is human nature as it is currently expressed and performed under capitalism, and human nature as it could be expressed and performed under the communist mode of production. Marx did not simply wish to claim that capitalism enforces a false picture of human nature. He also wished to show that human nature itself is malleable by class, history, and circumstance: molded by the world in which it is forged.

The world Marx lived in and analyzed was forever changed by the entrance of machines into production, and by one machine in particular: the steam engine. In Marx's later works, the theme of alienation becomes bound up with his understanding of technology. Alienation, Marx claimed, is made worse by the entrance of machines into production. Because machines automatically perform all the interesting parts of the work, they render the proletarian's activity dull and repetitive. Marx also shows how workers perceive steam technology as a dangerous competitor. Workers then revolt against technology—that is, against the means of production—and smash machines. By doing so, workers also smash the possible abolition of the human labor that those machines instantiated. Hence, these revolts partake in false consciousness, a false consciousness through which the worker hobbles himself or herself by destroying the technologies that are the accumulated real wealth of the industrial social world. In their revolt against the means of production, workers are alienated from the tools of material production, misrecognizing themselves, undermining the production of great wealth, and repudiating the accumulated science that is the distinguishing mark of the human species' progressive conquest of natural scarcity.

Marx also understood that steam technology changes the way in which human embodiment is constructed, experienced, and portrayed. In the age of the steam engine, human embodiment is likened to mechanical embodiment, and human labor is described in the terms of energetic conversion. These energetic terms undermine the older Hegelian notion of labor in which Spirit, as a qualitatively different kind of force from Nature, shapes Nature and leaves its imprint. Energetic science also undermines all qualitative differences between animal, human, and machine.[2]

In this book, I chart the path along which Marx's researches into science and technology developed in tandem with his deepening understanding of capitalist alienation. At the end of this development, Marx seems to offer a view of human nature and human labor that is incompatible with his early, humanist concepts. The humanist Marx was dependent on the view of human nature that included a notion of Spirit, or essence, that situated the human being as a force different in kind from the natural world, a force that humanizes or spiritualizes nature. The scientific Marx, in contrast, adopted the view of a human nature that is fully assimilated to the natural world, whose activity is indifferent from—and interchangeable with—that of machines, animals, and nature itself.

I trace the consequences of Marx's adoption of the scientific materialist notions of human embodiment for his accounts of labor, revolution, and alienation. Form-giving human labor becomes mere labor-power, a point where energy is transferred, but little more. Revolution becomes an act of structural inevitability rather than political will, a structural inevitability so strong that the meaning of human political will is erased. And alienation, reliant on a humanist notion of lost essence, becomes an impossible concept to explain for two reasons. First, there is nothing distinctive about the human essence that can be lost. Second, there is no reliable position outside of the norms of alienated world through which alienation can be diagnosed, let alone overcome.

But before concluding that Marx gave up his concept of alienation, we must remember the main lines of Marx's critique of ideology. Marx argued that concepts are products of material conditions. Marx therefore linked the concepts of the scientific materialists—and especially their reduction of the human body to a thermodynamic machine—to the structure of capitalism itself, and especially to its requirement that everything be quantifiable in terms of its value for production.

Marx's most mature expression of his critique of alienation is *Capital*, a work that we have only just begun to understand, because it requires a complex hermeneutic. In *Capital*, Marx attempted to reveal those forms of life peculiar to capitalist alienation from within the norms established by this alienation: that is, in an environment in which alienation has become so definitive and real that it disappears as a concept and term of analysis. This method reflects a still more developed notion of alienation than that which characterizes Marx's early works. In its most developed form, alienation is so complete as to occlude any concepts not commensurate with the functioning of the capitalist world.

Because Marx tries, in *Capital*, to stay within the conceptual framework offered by the capitalist world to better explain the concepts of this world, the formulas he offers must be understood with recourse only to the capitalist world. It is the capitalist world that reduces labor to labor-power; that eliminates human agency from political revolution; and that makes alienation unthinkable because there is no longer any human essence to lose.

Capitalism denigrates and demoralizes human prominence ideologically as well as materially. Humans become a calculable resource like any other within the economy. Within this economy, resources are all subject to exchange-value, and must therefore be made calculable in terms of one another. An ontological leveling occurs within capitalist conceptuality in order to make this possible. Forces previously separable by kind are seen as similar. Human force must be quantifiable and exchangeable. Scientific materialism and its empiricist and positivist companions, with their proud inattention to conceptuality, metaphysics, or teleology in shaping human perceptions of scientific facts, offer such a framework.

Beginning with the discovery of the 1844 Manuscripts and continuing in the wake of the publication of the *Grundrisse* after Stalin's death in 1953, some scholars have charted humanist and scientific periods in Marx's work (Althusser 1969). The scientific period, encompassing much of Marx's work subsequent to 1861 and including all of *Capital*, has been indicted for its inattention to the problem of human will in the face of materialist determination. But according to my interpretation, the much-famed split between a humanist and a structuralist, scientific Marx is less a split within Marx's work than a commentary on the forms of thought available prior to capitalism and within it. Capitalism, not Marx, invalidates the earlier humanist conceptual framework.

Thus, Marx is not confused when he mobilizes seemingly contradictory humanist and scientific concepts. Rather, he is involved in a broad and sweeping interpretive framework in order to show how scientific concepts are conditioned by capitalist ideology. He chose to mirror the transition from a precapitalist to a capitalist world in his text, so that we may see the received world as historical, and not as natural. By positioning himself critically within capitalism, he tries to avoid being uncritically caught up in the systems of thought that capitalism mandates. His strategy is, perhaps, overly subtle, requiring a reader who does not take *Capital* and its concepts at face value, but understands them as a response to the capitalist world.

The questions that Marx's method in *Capital* raises are troubling: What is the reality of alienation and how is that reality mediated to us? If, as alienated, we stay within the norms of capitalist conceptuality, do we not lose all possible resources for criticizing these norms? Are we reduced to pointing out that workers must be fed in order to work, or might we still make a claim about the inherent worth of human activity that is not subject to the dictates of instrumentality? Alternatively, why might it be in capitalism's interest not to hide our alienation from us, but to show it to us in scientific form? In accepting our alienation as a natural and ineluctable part of the human condition, our energies of resistance are organized, and then neutralized, along lines certain to pose no real threat to capitalism's operation. So long as the norms of capitalism appear as features of the natural world, human beings need take no social and political responsibility for these norms. Again, a symptom of this is the way social and political issues are increasingly absorbed, resolved, and regulated by scientific discourse.

Marx seemed to suggest in his early works that capitalism may unwittingly produce critical energy and perspectives, and, in this case, also unleash forces beyond its control: the *Communist Manifesto* deploys the image of a system of production that produces its own gravediggers, including thinkers like Marx. But Marx's method in *Capital* of portraying capitalism as the totalizing closure of the real would seem to be flawed were the solution this simple.

Is capitalism truly hegemonic? The late Marx's hermeneutic produces a classic circle, for if we were fully enclosed within capitalist alienation, and thus fully enclosed within ideology, Marx would be unable to account for the genesis of his own and other criticisms of the capitalist mode of production. Perhaps an adequate account of capitalism, then, requires us to observe that capitalist conceptuality is not particularly coherent, or even that capitalism enables explicitly contradictory modes of thought. We see an example of this in the way a better understanding of the human body's energy economy can be used both to exploit workers and to defend them from exploitation.

Despite his claims to have eliminated noncapitalist concepts in *Capital*, and to have generated an account of the capitalist mode of production and its overcoming from within this conceptual closure, Marx continually relied on claims about an authentic human essence that the capitalist scientific worldview claimed to have erased. In particular, he appeals to the term "human." This term appears as a marker for labor, the free play of the faculty of imagination beyond material determination, and an incitement to moral indignation. Marx also appeals to "use-value," the inherent worth of a thing that serves as the regulative ideal of exchange. Capitalism and its scientific materialist ideology struggle to eliminate the meaningfulness of these concepts, because ostensibly everything can be quantified in terms of everything else. But Marx seemed not to have eliminated them even when he claimed to have eliminated all meaningfulness not coherent to capitalism.

Hence, it is tempting to be critical of Marx for rehearsing a nostalgic and antiquated humanism derived from the classical and feudal periods, a humanism that relied on the notion of an authentic human essence that is lost in the modern qua capitalist world. In *Capital*, Marx seems to rely on a historically deracinated, feudal, or even classical notion of human essence as a foil for the degraded human essence characteristic of the capitalist mode. Marx's account would then be subject to the contemporary feminist and postcolonial critics that have deconstructed the concept of the human peculiar to the classical, mediaeval, and modern philosophies of the Western tradition. These critics stress how the concept of the human itself was born with a sexist pedigree—and how, beginning in the mediaeval period, it was stamped with a specifically racist one.[3]

Were this form of anachronistic humanism characteristic of Marx's own thinking, then his normative vision of unalienated labor would be a call to return to the purity of these lost historical essences. His thought would be a species of romanticism. Insofar as Marx's thought was determined by the theme of purity and its political corollary—a revolution to end all revolutions and to restore this lost human essence—he could even be read as a reactionary. His thought would be nostalgia, and perhaps even a dangerous nostalgia, for a concept of the human forged by and in the norms of an unequal world.

But if we read carefully, we find that Marx does not express this uncritical longing for the features of the precapitalist world, nor for the forms of humanity that it inaugurated. Though critical of capitalism, Marx never retreats from the insight that bourgeois revolutions were emancipatory improvements of the human condition, great steps forward: indeed, the greatest possible steps "within the hitherto existing world order," even if they were not "the final forms of human emancipation" that would be present in some possible world.[4] Nor does Marx retreat from an account of all nature, including human nature, as essentially historical: shaped by material conditions and by the resultant capacities of human knowing and action.[5]

This leads me to the following interpretation of Marx's humanism. Perhaps the reactionary and romantic features of this humanism, like the scientific materialism with which they all-too-readily contrast, are also a product of the capitalist world, and not simply an importation from the explanatory systems of earlier, obsolete worldviews. Using this interpretation, it would be capitalism, not Marx, which produces a reactionary and romantic humanist nostalgia for the feudal world. Capitalism produces this romantic humanism in contrast to the scientific discourse that it also unleashes. For this reason, nineteenth-century romantic humanism is not simply a prolonged survival of the systems of thought that characterized an earlier historical period. Instead, it is one of the disavowed products of capitalism itself. I call it capitalist humanism. Marx's use of this humanism, like his use of scientific materialism, would then be a performance: a performance designed to show that capitalism cannot account for its own activity without recourse to the humanistic notions that it supposedly banishes.

Capitalist humanism is an example of what feminist philosopher Donna Haraway, following Chela Sandoval, calls an "oppositional ideology." An oppositional ideology appears in its fullest form only in its mythical opposition to a given, fully modern reality. Of twentieth-century ecofeminism, Haraway (1991) writes,

[The] symbolic systems and the related positions of ecofeminism and feminist paganism, replete with organicisms, can only be understood in Sandoval's terms as oppositional ideologies fitting the late twentieth century. They would simply bewilder anyone not preoccupied with the machines and consciousness of late capitalism (174).

Applying her insights to a preceding historical period, we might write that the symbolic systems of romantic humanism, replete with appeals to the feudal and classical periods and the model of agrarian labor, can only be understood as oppositional ideologies fitting the mid-nineteenth century. They would bewilder anyone not preoccupied with the machines, changes in labor and nature, and the resultant consciousness of early capitalism. Scientific materialism and romanticism work together in this consciousness, and therefore in the capitalist mode of production.[6]

Cultural ideals are notoriously complex. Haraway and Sandoval are not alone in noting that the ideals created by a culture are of at least two types: expressive and oppositional. Expressive ideals capture something essentially true about the culture's operation. An oppositional ideal captures something essential about what a culture lacks and what it wishes it had. Oppositional ideals are produced in cultures as a species of wish-fulfillment, often in response to expressive ideals, with which they contrast. In my account of the nineteenth century, scientific materialism is an expressive ideal. Romantic and reactionary capitalist humanism, on the other hand, is an oppositional ideal.[7]

In the later chapters of this book, I chart the problems of the narrow norms by which capitalist humanism is regulated, especially in its exclusion of women, non-whites, and Jewish peoples. However, Marx's own humanism has already undergone some critical scrutiny and revision. Unlike his philosophical predecessors, Marx at least attempts to include women and the racially marked subjects of the US South in the concept of liberated humanity on which he insists. That is, the humanism of communism is based on an enlarged notion of what the concept "human" is and what it encompasses; it is not a reactionary capitalist humanism.

In comparison with the nineteenth-century society in which it was written, governed by waves of patriarchal reaction to bourgeois revolutions, Marx's vision of a liberated society is thus futural in the extreme. Perhaps it is a vision even more relevant to our world than it was to Marx's. From this perspective, despite the immediate notoriety of Marx's work, its effects on the political developments of the twentieth century, and its supposed defeat in the aftermath of what is called the "communist collapse," his work is enduringly—and increasingly—relevant to the twenty-first century and its problems of globalization, environmental degradation, and still more widespread labors, both waged and nonwaged.

Marx's strategic and critical deployment, in *Capital*, of capitalist science and capitalist humanism performs the contradictions of the capitalist world's expressive and oppositional ideals. Remembering this will help us understand Marx's theory of machine technology as I present it in this book. Although it is clear that Marx is worried about the forms of labor and human embodiment unleashed by the modern, technological world, it is also clear that he thinks these will continue in the communist period of Modern Industry, and continue for the betterment of human society as a whole. He perceives the machine destruction called for by the Luddites, among others, as a form of romantically driven false consciousness. Capitalist life is already a step, if treacherous, towards liberation.

Marx's explicit thought, therefore, in no way points to a return to the norms of feudal labor. However, this does not mean that the norms of feudal labor, and especially the model of a single craftsman wielding a tool as the model for skilled labor, have not influenced Marx's thought. Marx's performance of capitalist science and capitalist humanism occurs both consciously and unconsciously: consciously, when he wishes to show how the norms of energetic science reinforce factory labor or how virulent and reactionary residues of the feudal world appear within capitalism; unconsciously, when the placing of Marx's thought in the capitalist world comes to mark and determine this thought. In both senses, however, we must understand Marx's science and his humanism to be a part of his performance of capitalism and capitalism's contradictions. Marx would not have expected his own thought to be entirely free from the historical markings of the period in which it was forged, and he would have counted on his interpreters to point these out when they occur. We would count ourselves lucky if some contemporary or future reader will take the trouble to point out similar blind spots in our own thought.

For this reason, when we read Marx, and especially when we read his later work, we must approach him with the same circumspection with which we approach figures like Kierkegaard or Nietzsche. Marx cannot simply write the truth of capitalism. Rather, he offers a strategic intervention into the world he has received, and that he wants to criticize immanently, knowing that he can only work within the concepts characteristic of this world. If, in *Capital*, Marx's thought performs both capitalist science and capitalist humanism, this is a mark of his immanent critique of the capitalist mode of production. It is also the final form of Marx's own thought, at its most philosophical.

Marx thereby demonstrates that rhetorical flexibility will be a crucial consideration of political reasoning. In *Capital*, Marx has elected to criticize the bourgeois world of capitalism from within the conceptual vocabulary characteristic of this world. This does not represent the final form of emancipatory conceptuality, that is, a set of concepts that tend towards human liberation. This book's central example of emancipatory conceptuality will be a notion of human activity not reducible to and encompassed by labor. Marx's work therefore represents a stage on the way to a fully emancipatory conceptuality. Although he glimpses this conceptuality, it is not yet part of the world with which he must reckon and reason.

Despite the conceptual constraints of *Capital*, Marx hardly wishes to view the human being as mere exchange-value in a system that will bring on a crisis. This would violate his commitment, under the surface of a politically expedient argument, to instill perspectives other than those available within capitalism. Thus, a deeply philosophical Marx appears in the cracks and interstices of *Capital*: in the references to Aristotle's doctrine of human priority and the degraded mode of life that will result from a society too squarely driven by economics, in the critique of exchange-value, and in the accounts of labor that emphasize the human imagination and the special characteristics of this force. These philosophical concerns are not part of the capitalist calculus, but that does not mean they are inconsiderable in Marx's later work, the main point of which was to show that they cannot appear in an exchange-value–driven world. The knowledge-practices of this world, including some forms of its science, threaten to eliminate these philosophical concepts, and yet they haunt Marx's late thought as they do the capitalist world.

Marx's strategic mobilization of the concepts of energeticist science in *Capital* should not lead us to conclude that he considers all science to be capitalist science, nor that all scientific concepts have been ideologically shaped by the capitalist conceptuality of resource quantification. This is because, for Marx, science need not be positivist or empirical. In fact, science for Marx is most truly "scientific" when it calls into question the suppositions of the empirical and positivist methodologies. Likewise, technology need not be capitalist technology, developed at the expense of working-class human beings and nature, and deployed for the end of perpetuating class oppression and maximizing profit. In other words, for Marx, science and technology are potentially liberatory forces allied to the expanded but still recognizably humanist project of resisting capitalism. But to see this clearly we must look outside of *Capital* and, in particular, at the way this text contrasts with Marx's earlier accounts.

For Marx, science is neither positivist nor empirical because his notion of science was derived from Hegel's notion of *Wissenschaft*, and thus from Hegel's attention to the role of available concepts in shaping scientific inquiry. Historicizing Hegel, Marx offers a genealogy of the concepts used in scientific inquiry, and finds these concepts to be shaped by the capitalist world.[8]

When Marx claimed that his own work *Capital* was a scientific work he meant it in two senses. *Capital* is scientific in a narrow sense, because it proves that the resource use of the capitalist system is unsustainable in quantifiable terms: for example, the fall in the rate of profit argues that profit cannot sustain itself at increasingly high levels as the capitalist system continues to develop. But, more importantly, *Capital* is scientific in a broad sense, because it identifies the concepts with which the capitalist world, including capitalist science, operates. These are the abstractions of the commodity, wage labor, value, the individualized *homo economicus*, the systems of exchange these constructs presuppose, and a medical physiology that assimilates humans, animals, and machines to a single model.

Marx disagreed with the ultimate quantification of the human experience operative in these concepts. Hence, he wished to use science, in the broad sense, to show the underpinnings of how science, in the narrow sense, operates in the capitalist world. He believes that this is better science, and that part of science's enlarged task is to account for the lineage of the concepts with which it operates. Science in the narrow sense has failed to account for its own conceptual presuppositions. As such, it suffers from an alienated epistemology. We see, in this idea from Marx, a theme that later will become pronounced in Thomas Kuhn's interdisciplinary work on science, and Donna Haraway's twentieth-century feminist philosophy of science and technology.

The broad and narrow meanings of science in Marx's work are coupled with analogous meanings of technology. Marx was one of the first modern thinkers to begin to understand technology as an abstract noun covering an abundance of devices, rather than simply understanding it as a referent for the class of objects called "machines." For Marx, there is technology in the narrow sense of its deployment within the capitalist world, and technology in the broader sense of a device that adds stature and power to human capacities. In a world dominated by exchange-value, humans and machines are interchangeable, and both are subject to an abstract calculation of their quantifiable value. In such a world, humans are less valuable than machines, because their energetic powers are paltry by comparison.

In a world in which the priority of human persons has been reinstated in the expanded way envisioned by Marx, however, technology could never develop in this direction. It would instead develop in directions perhaps unimaginable to us today. Technology would actualize a modest material wealth, change and ameliorate the forms of human communication, and amplify human embodiment, but it would never produce the contradictions capitalism exacerbates.[9] In these contradictions, workers are pitted against their own instruments of production, and the quest for a fair share of material resources and meaningful activity appears as strife between humans and machines.

Thus, in his account of science and technology as well as his politics, we can chart the ambivalence in Marx's relationship to Enlightenment thought. Without question, Marx accepted Enlightenment notions of rationality and scientific and political progress as superior to earlier feudal notions. What Marx could not accept is limiting these notions—including the forms of science, technology, and politics—to the bourgeois conceptuality that produced them. In this form, individual liberation is pursued at the expense of society as a whole. Scientific rationality is developed for some at the expense of its development in others, and science is delimited to a narrow methodology whose cultural shaping is left unexplored. Finally, technology is deployed for maximizing profit and value rather than for improving the material conditions of all.

For Marx, a society is only as free as its most unfree member, and social health is measured by a communitarian standard rather than by the standard of the outstanding individuals a given society might produce. Thus, the question is whether the Enlightenment's commitments to rationality and scientific, technological, and political progress can be maintained without the economic individual that is their central construct. Marx argued that they can, and in this way is both the last flower of Enlightenment thought as well as its trenchant critic.

1
Karl Marx's Concept of Alienation

In his later years, and especially in *Capital*, Marx stopped using the term "alienation," a term he used frequently in the 1840s and the 1850s. In his attempts to redefine and reconfigure the concept of alienation as the central experience of capitalist subjects, Marx amplified it with the concepts of commodity fetishism and machine labor. In this amplification, the concept of alienation comes to define a world determined solely by economics. The illusions produced by capitalist making come to determine the possible range of human thinking. However, commodity fetishism and machine labor are not so much new concepts as developments of the discourse of alienation in a new terrain, in a different world from the one described by bourgeois political theory. On this new terrain, Marx reintroduces a classic philosophical theme as a counterpoint to the unalloyed worship of labor characteristic of bourgeois political theory: the idea of social and personal illness consequent upon imbalances in economic life.

Marx's development of the theme of alienation into the themes of commodity fetishism and machine labor follows from his criticism of civil, or bourgeois, society and its rules of exchange, including those rules that mandate alienated labor and the alienated production of goods. Marx takes Hegel's and Locke's use of "alienation" to represent bourgeois society, or he takes their ideas themselves to be part of the alienated ruling ideas whose particular genealogy he wishes to unmask. At the same time, Marx's theory of revolution remains indebted to the structure of civil society and the assertion of its privileges, including the rights of labor, against the old feudal society. In this chapter, I show the development of Marx's theory of alienation not only into fetishism, but also into the alluring prospect of an end of arduous human labor, a prospect made possible by accumulated scientific and technological wealth. I also show which elements of Marx's thought extend beyond the bourgeois valorization of labor and which remained mired within this valorization.

I   Objectification, alienation, and estrangement: on Marx's Hegelian inheritance

Marx begins his analysis and redefinition of the terms "objectification" [*Vergegenständlichung*], "alienation" [*Entäusserung*], and "estrangement" [*Entfremdung*] in the *Economic and Philosophical Manuscripts of 1844* and continues it in the *Grundrisse* of 1857–1858. In particular, Marx makes a distinction between objectification and alienation/estrangement. Though he does not repeat the distinction in *Capital*, it is only against the backdrop of this distinction that can we understand his mature work, and especially his account of the role of the social productivity of science and technology.

The distinction Marx draws between objectification and alienation/estrangement is derived from his application of capitalist relations of distribution and production to the meaning of "objectification" and "alienation/estrangement." Thus the distinction between them will be of increasing importance, because alienation/estrangement will become the historically specific structure that capitalist production as a totalizing whole superimposes on ontological human objectification. In early Marx, a human being who works on the world objectifies his or her essence, leaving his or her mark on nature. Work is a means of self-actualization. We will see how this characteristic comes to be curtailed in the mode of capital, where work is alienated, activity stunted, and humanity in this sense eliminated.

In fact, Marx's project as a whole will lead to a reversal in the evaluation of work. Instead of being the mode through which humans actualize themselves, work becomes alienated labor, an indenture that is to be minimized—though not completely eliminated—in the communist mode of production. Because of the alienation inherent to productive activity, freedom will also be reversed from its Hegelian sense. Freedom will no longer be that which the subject achieves through work but the potential actualized in the time freed from labor.

For the early Marx, objectification is the most basic feature of all living human activity. Objectification involves the mixing of human force with passive matter, with human force and passive matter conceived as absolutely differing in kind. In this process, humans produce nature and elicit its implicit rationality. We make objects that bear the human imprint, and the fact that these objects are not immediately available for use is the hallmark of "conscious life activity." Unlike an animal, according to Marx, "man produces when he is free from physical need and truly produces only in freedom from such need;" human beings "produce not only themselves, but the whole of nature ... in accordance with the law of beauty." Moreover, human objectification is not immediately annexed to the producer's physical body; time and space intervene, allowing for a reflective moment in which "man freely confronts his own product."

For Marx, this objectification is not individual but social, a feature he describes via the concept of "species-being" [*Gattungswesen*]. He writes, "It is, therefore, in his fashioning of the objective that man really proves himself to be a species-being ... nature appears as his work and his reality ... and he can therefore contemplate himself in a world he himself has created." It is not individual objectifications that transform the world in this way, but the transformations the human species as a whole brings about in a progressive humanization and spiritualization of the natural world. I recognize myself not only in my own creations but also in those of my fellows, whose objectifications I also recognize as exhibiting the same human spirit as my own. I only know what I am in my species-capacity insofar as I am integrated into a social world of human objectification.

In a situation that begins with the unjust distribution of the fruits and tools of production, this objectification becomes alienated. Products are no longer the producer's to enjoy, much less to contemplate:

> [T]he object that labour produces, its product, stands opposed to it as *something alien*, as a power independent of the producer. The product of labour is labour embodied and made material in an object, it is the *objectification* of labour ... In the sphere of political economy, this realization of labour appears as a *loss of reality* for the worker, objectification as loss of and bondage to the object, and appropriation as estrangement, as *alienation*.
>
> (*Economic and Philosophical Manuscripts of 1844*, Section 5)

In the appropriations mandated by political economy, workers must work in order to live, must appropriate the necessities of physical life by selling their labor. In exchange, workers appropriate not the produce of their own labor, but money that they exchange for something else. In such alienation, the positive characteristics of human objectification, especially the features through which the product is able to be separated from an immediate assimilation to workers' bodies, are turned against these bodies.

But the transformation is still deeper. Marx claims that "estrangement manifests itself not only in the result, but also in the act of production, within the activity of production itself" (*Economic and Philosophical Manuscripts of 1844*, Section 5). This alienation is the transformation of objectifying life activity. Creative fulfillment of human activity becomes a hated and detested chore undertaken only to meet physical need. The problem is not only an inequality of distribution of the means and products of production: it is the mode of production as a whole and the kind of human action it mandates.

Marx's development of the distinction between objectification and alienation/estrangement in the ensuing years included increasing attention to describing alienation, not simply as a feature of capitalist distribution, but as a feature of life in capitalism as a whole. It is not only that the worker is not returned a just equivalent for the objectifying labor he or she has performed, but also that his or her activity is not one of self-actualization, undertaken in freedom from physical need. Consider the formulation of this distinction in Marx's *Grundrisse*:

> [In *Capital*], the emphasis comes to be placed not on the state of being *objectified* but on the state of being *alienated*, dispossessed, sold [*Der Ton wird gelegt nicht auf das Vergegenständlichtsein, sondern das Entfremdet-Entäussert-, Veräussertsein*]; on the condition that the monstrous objective power which social labour erected opposite itself as one of its moments belongs not to the worker, but to the personified conditions of production, i.e. to capital. To the extent that, from the standpoint of capital and wage labour, the creation of the objective body of activity happens in antithesis to the immediate labour capacity—that this process of objectification in fact appears as a process of dispossession from the standpoint of labour or as appropriation of alien labour from the standpoint of capital—to that extent, this twisting and inversion [*Verdrehung und Verkehrung*] is a *real phenomenon*, not a merely supposed one existing merely in the imagination of the workers and the capitalists. But obviously this process of inversion is a merely historical necessity . . . but in no way an *absolute* necessity of production
>
> (1973, 831–832, German and emphases in original;
> MECW 1987, 29, 209–210; MEGA^2 II, 1.2, 698).[1]

That is, in the mode of production that characterizes capitalism, the focus is not on production as human objectification, but on production as alienated human labor. The latter is then claimed by political economists as an absolute necessity of production, independent of history, and adopted as such by workers and capitalists alike. Later in *Capital* Marx will write, "The advance of capitalist production develops a working class, which by education, tradition, habit, looks upon the conditions of that mode of production as self-evident laws of Nature" (1887, 689).

Marx's characterization of alienation has also developed since the 1844 Manuscripts. In alienated labor, objectification has become "monstrous" [*ungeheuerlich*]: a telling adjective by which Marx often denotes alienated conditions in his later work. The locus of alienation is also no longer the isolated object, nor the distribution of products and tools, but "the personified conditions of production" as a whole. In these conditions, as we shall see, the worker is alienated (1) from the objects produced, (2) from the means of production (i.e. the tools and instruments through which production is carried out), and (3) from the process of objectification itself, because he or she finds that his or her practical life activity stunts, abuses, and undermines itself.[2]

In the passage that follows, Marx describes how the transition to capitalism causes an error to become rampant: the error of thinking that all objectification must take the historical form given to it in alienation.[3] This is an understandable error, because the whole of production has been twisted and inverted in such a way that the human creative essence is no longer celebrated. Rather, objectivity in this sense is buried under calcified notions that characterize all human activity as work, and all human work as a suffering undertaken only for survival. Marx wishes to unmask the supposed givenness and naturalness of this formulation in order to imagine a world in which things operate according to different principles of distribution of both the spoils and the means of production, and also in which human activity can be conceptualized outside labor's iron cage. In such a world, the activity of production will no longer be alienated, and the emphasis again will come to rest on objectification.

This use and development of "alienation" are unique to Marx, though they were intimated in Hegel. As Jean Hyppolite wrote of Hegel's *Phenomenology*, "The term estrangement (*Entfremdung*) is stronger than the term alienation (*Entäusserung*). It implies not only that the natural self gives itself up, alienates itself, but also that it becomes *alien* to itself" (1979, 385). This implies that the distinction Marx will wish to draw between objectification and alienation is in some way present in the *Phenomenology*, though for Hegel it may be present in the difference between estrangement and alienation rather than in the difference between objectification and estrangement/alienation, as it is in Marx's appropriation of the terms. We have seen how, in the above passage from the *Grundrisse*, Marx continues to employ both Hegelian terms in his reworking and synthesis of them, which makes his exact relationship to any Hegelian distinction between the terms difficult to trace.

Despite the distinctions in the Hegelian vocabulary between "objectification," "alienation," and "estrangement," the terms are often related in Hegel's discussions. In the *Phenomenology of Spirit*, Hegel even uses "objectification" and "estrangement" interchangeably to indicate the cycles of externalization and return that make up, first, consciousness's (and later self-consciousness's) dialectic with nature and human community, and, second, Spirit's dialectic with history. In this usage, the moment of return is inevitable for Spirit and not socially dependent on distribution or production. That which is estranged ineluctably returns enriched by the content of the negational tarry; it is only a matter of more or less time, to whose abstractions Spirit as a whole is ultimately indifferent. In the preface, Hegel writes,

> Spirit becomes object [*Gegenstand*] because it is just this movement of becoming an *other to itself* [*Gegenstand seines Selbst*], i.e. becoming an *object to itself*, and of suspending this otherness. And experience is the name we give to just this movement, in which the immediate, the *unexperienced*, i.e. the abstract, whether it be of sensuous [but still unsensed] being, or only thought of as simple, becomes alienated from itself [*sich entfremdet*] and then returns to itself from this alienation [*Entfremdung*]
> (Hegel 1977, para. 36; German from Hegel 1969, 38–39;
> emphases in original).

Instead of using "objectification" and "estrangement" interchangeably, Marx developed the concept of alienation/estrangement and reserved it for a specific use: in it, he incorporates a historically specific social form of production that refracts back the meaning of production as a whole. In giving this more economic sense to Hegel's terms, Marx has transformed them. This is why Schlomo Avineri claims that Hegel has no concept of "alienation/estrangement" distinct from "objectification" in the sense Marx will want to outline. The reason behind this, Avineri claims, is that Hegel's thought lacks the idea of a distribution of work within the capitalist system (1968, 97).[4]

Although this may correctly describe the above Hegelian usage in the *Phenomenology*, it obscures the way in which Hegel, in the texts on property from *The Philosophy of Right*, applies the term "estrangement" to describe the extortion of labor that occurs in historical systems like slavery and feudal serfdom. In *The Philosophy of Right*, Hegel even seems to foreshadow the distinction Marx will make between the concepts, or at least the beginnings of this distinction as it is founded on distribution. In *The Philosophy of Right*, Hegel uses a property-based notion of alienation/estrangement, in which the objectified essence of human self-mediation can precipitate a clash between human potentiality and its actual expression in the world. Hegel locates this possibility, as Marx will, in historical forms of labor in which the producer's products are appropriated by someone other than the producer. In the same passage, Hegel also gives a criticism of "superstition," which parallels the one Marx will later give of the "mystification" of consciousness. The relevant passages from *The Philosophy of Right* read as shown below:

> It is in this very concept of spirit as that which is what it is only *through itself* and as *infinite return into itself* from the natural immediacy of its existence that lies the possibility of an opposition, in that what the spirit is only *in itself* may differ from what it is *for itself* . . . . Herein lies the *possibility of the alienation of personality* and its substantial being . . . Examples of the alienation of personality are slavery, serfdom, disqualification from owning property, restrictions on freedom of ownership, etc. The alienation of intelligent rationality, of morality, ethical life, and religion, is encountered in superstition, when power and authority are granted to others to determine and prescribe what actions I should perform
>
> (Hegel 1991, 96; emphases added).

Nowhere in his 130-plus-page analysis of Hegel's *Philosophy of Right* does Marx address this passage.[5] This is instructive in what it tells us about the relationship between the two thinkers during Marx's early years. What the young Marx criticizes in Hegel he highlights, whereas what he has adopted or absorbed goes unmarked.

But there is also a real difference in how the two thinkers resolve the alienation/estrangement of the personality and the substantive being. Hegel is more optimistic than Marx about overcoming alienation/estrangement. Hegel also resolves alienation/estrangement, not socially and politically, as Marx will, but metaphysically, since this form of externalization is phenomenologically inadequate, and ultimately impossible. The external, in Hegel, can never remain external, and is degraded, inauthentic, and unfulfilled when it does so:

> The right to what is in essence inalienable is imprescriptible, for the act whereby I take possession of my personality and substantial essence and make myself a responsible being with moral and religious values and capable of holding rights removes these determinations from that very externality which alone made them capable of becoming the possession of someone else. When their externality is superseded in this way, the determination of time and all other reasons [*Gründe*] which can be derived from my previous consent or acceptance lose their validity. This return on my part into myself, whereby I make myself existent as Idea, as a person with rights and morality, supersedes the previous relationship and the wrong which I and the other party have done to my concept and reason [*Vernunft*] in treating the infinite existence [*Existenz*] of the self-consciousness as something external, and in allowing it to be so treated. This return into myself reveals the contradiction inherent in handing over to others my capacity for rights, my ethical life and religiosity
>
> (Hegel 1991, 96).

When Marx redefines Hegelian alienation/estrangement in the historically specific senses particular to capitalist production, this return into the self can no longer be self-evident and presupposed on the basis of the concept of human objectification. Instead, the alienation of the substantive being will continue until it is politically rectified; that is, this inauthentic expression of spirit will be much more tenacious than Hegel realizes. Thus Marx's particular use of "alienation" differs from Hegel's, but only in the breadth of its extent and in the way alienation/estrangement will come to be resolved, a modification consonant with Marx's critique of Hegel in the early 1840s. In this critique, as is well known, Marx claims to generate insight beginning with the practical and material world rather than the ideal world.

However, in a broader sense, Marx never leaves behind the structure that characterizes the inevitable return of Hegelian alienation/estrangement. Despite the historical disappointments suffered by the communist movements in Germany, France, and England in the mid-nineteenth century, Marx maintains his forecast of a political revolution through which alienation—as he has redefined it historically—will become nonmonstrous objectification. Alienation ends with the revolution, enriched by the accumulation of material wealth that occurred during alienation's monstrous reign. Because of this accumulation, the society both before and after the transition is socially and economically prepared for a new political configuration. All of Marx's work, including his theories of capitalist crisis through the fall in the rate of profit, a theme of his late work to which I will turn in the discussion of machines in Chapter 3, must be understood against this backdrop of his tenacious belief in this revolution, and with this a belief in the ability of the political to rectify the social.

The revolution has the power not only to restore the worker's activity, but with it to restore the essence of the human species as such to produce freely, and to produce itself as a free producer in nonalienating practical life activity. Revolution thus restores objectification and what alienation has taken away as a result of objectification's loss: spirit (i.e. personality). The effect will be a notion of human activity, or production, unlimited by the alienated constructions that make up the notions "labor" or "work." Marx's call to revolution thus extends beyond a critique of distribution to challenge the mode of production. It is not simply that the political realm finally becomes adequate to the economic substrate; rather, it challenges this economic substrate as alienated and alienating.

Politically, this means that Marx must distinguish the communist revolution from the preceding bourgeois revolutions, which *were* more simply ways that the political realm became an adequate expression of the economic substrate by mobilizing a labor-based theory of property and right. In the *Eighteenth Brumaire of Louis Bonaparte* (1851), Marx defends the inevitability of the communist revolution, and contrasts this revolution with the bourgeois revolutions that preceded it:

> Bourgeois revolutions, such as those of the 18th century, storm along from strength to strength; their dramatic effects outdo one another, people and events seem to have a jewel-like sparkle, ecstasy is the feeling of the day; but they are short lived, quickly attaining their zenith, and a lengthy hangover grips society before it soberly absorbs the burning lessons of such *Sturm and Drang*. By contrast, proletarian revolutions, such as those of the 19th century, engage in perpetual self-criticism, always stopping in their own tracks; they return to what is apparently complete in order to begin it anew, and

deride with savage brutality the inadequacies, weak points, and piti-
ful aspects of their first attempts. They seem to strike down their
adversary, only to have him draw new powers from the earth and
rise against them once more with the strength of a giant; again and
again they draw back from the prodigious scope of their own aims,
until a situation is created which makes impossible any reversion,
and circumstances themselves cry out: *Hic Rhodus, hic salta! Hier ist
Rose, hier tanze!*

(I; 1996, 35; MECW 1976, 11, 106–107; MEGA^2 I, 11,
101–102).[6]

Marx means for the *Hic Rhodus, hic salta* citation, taken from the preface
to Hegel's *Philosophy of Right*, to be ironic. In Hegel's usage, the passage
is an injunction always to enjoy the present, recognizing the universal in it. This recognition of the present's rational structure reconciles
the philosopher to the actual and dissuades philosophy from "fancy[ing
that it] can transcend its contemporary world." Hegel especially warns
against "the obligation to construct *a state as it ought to be*" (Hegel 1991,
21, emphasis added). Marx's appeal to the formula, in contrast, is an
appeal to just such a transcendence and construction. Against the qui-
etism of Hegel's formula, he posits a revolutionary overcoming of the
present in the future. Philosophy is not content to remain a specula-
tive diagnosis; instead, philosophy plays an active role in the transition.
In this, Marx follows the French rather than the German model of the
Enlightenment (Kouvelakis 2003, 12–15).

But in another sense, the original intent of Hegel's passage holds.
Marx recognizes the rational universal in the repeated historical ruptures
of the nineteenth-century revolutions. Though Marx clearly does not
think we ought to enjoy the capitalist present, including its barbarous
child labor and bogus restoration governments, he may be committed to our need to pass through it. We may view the older Marx's
explanation of the harsh period of alienation as a kind of theodicy:
a necessary evil in the formation of "a situation which makes impossible any reversion" and which will no longer "draw back from the
scope of its own prodigious aims" but instead force an apocalyptic
transition.[7]

By the same token, the proletarian revolution must differ in kind
from the preceding bourgeois revolutions, which were its rough drafts.
These revolutions left the political sphere unmodified—there was no
permanent transition to democracy, nor was there universal suffrage.
Historically, the bourgeois always compromised in favor of a facile

republicanism that preserved the form of absolutist government even while progressively negating its content. This illuminates Marx's understanding of the French Revolution as an incomplete and ecstatic forerunner, a view best understood against the historical backdrop of the nineteenth-century restorations and renewals of aristocratic privilege and ideals that are the topic of the *Brumaire* as a whole. More than this, bourgeois revolutions based their criticism of the political sphere on the economic sphere, establishing a split between the state and civil society that was left untouched and which Marx was to criticize as an unfinished and incomplete antinomy.[8]

Marx's mature philosophy retains more than these Hegelian teleological schematics about the goal of alienation and the role of the rational universal in the actual as it will appear after the communist revolution. The historical period of alienation stockpiles the resources that a future society, liberated from work, requires for its sustenance. Marx also retains the Hegelian method, that is, dialectic. Marx reread sections of Hegel's *Science of Logic* while planning the *Grundrisse* and *Capital*.[9]

If Marx offers us a materialist *Phenomenology* in his philosophical anthropologies of the 1840s and early 1850s, in *Capital* he offers us a materialist *Logic* that isolates the alienated categories of political economy and shows their transformation into one another, beginning from the inner dynamic of the commodity. This can make *Capital* difficult to understand, because the presentation is framed by the assumption that we are fully within the mode of capitalist production, and thus locked into the alienated world. Marx makes this methodological indebtedness to Hegel explicit in the famous 1872 *Afterword* to the second German edition of *Capital*:

> The mystifying side of the Hegelian dialectic I criticized nearly thirty years ago, at a time when it was still the fashion. But just as I was working at the first volume of "*Das Kapital*," it was the good pleasure of the peevish, arrogant, mediocre Ἐπίγονοι who now talk large in cultured Germany, to treat Hegel in the same way as the brave Moses Mendelssohn in Lessing's time treated Spinoza, i.e., as a "dead dog." I therefore openly avowed myself the pupil of that mighty thinker, and even here and there, in the chapter of the theory on value, coquetted with the modes of expression peculiar to him. *The mystification which dialectic suffers in Hegel's hands by no means prevents him from being the first to present its general form of working in a comprehensive and conscious manner*. With him it is standing on its head. It

must be turned right side up again, if you would discover the rational kernel within the mystical shell

(MECW 1996, 19, 35; MEGA^2 II, 9, 24, 27; MEGA^2 II, 8, 55, emphasis added).[10]

We shall see that in his political as well as his more economically themed works, Marx leaves Hegel behind only through Hegel's own methods, using these methods to critique Hegel himself and to show how his concepts are a product of bourgeois historicity and bourgeois conceptuality. Philosophy is no longer exempt from the limited historical world it describes. Instead it is immersed, to the core of its conceptual life, in the practical exigencies through which this world is built up.

II Other origins of "alienation" and "objectification"

Marx's use of "alienation" and "objectification" are not exclusively indebted to Hegel. His usage is influenced by a broad array of philosophical sources. Some of these sources—such as Aristotle, Rousseau, and Adam Smith—themselves had a powerful influence on Hegel. Others, like Feuerbach, were influenced by Hegel. Marx knew all of these thinkers well from his philosophical training.

Drawing on this historical and conceptual inheritance, Marx avails himself of a notion of alienation that designates the economic world and sphere of exchange, names a sort of spiritual sickness, and powerfully connects this spiritual sickness to imbalances in the economic world.[11] This theme begins in Aristotle.

The most influential ancient use of "alienation" denotes an imbalance in household management in Aristotle, as I shall elaborate in the following subsection. Influential modern uses of the concept include Rousseau's concept of the general will and Adam Smith's economic use of the term to indicate any form of exchange. As for "objectification," Marx owes his use of the concept and term primarily to Feuerbach's theological anthropology, which was indebted to Hegel's notion of "Objective Spirit." Marx's use of "alienation" and "objectification" offers us a synthesis of the dimensions treated in these thinkers from the history of philosophy, and this in addition to the Hegelian determinations explored above. It is useful to review the accounts of alienation in these thinkers in order to understand the background against which the Aristotelian connection between exchange and spiritual sickness is developed and extended in Marx.

Aristotle: alienation and living well

To develop his account of alienation in capitalism, Marx cites from Aristotle's *Nichomacean Ethics, Book V,* and *Politics, Book I,* and, as we shall see in subsequent chapters, Marx also revisits the Aristotelian dream of self-moving tools. He pulls two central ideas from these texts: first, the definition of justice as an equal exchange; second, the proper purposes of the sphere of exchange in use. When exchange loses sight of use, it becomes monstrous and unnatural. The definition of justice establishes Marx's concept of alienation because it is founded on inequalities of distribution: first, property distribution; and second, how tools for making and establishing such a property are distributed. The meditation on tools will be most important, since it will allow Marx to use the concept of alienation to characterize the mode of production as a whole, the kinds of activities that unfold under it, and thus the notion of labor itself.

In the *Ethics*, Aristotle defines the just as "intermediate between a sort of gain and sort of loss . . . it consists in having an equal amount before and after the transaction" (Aristotle 1984, 1132^b20). The measure of this equality necessitates a standard of fungibility: "All goods must be measured by some one thing" (1133^b26). For Aristotle, this one thing is "demand" in nature; demand is represented by money in human convention.

Although praising the Aristotelian discovery of the need for a universal equivalent, Marx is quick to correct the Aristotelian standard of measure in his citation of the text in *Capital*, because in capitalism all goods are measured by the abstract quantity of human labor they embody. Aristotle, Marx reminds us, cannot have a concept of abstract labor because in his society all labor was not of equal quality:

> Greek society was founded upon slavery, and had, therefore, for its natural basis, the inequality of men and of their labour-powers. The secret of the expression of value, namely, that all kinds of labour are equal and equivalent, because, and so far as they are human labour in general, cannot be deciphered, until the notion of human equality has already acquired the fixity of a popular prejudice. This, however, is possible only in a society in which the great mass of the produce of labour takes the form of commodities, in which, consequently, the dominant relation between man and man, is that of owners of commodities
>
> (I.I.III.3, 1887, 65–66).[12]

Here Marx introduces the theme he will later develop as "commodity fetishism." We also see Marx's idea that the bourgeois notion of human equality is produced by the fungibility of human labor.

If in Aristotle exchange is one foundation for human association, it is hardly the primary or sole motivation for association, being, moreover, founded exclusively on human need (1133^{b}7–18). In capitalism, however, all human association will come to be mediated through labor's expression in commodities on the market. When this occurs, humans identify themselves exclusively either with the kind of labor they undertake for sale in this format or, in later stages, with what they are able to purchase, with the commodities they are able to command and display.

The tendency of exchange to go beyond its proper bounds in the human life is the theme of the second idea Marx derives from Aristotle. In the *Politics*, Aristotle writes,

> Of everything which we posses there are two uses: both belong to the thing as such, but not in the same manner, for one is the proper, and the other the improper use of it. For example, a shoe is used for wear, and is used for exchange; both are uses of the shoe. He who gives a shoe in exchange for money or food to him who wants one, does indeed use the shoe as a shoe, but this is not its proper use, for a shoe is not made to be an object of barter
>
> (1257^{a}8–12).

To interpret this distinction using another Aristotelian schema, in its improper use, the shoe does not correspond to the final cause, that for the sake of which it is produced: the protection of the foot, or walking. This distinction serves as the basis for Aristotle's indictment of the retail trade and the illusions about household management to which it gives rise:

> The same [distinction] may be [made for] all possessions, for the art of exchange extends to all of them, and it arises at first from what is natural, from the circumstance that some have too little, others too much. Hence we may infer that retail trade is not a natural part of the art of getting wealth; had it been so, men would have ceased to exchange when they had enough ... the art of wealth-getting which consists in household management ... has a limit; the unlimited acquisition of wealth is not its business. And therefore, from one point of view, all riches have a limit. Nevertheless, as a

matter of fact, we find the opposite to be the case; for all getters of wealth increase their hoard of coin without limit. The source of the confusion is the near connection between the two kinds of wealth getting; in both, the instrument is the same, although the use is different, and so they pass into one another; for each is a use of the same property, but with a difference: accumulation is the end in one case, but there is a further end in the other. Hence some persons are led to believe that getting wealth is the object of household management, and the whole idea of their lives is that they ought either to increase their money without limit, or at any rate not to lose it. The origin of this disposition in men is that they are intent upon living only, and not upon living well

(1257^{a}11–19; 31–41).

The influence of this distinction on Marx is evident from the *Grundrisse* onward: it is the basis of Marx's distinction between use and exchange-value, a foundational distinction for Marx, and one to which I will refer throughout this work.

In its separation from use-value, exchange-value will continue to be an alienated and deficient mode of object-relations. The lack of limits to capital's circulation will become an object of critique for Marx, and later the target of his prediction of systemic crisis. If we superimpose Marx's distinction between alienation and objectification back on Aristotle's distinction, we understand that the first kind of relationship to the material object, for the purpose of use, is the result of objectification, whereas the second kind of relationship to the material object, in which exchange becomes the goal of the process, opens the door to alienation.

Rousseau: alienation and the general will

The concept of alienation also has a foundation in social contract theory, and the political determinations of the concept emerge when we consider this foundation. The central concept of Rousseau's *Social Contract* (1762) is that of the "general will."[13] It is significant that this will requires "the total *alienation* to the whole community of each associate with all his rights" (Rousseau 2002, 163, Bk I, chapter 6, emphasis added). Rousseau calls this alienation the social contract. Later in the text, he qualifies its extension: "We agree that whatever part of his power, property, and liberty each person alienates by accepting the social compact is only what is useful and important to the community; but we must also agree that the sovereign alone is judge of what is important" (2002, 174, Bk II, chapter 4). This alienation is not without due recompense, for "each giving himself to all, gives himself to no one; and since there is no associate over whom we do not acquire the same rights which we concede to him over ourselves, we *gain the equivalent* of all that we lose, and more power to preserve what we have" (2002, 164, Bk I, chapter 6, emphasis added). In Rousseau, political alienation is connected to the economic theme of gain and loss, or distribution of goods, and it appeals to rationally deciding rather than coerced economic agents, even if the sovereign remains the judge of what is important. Everything is alienable, then, but not all at once.

The theme of spiritual sickness, "madness" in Rousseau's case, appears as the token of imbalances in exchange, this time not imbalances of goods, but imbalances of political right. Rousseau emphasizes the gains won through alienation into the general will to distinguish his form of alienation from that demanded by Grotius as a justification of absolutist divine right.[14] According to Rousseau, in Grotius's account, "an individual can alienate his freedom and become the slave of a master" (2002, 158, Bk I, chapter 4). But for Rousseau liberty is inalienable by nature, or at least it is inalienable without the return of a superior equivalent that constitutes liberty's own amplification. To challenge Grotius, Rousseau begins by defining alienation: "To alienate is to give or to sell" (2002, 158, Bk I, chapter 4). Even a slave, who "sells himself for subsistence," is more comprehensible than the Grotian subject, who gets neither subsistence from the king nor tranquility from his hostile relations with neighboring peoples. To expect such alienation "is to suppose a nation of fools; and madness does not confer rights" (2002, 158, Bk I, chapter 4).

The difference, then, is what the one who is doing the alienating stands to gain from this alienation of his[15] powers. Rousseau splits alienation into rational and irrational uses by political philosophy. If this philosophy appeals to an economically calculating agent as its base, it cannot appeal to an agent who would act irrationally or against his own self-interest. For Rousseau, only a rational public sovereignty in accordance with the general will meets the qualifications that cause men to leave the state of nature and form compacts. Mutual preservation must be its first law. Unlike the absolutist justifications of Hobbes and Grotius, which are founded on the right of the strongest (and therefore no right at all but a system of continual usurpation), Rousseau argues that "all human authority is established for the benefit of the governed" (2002, 157, Bk I, chapter 2). Anything else would simply be irrational.

Legislation's primary task in this society is to defend liberty and equality. Rousseau argues that the radical inequalities of nature are rectified in the convention of the general will; therefore men are equal in the situation established by the social contract. But class inequalities have the potential to disrupt liberty:

> [A]s to wealth, no citizen should be rich enough to be able to buy another, and none poor enough to be forced to sell himself.... If, then, you wish to give stability to the State, bring the two extremes as near together as possible; tolerate neither rich people nor beggars. These two conditions, naturally inseparable, are equally fatal to the general welfare
>
> (2002, 189, Bk II, chapter 11).

Like the friendship of the ancients, alienation is freely undertaken and properly recompensed among individuals only if these individuals are of roughly equal wealth and social standing. Rousseau thus foresees the problems class will pose to the liberal state. He does not, however, foresee the ways in which posing the economic agent as a political calculator will become an ideological construct of domination.[16]

John Locke and Adam Smith: objectification, alienation, property, and tools

In John Locke's theory of property, property is something I make by mixing my labor with some unowned natural substance. This making is founded in a still more primary property, the property of the body. Locke writes,

> [E]very Man has a *Property* in his own *Person*. This no Body has any Right to but himself. The *Labour* of his Body, and the *Work* of his Hands, we may say, are properly his. Whatsoever then he removes out of the State that Nature hath provided, and left it in, he hath mixed his *Labour* with, and joined to it something that is his own, and thereby makes it his *Property*. It being by him removed from the common state Nature placed it in, it hath by this *labour* something annexed to it, that excludes the common right of other Men. For this *Labour* being the unquestionable Property of the Labourer, no Man but he can have a right to what that is once joined to, at least where there is enough, and as good left in common for others
>
> (Locke 1960, 305).

When I mix my labor in the way outlined by Locke, I do not alienate it; instead, I objectify it for my own use. This objectification has its own rights and forever marks the material on which it acts as its own. This fundamental right of annexation is inalienable. For Locke, the possibility of alienation begins with the exchange of this objectified labor and with the possibility that its fundamental rights of annexation might not be respected.

Locke inherits the colonial construction that considers the expanses of American land as unowned and uncultivated. In the European and English cultural imaginations of Locke's time, the Americas represent a benevolent gift of nature. Worked up into a formula of property acquisition during the waves of colonization, this becomes the myth of an unowned, given, natural substance.

Locke is nonetheless revolutionary in signifying the laboring act as establishing a property. Imagine the oddity of his claim to a classical slave-holding society. More pertinently, imagine making it, as Locke did, to a feudal society for whom owning a property would have been antithetical to the practice of labor, not its outcome! The laboring subject scripted by Locke challenges a feudal society that rejects the idea that labor establishes a property, because property in feudal society is handed down through birth. Part of Locke's philosophical project is to characterize feudal relations as "artificial" and the laboring subject as "natural." By appealing to nature, Locke tries to reverse the power roles traditionally scripted by the performance or nonperformance of labor. It is therefore a mark of bourgeois political philosophies, like Locke's, to regard property as labor's natural recompense.

In *The Wealth of Nations*, Adam Smith inherits Locke's notion of natural property formation. Smith is not worried about the conventions by which a property is established, but rather by the more abstract question of labor's recompense. He locates this first in nature: "The produce of labour constitutes the natural recompense or wages of labour. In that original state of things which precedes both the appropriation of land and the accumulation of stock, the whole produce of labour belongs to the labourer. He has neither landlord nor master to share with him" (Smith 1976, 82, Bk VIII).

However, Smith goes on to challenge the scenario of the natural wage of labor in the use of the objects it produces. The givenness of land and tools that condition this natural wage, the use of the produced object, do not last "beyond the first introduction of the appropriation of land and the accumulation of stock... as soon as land becomes private property, the landlord demands a share of almost all the produce which the labourer can either raise or collect from it" (1976, 82, Bk VIII). The convention of private property poses a new problem for theorizing the role of labor in property formation: how does property come about when what is worked up is not an unowned natural given, but something owned by prior title or convention? To what degree is the product of my labor still mine?

The tool or tools by which one's labor is mixed are also given, or rather, unaccounted for, in Locke's formula. Tools are neither precisely part of the body of the labor mixer, nor found lying among other unowned natural substances. One could imagine an account of origins in which the tool is both one and then the other: the hand, as a part of the body, and the stick or stone, as a part of the natural environment. Property in tools would then come about in the same manner as any other property: the working up of the stick or stone through the labor of the human hand. But historical human tools have already developed far beyond this by the time of Locke and Smith. And the contest over to whom the tools of labor belong will become important in early capitalism—a mode of production in which tools are increasingly owned by manufacturing enterprises rather than by workers.

Because of this, Smith continues his critique of Locke's scenario by arguing that the "original state of things in which the labourer enjoyed the whole produce of his own labour…was at an end long before the most considerable improvements were made in the productive powers of labour" (1976, 82, Bk VIII). That is, the natural wage was at an end long before the introduction of the tools and machines that mark modern forms of production. Both of Smith's criticisms of Locke reflect the truth that humans do not labor individually in a natural plenitude, but socially and historically in environments where property—including property in tools—is already owned. Concurring with Locke on labor's fundamental rights of annexation, Smith solves these problems by proposing that labor be returned its equivalent in the form of a wage. This, then, is the shape of the theoretical problem about property formation that Marx inherits.

Like these figures from the British Enlightenment, the young Marx, emerging from a stubbornly feudal Germany, will retain this emphasis on the fundamental importance of the labor and the rights established by it. Prior to his critique of labor itself as the alien mode of activity peculiar to the capitalist mode of production, and his vision of overcoming labor as the major mode of human practical life in the later works, Marx is simply critical of the institution of private property and its political effects in undermining labor's entitlement to its produce and to its tools. In Marx's early works, the substance of capital's injustice is still determined by the amount of labor it extorts from the worker without the return of a just equivalent, not yet by the form taken by labor. But Marx also picks up on Smith's observations about social labor, and amplifies the challenges that Smith raised to Locke's individualist account.

Capitalism comes on in historical stages, and we miss something crucial when we imagine capitalism occurring all at once. These stages are the basis for Marx's distinction between the formal and the real subsumption of capital. The formal subsumption belongs to an early stage, in which the worker sells his or her products for money, providing his or her own tools. The formal subsumption begins to be converted to the real subsumption as the capitalist begins to own these tools and to use them to exacerbate the division of labor, affecting the process of production, and causing workers to have to work together in factories in order to produce usable commodities. The real subsumption is complete when the process of production, or the way labor occurs, is transformed. In *The Economic Manuscripts of 1861–63*, Marx writes, "Adam Smith did not grasp the *division of labour* as something peculiar to the capitalist mode of production; something whereby, in addition to machinery and simple cooperation, labour is transformed not only formally, but in its reality— through subsumption under capital" (MECW 1988, 30, 271, emphasis in original).[17]

Marx draws a causal connection between the improvements in labor's productive power and the social labor that nullifies the possibility of the natural wage. The improvements in labor's productive power are historically indebted to the unjust bourgeois system of private property and profit extortion. This system forces laborers to work in combination without rewarding them for the increased production in material wealth enabled by this combination.

The problem then shifts to a slightly different terrain. Marx points out that human social production has been accomplished through ongoing historical injustice. The Industrial Revolution's massive amplification of material wealth was founded on the exploitation of both individual and social labors, and also on the increasing ownership and concentration of the tools and other means of production in the hands of capital. Historically, human sociality in production has been brought about when the worker's labor is expropriated by the conventions of private property and accumulated stock; that is, it has come about in an alienated form. The benefit of human sociality for the productive process as a whole has been founded on an alienated distribution wherein labor is not returned its due.

Marx will want to keep the immense gains in the production of material wealth that are a result of human sociality—and even the division of labor. These are a result of objectified and transferable human skills. Marx calls for the elimination of only the mode of expropriation and the profit motive in which these were constituted historically. For in this configuration, the labor mixer is not returned an equivalent for his or her contribution to the production process, and the activity of labor is not one of self-actualization. The labor mixer has lost the double givenness of the Lockean condition: the ownership of the means of production in the form of land and tools. He or she owns nothing but an abstract labor. In order to effect the common, material world— and to survive—laborers are therefore indebted to what Smith calls "a master [who] advances them the materials of their work and their wages and maintenance till it be completed" (1976, 82, Bk VIII).

Marx will want to lift the modern means of production, combinations of workers, and division of labor from the exploitive mode of production through which they were historically constituted. Much of Marx's later work is an attempt to work out how this can be accomplished. In this later work, Marx develops the concept of alienation as a social indictment. Alienation is not simply due to the failure of receiving a just equivalent for one's labor, nor is it simply due to the concentration of private property and tools in a few hands. In the real subsumption, the failure of receiving a just equivalent for one's labor and the concentration of private property and tools in a few hands are accomplished facts. Rather, alienation is most completely accomplished in an environment where the performance of labor is portrayed as the natural state of the human being. That is, alienation has already been guaranteed in the very formulations of Locke and Smith. In an alienated world, one is entitled to social and political status because of the labor one performs, and not because of one's humanity.

Using this critique, Marx calls the very concept of "labor" and its supposed naturalism into question. He criticizes Locke and Smith for their reliance on bourgeois labor as a natural feature of human life, and especially for portraying labor as conferring social and political dignity. Of Ricardo's development of Smith, Marx writes, "The bourgeois form of labour is regarded by Ricardo as the eternal natural form of social labour" (Marx 1970, 61, quoted in Postone 1993, 55).

In his later work, Marx claims that the category of labor is the product of an alienated society. In their claims about labor and the formation of property, Locke and Smith misunderstand a certain alienated mode of production as eternal and natural. Marx shows that Locke and Smith script a subject that occurs through the socially and politically foundational acts of laboring and exchanging this labor in the market. But Marx argues that this form of subjectivity corresponds to the historical situation of the bourgeois era rather than being the natural ontology of the human subject. This is why Marx can accuse Locke and Smith of ontologizing bourgeois labor as the natural human condition.

Instead of arguing for labor as a means of entitlement—that is, for freedom through labor—as he does in his early works, Marx increasingly argues for freedom from alienating capitalist labor as a degraded mode of practical activity. Marx develops the distinction between "objectification" (as the ontological interface between human beings and nature) and "alienation" (as the form this takes in capitalist labor). As Postone (1993) puts it, Marx's late work is increasingly "a critique of labor in capitalism" and not "a critique of capitalism from the standpoint of labor" (5).

In his late work, Marx distances himself from his bourgeois predecessors, and from the grounds of property-producing labor on which they stake their claims to social and political power. He also frames their emphasis on the importance of labor as an intrinsic part of capitalist ideology. At the same time, Marx retains the notion of the exchange of equivalents for one's labor and some of the ideas of labor as a mode of ontological self-creation in his later work. In Marx, labor is said in many ways. As we shall see, for Marx, the new themes that challenge the bourgeois model of Locke and Smith arise alongside it rather than fully displacing it and totally eliminating the critique of capitalism from the standpoint of labor.

Feuerbach: alienation and the gods

Thus, alienation is both an economic and a political concept. It is also a theological concept. For Marx, the gods are a projected version of the human essence: myths that stand over and dominate their actual creators. As we have seen, Marx derives this strain of his thinking from Ludwig Feuerbach, a left Hegelian whose break from Hegel's absolute idealism occurred through an anthropological critique of Christianity.

Feuerbach (1957) describes the structure of objectification in the making of myth: "Man is nothing without an object.... But the object to which a subject essentially, necessarily, relates is nothing else than this subject's own, but objective, nature.... In the object which he contemplates, therefore, man becomes acquainted with himself; consciousness of the objective is the self-consciousness of man" (4–5). What is true here of mythmaking in Feuerbach will be true *a fortiori* for material making in Marx. In material making, human self-consciousness is accomplished through the social act of objectification. As a species with no fixed ahistorical essence accomplished apart from this making, humans thereby establish their essence as historical and material. If the social act of objectification becomes impoverished and alienated, as it does in labor, so too will the human essence it defines.

Feuerbach is not yet concerned with this extension of his metaphor to human labor, but mainly with its theological consequences: the existence of the projected human objectification in the myth of God. This is the basis of his criticism of predication. He writes, "the positive final predicates which [a human] give[s] God are always determinations or qualities drawn from [his species], his own nature—qualities in which he in truth only images and projects himself" (Feuerbach 1957, 11). In statements of the form "God is X,"

> what the subject is lies only in the predicate. The predicate is the *truth* of the subject—the subject only the personified, existing predicate, the predicate conceived of as existing. Subject and predicate are distinguished only as existence and essence. The negation of the predicates is therefore the negation of the subject
>
> (19, emphasis in original).

As a whole, Feuerbach's *The Essence of Christianity* shows how that which historically has been predicated of and attributed to God derives from the human faculties, characteristics, and qualities of the peoples producing the God or gods in question. The chastity of monks and the object that they deny themselves are projected onto the Virgin Mary; the deified virtues, states of mind, and passions of the Greeks are projected onto the Pantheon; and intellect, will, morality, and judgment become the prominent features of the Protestant Christian God.

Feuerbach finds this structure of inverted predication worrisome when it impoverishes human agency by claiming that internal characteristics of the human species have been externally imposed, a radical act of self-negation. He writes, "To enrich God, man must become poor; that God must be all, man must be nothing" (1957, 26). In religion, "Man ... projects his being into objectivity, and then again makes himself an object to this projected image of himself thus converted into a subject; he thinks of himself as an object to himself, but as the object of an object, of another being than himself" (29–30).

Feuerbach uses "alienation" and "objectification" to describe this projection and conversion. He defines "the element of alienation" precisely as "setting something over and above man that should be man's" (quoted in Gregory 1977, 4).[18] In his appropriation of Hegel's concept of alienation, Feuerbach also claims that Hegel knows no true externalization. In Feuerbach's 1839 critique of Hegel, he writes that in Hegel

> the alienation of the Idea is only a *pretence*, so to speak; it [alienates itself from itself], but not seriously; it is merely playing…. The Idea begets and testifies to itself not in a real other—which could only be the empirical, concrete perception of the understanding—it begets itself out of a formal, apparent contradiction
>
> (quoted in Gregory 1977, 23).

Hegel's concept of spirit's alienation in nature is not an authentic reckoning with a force that may be radically different from spirit and even determine it in some of its essential characteristics. In 1826, Feuerbach took leave of the great thinker with a comment that foreshadows this critique: Feuerbach announced to Hegel the "need to plunge into the direct opposite [of your philosophy]. Now I shall study anatomy" (quoted in Gregory 1977, 15).

Although Marx adopts much of the substance of the Feuerbachian critique unchanged, he will ultimately do this most interestingly on the terrain of the economic rather than the physical sciences, completing the turn Feuerbach foreshadows in his own work, but which, despite his boasting to Hegel, he did not complete. An early step in this appropriation is Marx's application of his distinction between alienation and objectification to Feuerbach's account of religion. In this application, the human objectification in the gods is not alienated, or is no longer alienated, if it knows itself to be such. However, human objectification that fails to recognize itself in the projection is and remains alienated. To use Hegelian language, it remains for-itself without ever becoming in-and-for-itself. Recognition moves the alienated object back to a merely objectified status that is owned by the human being who has projected it as his or her own. It can then be read as a sign that allows the philosophical anthropologist to determine a particular people's historical stage in the progression of humanity. Feuerbach (1957) writes, "That which to a later age or a cultured people is given by nature or reason, is to an earlier age, or to a yet uncultured people, given by God. Every tendency of man, however natural—even the impulse to cleanliness, was conceived by the Israelites as a positive divine ordinance" (31) and "Where man inhabits houses, he also encloses his gods in temples. The temple is only a manifestation of the value which man attaches to beautiful buildings. Temples in honour of religion are in truth temples in honor of architecture" (20).

Marx writes,

> If I *know* religion as *alienated* human self-consciousness, then what I know in it as religion is not my self-consciousness, but my alienated self-consciousness confirmed in it. I therefore know my self-consciousness that belongs to itself, to its very nature, confirmed not in *religion* but rather in *annihilated* and *superseded* religion
>
> (*Economic and Philosophical Manuscripts of 1844*, XXIX; MECW 1975, 3, 339, emphases in original).

As we shall see, Marx ultimately has little interest in the importance of this critique for Christianity. But he has a great deal of interest in the structure of projection and its concomitant inversion of subject and predicate. During these same years, he begins to use this schema to explain not the theological world, but first the political realm, especially as expressed in Hegel's philosophy, and then the capitalist economic realm, especially as expressed in commodities.

III Marx's account of alienation: from early to late

Drawing on these historical sources, Marx's full account of alienation develops over the course of his works, both early and late. His complete account of alienation has at least five overlapping dimensions: theological, political, psychological, economic, and technological. For each dimension, there is a corresponding metaphysical object into which the human essence is alienated. For Marx, these objects are produced by human beings themselves, yet come to dominate humans as alien powers over which they have no control. These objects are God (and related theological fictions), the state, ruling class ideology, and, finally, the commodity and the industrial machine.

Combined, these structures give rise to alienation in its most general sense: through them the alienation of the human being from his or her fellow human beings is accomplished. As a whole, Marx's critical project shows the material, human roots of each of these objects, demystifying its metaphysical status and thereby alleviating its alienating power. But a critical explanation will not be enough to do this in a world constituted by and in alienated forms. Philosophy will also have to come out of its explanatory role and enter the political realm as an agitator: Marx's famed eleventh thesis on Feuerbach is an injunction to change the world rather than merely to continue interpreting it.[19]

Marx thus makes a shift from the world of human ideas to the world of human practice. Although Feuerbach has offered an explanation of the mythical human projection that occurs in religious practice, he has not offered an explanation of the material human projection that occurs in production. Feuerbach's prescription for change is also intellectual: disalienation will be a matter of recognition rather than of reordering the world in a form altered by the substance of the recognition, or of living in such a way as to place the human being at the apex of creation. Marx's project will be to extend Feuerbach's criticism to the terrain of practice and show the alienation that occurs in this terrain, in the act that becomes for Marx more fundamental than either intercourse with the gods or self-consciousness, that is "production."[20]

The sites within production that the alienated human essence occupies in Marx's later texts are the commodity and the industrial machine. I will discuss them in subsequent sections. But first, let us dwell for a moment on God, the state, and ruling class ideology. The politicized structure of human alienation in these characteristic targets of the young Marx's critical eye forms the starting point for his subsequent accounts of alienation. It also explains how the structure of alienation transitions, in Marx, from the theoretical to the practical realm, since in capitalism alienation will characterize productive life as a whole. We will then be in a position to understand Marx's characterization of the theoretical realm as a reflection of a practical realm that, in the bourgeois era, reinforces these alienated norms.

Theological alienation: surpassing the critique of religion

Even Feuerbach took his own work to demonstrate that Christianity had become an historical exercise, and the real interests of the age lay elsewhere. In his 1843 preface to the *Essence of Christianity*, he writes,

> Christianity has in fact long vanished, not only from the reason but from the life of mankind... it is nothing more than an *idée fixe*, in flagrant contradiction with our fire and life assurance companies, our railroads and steam-carriages, our picture and sculpture galleries, our military and industrial schools, our theaters and scientific museums
>
> (1957, xliv).

Marx will take this insight a step further, questioning not only Christianity but also the real interest in criticizing it further. Although for Marx "the criticism of religion is the premise of all criticism," it functions as such only as a preliminary, propaedeutic exercise. Moreover, Marx thinks that "[f]or Germany, the criticism of religion is in the main complete" (*Contribution to the Critique of Hegel's Philosophy of Law*, Introduction; MECW 1975, 3, 175). Stathis Kouvelakis rightly claims that "by the time Marx joined the *Rheinische Zeitung*, he was already convinced that it was necessary to turn from the criticism of religion to political criticism" (2003, 289).

Marx displaces the structures of Feuerbachian objectification and alienation into two other domains: the political and the economic.[21] The first domain will encompass Marx's critique of the Hegelian *Philosophy of Right* (1843) and the *Economic and Philosophical Manuscripts of 1844*; the second, beginning already in the latter text, will encompass the work that occupies him for the rest of his life. Marx gets both his political and his economic critiques off the ground by reference to the pattern of theological alienation.

Let us look at three characteristic examples, two in which Marx uses theological alienation as a model for political alienation, and one in which Marx uses theological alienation as a model for economic alienation. Marx writes, "Sovereignty of the monarch or sovereignty of the people—that is the question...*It is the same with the question: 'Is God sovereign, or man?' One of the two is an untruth, even if an existing untruth*" (MECW 1975, 3, 28, emphasis added).

Here God is like the monarch's sovereignty: it is really the people's sovereignty that is expressed, but related to it in an alien form. Marx's appeal is directly to Rousseau. Or again, with respect to democracy, Marx writes,

> Democracy is the solved *riddle* of all constitutions. Here, not merely *implicitly* and in essence but *existing* in reality, the constitution is constantly brought back to its actual basis, the *actual human being*, the *actual people*, and is established as the peoples' *own work*. The constitution appears as what it is, a free product of man.... Hegel starts from the state and makes man the subjectified state; democracy starts from man and makes the state *objectified* man. **Just as it is not religion which creates man but man who creates religion, so it is not the constitution which creates the people but the people which creates the constitution**
> (MECW 1975, 3, 29, emphasis in original, bold emphasis added).

Here the parallel is between religion and the constitution. Note also how the language of objectification comes to represent the nonalienated democratic relationship between the human being and the state.

Marx soon modulates these realizations about the political realm into insights about the economic realm. In the *Economic and Philosophical Manuscripts of 1844* he writes,

> All these consequences are contained in the definition that the worker is related to the *product of his labor* as to an *alien* object. *For on this premise it is clear that the more the worker spends himself, the more powerful the alien objective world becomes which he creates over-against himself, the poorer he himself—his inner world—becomes, the less belongs to him as his own. **It is the same in religion. The more man puts into God, the less he retains in himself. The worker puts his life into the object, but now his life no longer belongs to him but to the object***
> (MECW 1975, 3, 272–273; Here Tucker 1978, 72; MEGA^2 I, 2, 236, emphasis in original, bold emphasis added).

Marx is using Feuerbach's religious critique and even his language to develop the concepts that will become his critique of commodity fetishism in *Capital* (MECW 1996, 35, 81–94; MEGA^2 II, 9, 61–73, I.I.I.4; MEGA^2 II, 8, 100–111). Twenty years later, Marx will make the same point more succinctly in *Capital*: "As in religion, man is governed by the products of his own brain, so in capitalistic production, he is governed by the products of his own hand" (MECW 1996, 35, 616; MEGA^2 II, 9, 538; I.VII.XXV.1; MEGA^2 II, 8, 584). Alienation is the means through which the worker's activity not only becomes the private property of someone else, but also becomes miserable and stunting labor, and his or her products glorious and actualized. Thus, property, sovereignty, and the state are the practical alienated analogues of God. In each of them, the human being worships his or her own essence, but in an alienated form.

Mystification: political alienation and the state

Hegel praises Rousseau for recognizing the will as the intellectual principle of human association. Then he claims that Rousseau paid too much attention to the will's subjective and affective features and too little to its rational, universal features. This critique is possible only following Kant, who, inspired by Rousseau, divided the will into parts, some of which were closer to reason and some of which were closer to the affective capacities of the human body. The critique allows Hegel to retain the idea of the will, but to blame Rousseau for the form his doctrine assumed in the French Revolution. Hegel writes,

> The definition of right which I have quoted embodies the view, especially popular since Rousseau, according to which the substantial basis and primary factor is supposed to be not the will as rational will which has being in and for itself or the spirit as *true* spirit, but will and spirit as the *particular* individual, as the will of the single person [*des Einzelnen*] in his distinctive arbitrariness. Once this principle is accepted, the rational can of course appear only as a limitation on the freedom in question, and not as an immanent rationality, but only as an external and formal universal. This view is devoid of any speculative thought and is refuted by the philosophic concept, and at the same time has produced phenomena [*Erscheinungen*] in people's minds and in the actual world whose terrifying nature is matched only by the shallowness of the thoughts on which they are based
> (Hegel 1991, 58).[22]

Hegel misreads Rousseau here, because the latter believes he is appealing to the height of the rational principles in the individual contracting wills, and not to their arbitrariness, opinion, and caprice. For Rousseau, this rationality is the expression of survival and liberty, and it indicates the acceptance of the civil institution of equality before the law.

At the very least, Hegel appeals to a rationality of a different sort, namely that which is inculcated by education in the upper echelons of civil society. This is very clear in *The Philosophy of Right*. For Hegel, civil servants are the universal class whose job it is to reconcile individual interests with those of the state. Their educated wills are superior to those of others in recognizing the rational universal: it is they who move in the Idea and the Concept and translate its dictates back down through the social body. Marx's critique of Hegel undermines the authority of this class, and leads us back to Rousseau's notion of rationality rather than Hegel's.

According to Marx, in Hegel's use of "the philosophic concept" that he claims is lacking above, Hegel offers only

> [A] manifest piece of mystification ... the various [state] authorities are therefore not determined by their "own nature," but by a nature alien to them. Likewise the *necessity* is not derived from their own essence, still less critically established. Rather, their fate is predetermined by the "nature of the concept." ... The soul of objects, in

this case the state, is cut and dried, predestined, prior to its body, which is really mere appearance.... "Idea" and "concept" are here hypostasized abstractions

(MECW 1975, 3, 14–15).

In this text of Marx's, the terms "mystification" [*Mystifikation*] and "abstraction" [*Abstraktion*] often come to replace "alienation"; they stand in for "alienation" as theoretical counterparts, confirmations, and extensions of this concept, as they will continue to do throughout Marx's later writings.

Marx believes Hegel generalized the rules of the modern state into eternal truths of right. Thus his critique of Hegel has a larger target than the philosopher himself, for behind Hegel stands modern government, and especially its Prussian, absolutist, and therefore alien form that dictates policy from the top down, or from the state via the upper echelons of civil/bourgeois society. The bourgeois critique of right works to install civil society as a sphere of social power. Bourgeois society demands that political influence should proceed from civil society to the state rather than vice versa. Marx will want to critique this constellation in turn, drawing attention to the increasing powers of civil/bourgeois society as a system not of emancipation, but of domination.[23]

The bourgeois class and the civil society it represented had gained increasing political power even in the gradual transitions of the German world, a phenomenon brought on by the increased importance of industry. In republican government, a split is postulated between civil society and political society. In the abstractions of political society, inequalities of wealth and class are neutralized; in the concretions of civil society, they are maintained, though ostensibly they are without political significance. The retention of this split is why, for Marx, "*Political* emancipation is, of course, a big step forward ... [but] it is not the final form of human emancipation in general [but only] the final form of human emancipation *within* the hitherto existing world order" (MECW 1975, 5, 155). Although initially revolutionary, bourgeois society, especially in its vibrant contradistinction to political society, comes to pose its own dangers.

The chief of these is the appearance of bourgeois civil society not as a social and historical form, but as the natural truth of the human being. Marx writes,

Man as a member of civil society, unpolitical man, inevitably appears, however, as the natural man.... The political revolution resolves civil life into its component parts, without revolutionizing these components themselves or subjecting them to criticism. It regards civil society, the world of needs, labour, private interests, civil law, as the basis of its existence, as a precondition not requiring further substantiation and therefore as its natural basis. Finally, man as a member of civil society is held to be man in the proper sense, *homme* as distinct from *citoyen*, because he is man in his sensuous, immediate, individual existence whereas political man is only abstract, artificial man, man as allegorical, juridical person. The real man is recognized only in the shape of the egoistic individual, the true man is recognized only in the shape of the abstract citizen

(MECW 1975, 3, 167).

This natural appearance of civil society becomes the new "supreme practical expression of human self-alienation," the interests of which contrive against "human emancipation" (MECW 1975, 3, 167). For Marx, human emancipation is stymied by civil society. First, civil society has an unrecognized presupposition for its functioning in a class that produces but creates no property for itself: the proletariat. This class does not participate in civil society as the natural property holder assumed by the naturalized and individualized constructions of the bourgeois philosophers, and this class therefore owns neither the means of economic nor social production. Already in his critique of Hegel's philosophy of the state, Marx has referred to a "lack of property and the estate of direct labour, of concrete labour" that "form not so much an estate of civil society as the ground upon which its circles rest and move" (MECW 1975, 3, 80).

Second, in civil society a contradiction develops between what Marx calls "politics and the power of money in general. Although theoretically the former is superior to the latter, in actual fact politics has become the serf of financial power" (MECW 1975, 3, 171). In general, we may regard this as the historical example of bourgeois legislatures that have gotten the upper hand. In this situation, the political will that is supposed to express the people as a whole again becomes limited to its propertied part. The old political alienation of the absolutist state is transformed into the new economic alienation of the republican state.

Having just mentioned the guillotine, Marx reminds us that "at times of special self-confidence" (MECW 1975, 3, 156) political life revolutionizes the civil society that reformist (but nonrevolutionary) change leaves untouched. When this happens, "political life seeks to repress its prerequisite, civil society and the elements composing this society, and to constitute itself as the real species-life of man devoid of contradictions" (MECW 1975, 3, 156) But this is also a dialectical circle, because

> it can achieve this only by coming into violent contradiction with its own conditions of life, only by declaring the revolution to be permanent, and therefore the political drama necessarily ends with the re-establishment of religion, private, property, and all elements of civil society, just as war ends with peace
>
> (MECW 1975, 3, 156).

Such for Marx is the alienated modern state's insuperable division into the political and the civil: in revolution and restoration, it swings between the two principles in an interminable historical antinomy. Marx will, nonetheless, repeat the revolutionary political gesture as the only possible outcome of the new, economic alienation. This, along with labor as a mode of self-creation, is the residue of the bourgeois mode of valuation in his thought.

Marx's real goal, and here he has moved beyond the Rousseauian framework, is to challenge the dualistic structure of civil and political society as an antinomy. Marx also unmasks the supposed naturalness of the human being that this dualism postulates: a human being who gets his or her worth and his or her rights in the alienated forms of labor, property-formation, and exchange, and who exists as an isolated individual whose interests are to protect these actions. Marx will wish to challenge the concept of human nature that results from capitalist enframing, and the political claims that are made on its basis, including the concept of being determined by labor. At the very least, Marx wants to change the kind of accounts that are given of human nature, and to reveal that the notion of human nature particular to bourgeois life results from the given historical forms of the reigning system of objectification as alienation. Here he moves beyond the bourgeois critique that finds its political ground in labor and its political redemption in revolution. The concern of Marx's later work will be to ground liberation not in labor, but in freedom from labor.

Marx's later economic work treats the bourgeois revolutions by which civil society gets the upper hand as though they were completely accomplished historical facts rather than complex processes society continued to undergo.[24] His justification for this is economic. Because, for Marx, the reigning modes of production had shifted to those of the bourgeoisie, he increasingly interprets political shifts as mere epiphenomena of economic realities.[25] However, this neglects the feudal aristocracy's political influence despite the waning economic powers of the class.

Contemporary historians now speak of "the 'persistence of the old regime' down to the First World War period, which saw the beginnings of its dissolution" (Mayer 1981, in Kouvelakis 2003, 38). The political influence of the *ancien régime* lasted until well after Marx's death in 1883. In other words, it persisted until the moment often regarded by historians as the defeat of Marx's political vision: the demise of the Second International, when workers went to fight against one another in the service of their respective nation states. This would mean that the death blow to the feudal aristocracy was dealt at approximately the same time the worker's movement, at least in the pan-European revolutionary form Marx envisioned, fell apart.

This would explain the tendency in first-generation Marxism, and among workers' movements, to see Marx's work as a defense of labor's priority rather than a critique of labor as alienating. But if Marx were defending the rights and priority of labor, his argument would ultimately differ little from Locke's and Smith's. The historical incompletion of the bourgeois revolutions thus affected how Marx himself was interpreted. His more trenchant insights about labor's historical and alienating specificity are buried by the appeals to the rights of labor that characterize the modern era. Political revolution may be inevitably linked to only one structure in modernity, and that structure is the bourgeois overcoming of feudalism, an overcoming based on labor's entitlements to the fruits of its produce.[26]

Perhaps Marx's appeal to revolution suggests that his political conceptual apparatus remains mired in a structure that other aspects of his analysis have surpassed, that is, the political structure issuing from the overcoming of a feudal order. We will see how this appeal changes form in his later work. Because the older Marx is dealing with a political context where the communist revolutions of the nineteenth century have been defeated, he reconceptualizes the revolution he forecasts. The revolution is not a product of particularized agent-based political action or justice. Instead, it occurs because of the inevitable crisis and collapse of the system of production.

As I shall argue in Chapter 2, Marx's notion of revolution changes in his later work. Revolution occurs not through the willful agency of the proletariat, but through the crisis in the system of the production. I shall argue that this change in conceptualization of the revolution is dependent on the major discourse of decline that dominated late-nineteenth-century scientific thought: it is one of a species of political theory that popularized the thermodynamic notion of entropy.

Psychological alienation: false consciousness and the indictment of German philosophy

Marx's nearly lifelong participation in and agitation for a free press should be viewed against the backdrop of his claim that philosophy should not only explain the world, but also change it. Kant's and Hegel's philosophies, although proto-revolutionary in certain ways, demonstrate an undeniable fear of the uncultivated masses. Hegel's fears are apparent in his critique of Rousseau. Kant writes, "It is certainly agreeable to think up political constitutions which meet the requirements of reason (particularly in matters of right). But it is foolhardy to put them forward seriously, and *punishable* to incite the people to do away with the existing constitution" (from "The Contest of Faculties," quoted in Kouvelakis 2003, 14, emphasis in original). Less ambiguously, Kant writes,

> The only qualification required of a citizen (apart, of course, from being an adult male) is that he must be his *own master* (*sui juris*), and must have some *property* (which can include any skill, trade, fine art, or science) to support himself.... The domestic servant, the shop assistant, the labourer, or even the barber, are merely labourers (*operarii*) not *artists* (*artifices*, in the wider sense) or members of the state, and are thus unqualified to be citizens
> (from "On the Common Saying," quoted in Kouvelakis 2003, 22).

Correspondingly, the form in which Kant and Hegel write philosophy is that of a learned treatise aimed at the learned, upper bourgeoisie. According to Kouvelakis (2003), in this manner Kant and Hegel both demonstrate the upper-class German reception of the French Revolution, a reception that greeted the revolution with excitement and interest, yet limited the expression of this interest to certain safe domains, and never wished to see the liberties attending this revolution extended to the masses of their own country.

Kouvelakis (2003) thinks that fear in Kant and Hegel is not simply due to the pressures from Prussian censors. He writes, "For Hegel, as for Kant, intellectuals are privileged mediators of the universal" (40). We have seen how this affected Hegel's political conception of the relationship between the state and civil society, a relationship which is placed in the hands of intellectual mediators. Even in absolutist Prussia, certain privileges were extended to the intellectual class so long as this class only advocated for reformist rationalism in the proper circles and in the proper format:

> So defined, the maxim of publicity reinforces the terms of compromise between the intelligentsia and the established order by preventively eliminating the temptation to engage in illegal activity; it also forestalls the emergence of an organic bond between intellectuals and subaltern classes. Even if this presents certain disadvantages for the rulers, it remains preferable, from their own standpoint, to accept a public sphere carefully confined to bourgeois strata rather than to eliminate the legal margin for free expression at the risk of seeing it informally or secretly extended to the lower orders, a development that would have the additional consequence of transforming the philosophers who would bear the brunt of repression into subversive propagandists and agitators
>
> (Kouvelakis 2003, 19).

Conversely, Marx uses philosophy, not only in long treatises like *Capital*, but also in his newspaper articles; by the time he has gone into exile in France, he has even become something of a pamphleteer. This reflects a use of philosophy that is different from Kant's and Hegel's. Kouvelakis (2003) reminds us that even prior to Marx's 1843 turn from Rheinish liberalism to French radicalism, he "devoted his theoretical and practical efforts to winning recognition for the idea that a free press is the defining feature of a [nonalienated] civil society" (261). Under the pressures of Prussian censors and the intellectual community as a whole, Marx fought for freedom of the press and the popularization of philosophical truths. In his essay "Freedom of the Press," and other anonymous leading articles written for the *Neue Rheinische Zeitung* prior to its demise in 1843, Marx gives philosophy a new task:

> [A]lthough philosophy "had even *protested against the newspapers* as an unsuitable arena," it had at last been forced "to break its silence," and "become a newspaper correspondent." In this way, it made its way "into salons, priests' studies, editorial offices of newspapers and court antechambers." It is only in this way that "philosophy becomes worldly and the world became philosophical." ... It is no longer one system struggling against others but "philosophy in general in relation to the world." Internally, by its content, philosophy has, of course, always represented "the intellectual quintessence of

its time" but when this internal content meets an external manifestation adequate to it [i.e., the free press], it enters into contact and interaction with "the real world of its day"

(Marx, quoted in Kouvelakis 2003, 259, emphasis in original).

Marx's agitation for the use of philosophy in the free press comes as a triple corrective: first, to the refinement and isolation of philosophical ideas in the ruling classes; second, to the subsequent impoverishments and mystifications of philosophy; finally, to the problem of lower classes confronted by a philosophical expression that does not represent them. This triple corrective brings me to Marx's formulation of the problem of psychological alienation.

The most striking formulation of psychological alienation, or false consciousness, occurs in *German Ideology* (1845). By distinguishing alienation from its Hegelian use in the ideal realm and looking at its expression in the material realm—which for Marx during this period increasingly comes to mean the economic and technical realm of production—Marx is able to trace a relationship between these two realms. Ideas are politicized by their origins in the ruling class. He writes,

> The ideas of the ruling class are in every epoch the ruling ideas, i.e. the class which is the ruling material force of society, is at the same time its ruling intellectual force. The class which has the means of material production at its disposal has control at the same time over the means of mental production, so that thereby, generally speaking, the ideas of those who lack the means of mental production are subject to it
>
> (Part I, *Feuerbach: Opposition of the Materialist and Idealist Outlooks*; B. The Illusion of the Epoch; Section 3, Ruling Class and Ruling Ideas).

In this way, the technical alienation of the workers from the means of production that characterizes the real subsumption of capital inaugurates the alienation of the proletarian class in a much broader sense. Because of its material alienation, the proletariat engages only in those mental productions that are in the service of the status quo.

These mental productions include the ideas the proletariat forms and circulates about itself. Because material and mental means of production are the same, working-class subjectivity is scripted by the conceptualizations of those who do not participate in it, but view it from above.

Alienation is thus broadened: as a worker, I am alienated not only from the product and the means of production, and not only from my life activity into a form of barbarous and detested labor, but also from my own thoughts and self-conception. If I find that my experience does not correspond to stereotypes about my social class, I lack the vocabulary and other forms of social power that might help me to articulate this. Alienation in this sense, although not losing its economic and technical roots, becomes broadly psychological, and the basis for the concept of false-consciousness. The chief ruling ideas of the capitalist age will include the illusion of an individual producer whose subjectivity and sociality are founded in the acts of labor and exchange.

As Marx develops the discourse of alienation into the psychological realm of self-conception, he also expands the sphere of its grip. Alienation moves from simply being a feature that characterizes unequal distribution of the means or products of labor (or from simply being the advance of particularistic over general interests) to being a feature that characterizes social life as a whole, including notions of the human self or person. In this way, Marx's use of the concept of alienation is developed considerably beyond what we find in any previous thinker. We will see this more clearly in Marx's doctrine of the commodity fetish, and in his characterization of labor with machines.

IV   The alienated object of production: commodity fetishism

In the *Economic and Philosophical Manuscripts of 1844*, Marx has already begun to use the concept of a commodity. This use is not yet fully critical in the way it will become in his later works, where it indicates a product peculiar to the capitalist mode of production. In this early text, Marx writes of workers:

> On the basis of political economy itself, in its own words, we have shown that the worker sinks to the level of a commodity and becomes indeed the most wretched of commodities; that the wretchedness of the worker is in inverse proportion to the power and magnitude of his production; that the necessary form of competition is the accumulation of capital in a few hands, and thus the restoration of monopoly in a more terrible form; and that finally...the whole of society must fall apart into two classes—the *property owners* and the *propertyless workers*
>
> (MECW 1975, 3, 270, emphasis in original).

The worker not only moves in a material world increasingly made up of commodities, the worker *is* a commodity himself or herself. This occurs because he or she owns nothing but labor to sell, and thus can be bought. Here the problem of economic alienation is still posed in terms of class struggle—a problem that can be solved by the distribution and redistribution of the tools and spoils of production.

But this is not the final form of the problem in Marx. Instead, his mature reflections on the problem of economic alienation have a much broader target: the system of labor as a totality and its valorization of production and productivity, what I will call its "productivist metaphysic." Marx's later work remains concerned with capitalism's inequalities of distribution and divisions into classes delineated by their relationship to the means of production. And to the end of his life, Marx is convinced that class-based revolution is imminent. But Marx also becomes more concerned about capital's operation as a totalizing social program, with a system of ideological rules that alienates all forms of human objectification from the moment of their very conception as labor. Capitalist making is echoed and subtended in capitalist thinking.

In his development of commodity fetishism, Marx wants to show something that cannot be seen as long as one stays within the norms of bourgeois society, and one risks staying within these norms when continuing to use a precritical concept of alienation. As David Rasmussen (1975) puts it,

> In its classical modern context alienation applies to an act of exchange.... Behind this basic act of mutual appropriation lies the idealistic subject of modern society.... Marx, regarding this theory of exchange, never tired of pointing out that as long as one restricted one's attention to this act of exchange between individual subjects, it would appear to demonstrate the basic value structure of modern society, namely freedom, equality, and right of association.... "Alienation" could descriptively characterize the experience of individuals within a society; it could not characterize the experience of the society as a totality. The theoretical point of departure for Marx is commodity fetishism.... Through the exploration of the commodity, the relations of a society as a totality are made apparent (54).

For Marx, it is not simply that there is something wrong with freedom, equality, or the right of association: these are themselves "a big step forward" from the absolutist and feudal constructs they replace. But these dogmas of modern revolutions are products of bourgeois labor. They derive political sovereignty and personal autonomy from labor and therefore cannot represent "the final form of human emancipation." Instead, the emancipatory discourse of one historical era becomes the historical fetter of its successor. Bourgeois societies are subject to certain illusions that differ from those of their feudal predecessors and are potentially more damaging, because relations of domination are not expressed directly but masked under neutral forms of economic life as natural laws.[27]

Chief among the illusions of bourgeois society is the "idealistic subject" Rasmussen refers to above and its characteristic idealistic acts of labor and exchange. The subject's properties are then taken as those that naturally and ahistorically belong to human beings. They include the property of a radical and, from Marx's perspective, false individuality. This individuality founds the subject in the social and political acts of laboring and exchanging this labor in the market. As we have seen in the account of Locke, the very naturalness of this subject was carefully scripted by bourgeois philosophers, crafted to challenge the "artificial" feudal society that rejected the idea that labor established a property, because property was handed down through blood and birth. But regarding this laboring subject as natural precludes the move Marx wants to make of seeing this subject itself as scripted and of grasping the rules and values of the society that produced it.

Marx wants to denature the bourgeois object (or commodity [*die Ware*]) along with the bourgeois subject. Marx inherits the concept of a commodity from Smith and Ricardo. They use the term "commodity" to encompass all material wealth, and thus do not recognize its limitation as the particular form of wealth in a capitalist society. Marx calls this usage of "commodity" a "fetish" that elevates a particularized form of material wealth tied to the capitalist mode of production to a natural and transhistorical status.

As Terrell Carver (1975) explains, the concept of fetishism entered European intellectual life with the anonymous publication of Charles de Brosses's *Le Culte des dieux fetishes* (1785) in Paris, which Marx read in German translation in 1842 (50). Carver continues, "Marx used the word 'fetish' in this eighteenth and nineteenth century sense ... [as a]n inanimate object worshipped by savages on account of its supposed inherent magical powers, or as being animated by a spirit" (51). Marx means to claim that in capitalism, commodities are worshipped as the eternal form of human wealth when in fact they represent only its capitalistic instantiation. The real demystification of the commodity, therefore, is not simply to link it to the bourgeois laboring subject that produced it, but to link both constructs to a historical and alienated form of production.[28]

The commodity is the first of the categories Marx unfolds in *Capital* using the model of Hegel's logic, or the category from which all subsequent categories will be generated.[29] Marx's first move in defining the commodity is to return to Aristotle's distinction between use-value and exchange-value. Use-value is the enjoyment of a thing that we use, a concept I will also refer to as "material wealth." Exchange-value is an abstract calculation of what can be returned for a thing when we exchange it for other goods, a concept Marx also refers to as "bourgeois value."

Marx builds a second distinction on this distinction: Labor differs depending upon whether it produces use-value (and thus material wealth) or exchange-value (and profit). The first sort of labor is concrete, qualitative labor; the second is the quantitatively measurable labor Marx will refer to as "abstract labor."[30] In a letter to Engels in August 1867, Marx writes that "what is best about my book is 1. (*all* understanding of the facts depends on this) *the double character of labour*, depending on whether it expresses itself in use-value or exchange-value" (quoted in Postone 1993, 55, emphasis in original). The latter is alienated, whereas the former is merely objectified. Marx then defines "labor" as tending toward the latter in the capitalist mode of production. Abstract labor is not merely an *abstraction* in this mode. Because of the advancing division of labor that characterizes real subsumption, the worker's labor is partial and does not produce a complete use-value.[31]

This means that Marx's critique of distribution—and especially of the distribution of the means of production—forms a feedback loop with the mode of production as a whole. In the section in *Capital* on commodity fetishism, Marx makes it clear that the social tyranny of exchange-value is so comprehensive that it determines how things are made and even what is made. Thus, use-value and material wealth tend to operate as asymptotic structures of constantly diminishing social importance for the mode of production.

Capitalism does not care if it produces quantities for use; it cares about producing profit. Marx writes,

> this division of a product into a useful thing and [an exchange-]value becomes practically important, only when exchange has acquired such an extension that useful articles are produced for the purpose

of being exchanged, and their character as [exchange] values has therefore to be taken into account beforehand, during production

(I.I.I.4;1867, 78).

This means that the very form of what we are allowed to use must have been profitable, that nonprofitable human objectification never appears, and that use-value and material wealth are progressively eliminated.

We must rely on our ability to glimpse use-values and material wealth in imaginations increasingly closed down and bracketed by a world created for profit. In remaking nature, the human being remakes his or her essence. In remaking nature exclusively for profit, the human being determines this essence as alienated: just as the possibility for material wealth depends on the profitability of the things produced, human activity is valued in terms of this same profitability.[32]

Overall, capitalist society fails to recognize the value of human activity in the products or results of labor, commodities that it fetishizes in order to celebrate abstract labor while degrading concrete labor. For Marx, the animating spirit of the commodity is the concrete labor that went into its production. But this labor comes to be recognized in its abstract form for the first time in the exchange and fungibility of commodities, which are thereby separated from the qualitatively differentiated concrete labor that produced them. This is why commodity fetishism is convincing: in commodity exchange—and later, in the commodity production of an advanced division of labor—concrete labor is socially actualized for the first time, and actualized only as abstract.

Marx calls the discovery of the labor theory of commodity value, which he draws from Smith and Ricardo, a scientific discovery. The discovery operates in the same way that the chemical decomposition of the atmosphere's component gases demonstrates something about the atmosphere, but something of which the breather is unaware (I.I.I.4; 79). The concrete labor in the commodity, like the percentage of nitrogen in the air, can be rationally but not really distinguished. The concrete labor without which commodities would be impossible is invisible to the capitalist society, which operates not scientifically but perceptually. For this society, magical properties inhere in commodities along with abstract labor, and the society thus projects the powers of the creator onto the created. The commodity, as the first expression of abstract labor, conditions the world of exchange-value to which concrete labor is made subject. In his most succinct definition of the commodity fetish, Marx writes, "the mutual relations of the producers … take the form of a social relation between the products. A commodity is therefore a mysterious thing, simply because in it the social character of men's labour appears to them as an objective character stamped upon that labour" (I.I.I.4; 1867, 77).

Marx's concern is not to return us to the labor theory of value characteristic of the political economists.[33] Instead, he wants to focus on the social alienation that produces the illusion of the commodity fetish, the program of abstract labor, and the tyranny of exchange-value. This is a much broader critical attitude. The commodity fetish is not simply debunked by the discovery that commodities are made of labor. If it were, it could be debunked by a sober reading of Ricardo and Smith, each of whom espouses a labor theory of value. Marx criticizes these thinkers and their constructions: "they lay all their emphasis on the aspect—*exchange-value*—and the *modernity* of their point of view consists in this" (*Economic Manuscripts of 1861–3*; MECW 1988, 30, 272, emphasis in original).

Both the political and the religious structures of "alienation" recur in Marx's economic use of "fetishism."[34] Fetishism is a kind of idolatry of the human essence, implanted by human objectification. In alienated capitalist production, this objectification is misunderstood. Human essence is seen as a property belonging to the commodity rather than to its creator. Despite his explicit wish to move on from the religious illusion to the economic illusion, we find that Marx's concept of the commodity fetish has clear religious overtones, those of a kind of natural, animistic religion as well as those peculiar to Christianity. Marx has powerfully likened the economic discourse of his day to that of a totalizing ideological religious program.[35]

Marx's development of the concept of alienation in his criticism of the commodity fetish actually allows him to develop the critique of religion far beyond the expressions of this critique in Feuerbach. Christianity, and Protestant Christianity in particular, comes to represent the most fitting form of religion not for maintaining the theological illusion, nor for maintaining the illusion of political absolutism, but for maintaining the capitalist illusion that takes the isolated human being, with a personhood founded on labor and exchange, as its starting point. Marx writes,

> [F]or a society based on the production of commodities, in which the producers enter into social relations with one another by treating their products as commodities and [exchange] values, whereby they reduce their individual private labor to the standard of homogenous human labour—for such a society, Christianity with its *cultus*

of abstract man, more especially in its bourgeois developments, Protestantism, Deism, &c is the most fitting form of religion

(I.I.I.4; 1867, 83).

In this account, religion changes form according to the more fundamental schema of the productivist metaphysic. The religious illusions support a different ideology: no longer one that subordinates the human being to God, but one that subordinates him or her to nature, to work, and to instrumental rationality.[36]

We have seen how the alienated object of production points, in its very definition, outside itself to an alienated process of production. The bifurcation of the commodity into use-value and exchange-value points to the bifurcation of labor into concrete and abstract. So too, the bifurcation between material wealth and bourgeois value, or profit, becomes exacerbated in capitalist production. This leads to bizarre phenomena in which material wealth can be destroyed in cases where there is a danger of bourgeois value being compromised.

Nowhere is this more evident than in the capitalist treatment of science and technology. Industrial machines have the potential to produce greater material wealth while limiting labor time. But machines, and technology more generally, are nonoptimally employed in the totalizing mode that values profit, or exchange-value, and not material wealth. This causes machines to become the means for extorting profit. They are therefore fetishized subjects in which the social relations of production come to be recognized in a material object. Machines are also marked in their very materiality by the political conditions of the mode of production that produces them.[37] Thus, machine fetishism relates not to the inert goods of consumption but to the lively means of production. This liveliness comes from past generations of accumulated living human labor and current objectifications of the state of human knowledge as a whole; that is, it comes from history and from science.

V   The alienated means of production: machine fetishism[38]

Under capitalism, alienation is not merely a feature of the distribution of social wealth. Alienation determines production, that is, the form taken by human activity under capitalism as labor. Because of this, alienation cannot be remedied and redeemed simply by a redistribution of commodities mathematically proportional to the labor invested in production. Although such redistribution might redress deep material inequalities of a capitalist society, it would not redress the basis of a society that makes alienating labor the foundation of all entitlement, both physical and political. In such an equation, it is still work that entitles one to sustenance and to political status. But workers are involved for basic entitlements in a mode of human activity that cripples and stunts human development. If one is authorized to work more in order to earn more, this does not fix the problem of the impoverished form taken by human activity.

Communist transformation and restoration of human activity therefore implies not simply the rectification of inequalities of distribution, but a fundamental change in the mode of production. Alienation is not simply an indictment of a society that does not return to the worker a just equivalent for the labor he or she has performed, though certainly capitalism is marked by this sort of injustice.[39] Alienation is the indictment of a society that mandates a crippled and stunted notion of human activity for the vast majority: for anyone who labors in order to live, for anyone whose labor is only instrumental, and, moreover, instrumental for so mean a definition of human sustenance.

In capitalism, workers neither own nor understand the means of production, or the tools and instruments with which they work. Increasingly in the capitalist era, sophisticated and complicated machines are introduced. These absorb the worker's functionality and, Marx will claim, deprive the human activity of production in labor of all interest. This leads to what I will call the theme of "technological alienation" in Marx's work. Technological alienation is a situation in which the practical life activity of the vast majority of human beings is undertaken as labor on machines that they neither own nor understand. Such labor is characterized by the reduction of the worker to an extremely partial use of his or her faculties. In addition, it is characterized by the repetition of a single function for long periods.

In technological alienation, human beings are not only dominated by the commodities they produce; the very tools with which human beings labor dominate them. The means (or instruments) of production [*Produktionsmittel*] is a broad category in Marx that includes the tools, land, and raw material that are owned, by convention, as private property in the alienated mode of production known as capital. Marx writes, "Instruments of production properly so called, such as tools, machinery, buildings, serve again and again for longer or shorter periods during repeated processes of production" (1865, *Wages, Price, and Profit*, Chapter 2).[40] But I wish to focus on how the tools specifically, which in the nineteenth century included the widespread introduction of machines into industrial production, come to dominate their human creators and operators. The private property of the capitalist class that Marx has underscored in his account of economic alienation reappears, this time not as articles of consumption nor private property in land, though these certainly continue to exercise domination, but as the mechanical means of production of industry and culture themselves.

In this mode of production, these means (i.e. machines) extort exchange-value on an ever-increasing scale through labor's intensification (see Chapters 3, 4, and 5). More importantly, from Marx's perspective, machines deprive work of interest and character and therefore stunt human development when the bulk of practical life activity is labor undertaken with machines. As they are progressively introduced to all aspects of productive labor, machines increase the scope of technological alienation. As different fields of production are automated, and as those previously automated come to be more intensively automated, workers are reduced to more and more partial operations. Technological alienation comes to be an increasingly dominant description of capitalist society as a whole.

Machine fetishism is a product of technological alienation. Not only do workers use means of production that seem to operate by mystical and occult properties incomprehensible to the workers themselves, these machines increasingly display the very functions of which the worker is progressively deprived: mobility, diversification of task, and skill. The alienation expressed by commodity fetishism in the sphere of exchange is expressed by machine fetishism in the sphere of production. In both cases, the occult qualities ascribed to objects result not from the objects themselves, especially considered from the perspective of their use-values, but from the specific illusion that results when their exchange-values determine the use-values and the form and amounts in which they are produced. As we shall see, the capitalist's sacrifice of machinery's potential production of material wealth to its production of profit means that machines are not optimized in the ways they could be and, moreover, that the only machines developed are those that maximize profit in some way.

In the Marxist corpus, the theme of technological alienation is developed in the 1850s and appears in the *Grundrisse* before appearing in more polished form in *Capital*. The machine is the final "metaphysical object" of the Marxist account of alienation, occupying the same structural position as God in Feuerbach or the absolutist state in Rousseau. Relationships with machines and other means of production in capitalism are correspondingly mythologized, and in no less baroque a fashion than God and the state.

This is why, beginning in the seventeenth century, and especially with Hobbes, we have seen a certain conjunction, in political rhetoric, of the themes of machinery and domination. The state is referred to as a machine, its operations as mechanical. By the nineteenth century, machines—and, in more general sense, science and technology—have become categories of pronounced and increasing importance for philosophers and political and social theorists.[41] In Chapter 2, I will discuss the widespread effects of the introduction of machines on the notions of human labor, human embodiment, and human participation in nature, and also on descriptions of human political configurations.

As we will see, the theme of technology is of increasing importance in the content of Marx's texts subsequent to the 1840s, and during these years Marx's account of machines undergoes substantial additions and conceptual modifications. In *The German Ideology*, machines, like money, are seen as destructive forces under what Marx calls "existing relationships," a concept that will be replaced in *Capital* by that of the "mode of production."[42] In the *Communist Manifesto* (1848), machines—and, especially, the comparisons of workers to machines—are the subject of scattered hostile remarks. Marx's main concern is to combat the triumphant pronouncements of the utopian socialists that machines herald the end of labor, and to warn about the acculturation of workers to act as mere machines, an acculturation that occurs as work with machines turns workers into machines themselves (MECW 1976, 6, 501; MEW 1959, 4, 477). He will develop this insight in subsequent years with his theories of the division of labor and the habituation of workers to industrial life, but in the *Communist Manifesto* Marx presents only the negative aspects of machine labor without making it clear how machine production of material wealth could also be a positive good in a different mode of production. The manuscripts written in the early 1850s (known as the *Grundrisse*) treat machines at greater length, but they are not yet organized under a single heading or presented systematically. Machines become a developed topic only in the *Economic Manuscripts of 1861–63*. Following this, a full chapter in Volume I of the 1867 edition of *Capital* is devoted to the analysis of machines as such.

Let me emphasize that machines come into focus as an object of analysis for Marx himself during the years in which he turns to studying political economy. Even in the short ten years that separate the *Grundrisse* from the first edition of *Capital*, machines change from a secondary theme that runs alongside other, more pivotal terms to a primary one. Marx's theory enlarges its frameworks to encompass an account of machinery that plays a major part. This lineage, apparent from the study of the *Communist Manifesto*, the *Grundrisse*, and *Capital*, in conjunction with Marx's manuscripts from these years, shows how, for Marx, technology figures in economic—and therefore political—life.[43] As Marx develops these theses on the social productivity of science, the connections between economic and political alienation also become explicit.

But Marx's studies of technology also have a more subtle effect on the key terms of his analysis. Marx's notions of "labor," "nature," and "revolution" also undergo crucial modifications and development following his researches on technology and machines. Marx's contact with the ideas of the second generation of German scientific materialists (see Chapter 2) causes him to superimpose a thermodynamic model of labor on the ontological model of labor he inherits from Hegel. In this thermodynamic model, humans are set into continuity with machines and nature rather than set in opposition to them. Unlike the ontological notion of labor—an objectifying, self-creating expression of the human being and progressive spiritualization of the natural world—the thermodynamic model of labor emphasizes human force as one species of natural force. Instead of human beings working on the world, nature works on itself. In his later work, Marx's simultaneous use of the older ontological and newer thermodynamic notions of labor led to confusions about the role labor plays in his account. In truth, all the commentators are right, because labor plays at least a double and opposing role: it is both that which distinguishes the human being as human, and that which eliminates the specific difference of the human being from the rest of nature.

Moreover, Marx's turn to the themes of science and technology in his later work reflect some fundamental transitions in the nineteenth-century notion of labor, transitions that are not limited to what is going on in Marx's texts. Conceptually, labor is transformed from the act of self-creation into an alienated activity that is to be at all costs minimized in favor of free time. The individual develops not in doing labor, as with Locke, but in liberation from it. Social and political status begins to be derived not from work, but from leisure—a fundamental reversal of the bourgeois mode of valuation.

Marx's development of the meaning of the social productivity of science and technology is underscored by his understanding of alienation and objectification and his diagnosis that although machines originated and played a role in alienated production, they could and would also play a role in simply objectified production. This causes him to stress different things in his account of machines, depending upon whether he is addressing the context of alienation or that of objectification. In the latter context, Marx becomes increasingly sympathetic to the socialist utopian scenario in which machines perform arduous labor instead of human beings. Unlike the socialist utopians, he is concerned about grounding this possibility with more than fantastic scenarios.

In my description of Marx's account of the social role of science and technology in Chapters 2 through 5, I follow Moishe Postone's stress on the continued importance of the theme of alienation to the later Marx. Postone writes that in Marx's later texts, "the developed theory of alienation implies that Marx saw the negation of the structural core of capitalism as allowing for the appropriation by people of the powers and knowledge that had been historically constituted in alienated form" (1993, 31). That is, the revolutionary reappropriation will involve the recognition and seizure of powers that belonged to the metaphysical abstractions during the period of capitalist accumulation, including, perhaps especially, the knowledge of science and technology. Through this transition, alienation becomes simple objectification, which, as we have seen, is an analogous structure that is not normatively negative so long as it operates within proper limits. In Marx, these limits are still those of Aristotle: the injunction to respect the priority of human enjoyment over profitability, and a warning against a productivist metaphysic in which exchange-value has definitively gained the upper hand.

2
Machines and the Transformation of Work

After 1848, Marx's work begins to be influenced by political economy's treatment of machines and by the related energeticist concepts of the nascent science of thermodynamics. These influences shape and transform some of Marx's basic premises about the interaction between human beings and the natural world. This transformation changes the meaning of two basic concepts of Marx's later political philosophy: the concept of labor, or work, and the concept of revolution. In this later political philosophy, Marx's key concepts are themselves undergoing a revision of sense.

In this chapter, I investigate the shifts of thermodynamic thinking, its source in scientific materialism, Marx's contact with this source, and the implications for Marx's later political philosophy. I conclude that Marx's later work does not fully or uncritically integrate the new scientific paradigm. Instead, Marx's work deploys both the older and the newer models of labor, and the older and the newer models of revolutionary political action. These tensions are often behind the disputes and inconsistencies frequently attributed to Marx's later work.

The science of thermodynamics precipitates a series of shifts that change how the activity of labor on the part of the worker is conceptualized, and thus change what "doing labor" means. Labor changes from a creative endeavor wrought by human spirit on inanimate nature, as conceived in Aristotle, Hegel, Smith, and Locke, into a mere conversion of energy in which nature goes to work on itself. Labor is no longer a spiritual, form-giving activity that infuses matter; it is merely a part of the transformations of a *natura naturans*. In a related change in thermodynamically influenced physiology, the notion of a vital force or animating spirit is progressively eliminated from explanations of human activity.

Prior to thermodynamics, labor was the sort of activity that emblematized and distinguished the human being, conferred his[1] position at the apex of the natural world, and brought with it political status. After thermodynamics, human labor is commensurable with other transformations wrought by the natural environment. Transformations brought about by machines, animals, or the power of wind and water can substitute for human labor. Labor now confers no particular dignity, political or otherwise, on the agent who undertakes it.

Thermodynamic science brings about what I will call the "energeticist model" of the interaction between humans and nature. In this model, human and natural forces are not distinct in kind. The human is not a spiritual or vital force at work in the natural, material world, transforming the latter in a form-giving way. Instead, concepts like "spiritual" and "vital" are progressively eliminated from scientific usage. Matter and form come to be seen as two expressions of a single kind of force: energy. Humans, nature, and machines all operate according to a single model—the model of energetic flow. Energy can be converted from a static material, to heat, to a mechanical activity, and back again. Such conversions subtend phenomena that were formerly portrayed as diverse and as operating according to different rules. In the energeticist model, the work of the steam engine, human labor, human intellection, natural events, animal actions, and even human political life are all portrayed in the same way, and they follow the same basic rule: the rule of energy transforming itself.

These conceptual changes in the meaning of labor may well derive from a material phenomenon. For the average worker in the nineteenth-century capitalist system, especially when this worker is compared with his or her agricultural and manufacturing forerunners, labor has a different meaning and plays a different role in lived experience. Labor is demoted in its conceptual importance for the crafting of human subjectivity in part because the work experience is radically transformed by the widespread introduction of machines in production. Whereas Locke was referring to a primarily agricultural labor schematized according to the construct of an individual human being wielding a tool, Marx must reckon with a primarily industrial labor that has all but eliminated this schema.

For this reason, in capitalism, abstract intellection becomes increasingly promoted as the sphere of the properly human. This is especially true of the intellectual operations of designing and maintaining machines: the scientific intellect of manipulating nature through design. The division of the labor of the body from the labor of the mind becomes evermore intensified in the capitalist era, even if both can be quantified energetically.[2] Concurrently, one's relationship to science and technology becomes evermore symbolic of one's relationship to power.

Marx's late texts and the commentaries and debates about them are marked by the fact that he runs the older and the newer meanings of labor—labor as ontological objectification of the human species and labor as energeticist transformation—alongside one another without always distinguishing between them. When he does draw a distinction, it is usually a moralizing one, in which the older, creative notion of labor is deployed as a criticism of the second, degraded, alienated notion. This locates Marx with the romantic, humanist resistance to the flattening of human beings, their instruments, their products, and nature itself onto an equitable ontological plane. Marx appeals to "human labor"; he appeals to "living labor"; he appeals to "labor in the form that stamps it as exclusively human" (*Capital* I.III.VII.1; 1867, 173). These appeals would make no sense had Marx not retained the older notion of a spiritual force that marks and distinguishes human products with the peculiar mark of the human essence. Even for the late Marx of *Capital*, this spiritual force is the faculty of the imagination. Marx thus repeats the *locus classicus* of the human essence common to nearly all of German idealism.

At the same time, Marx undermines the traditional source of such appeals to human spirit by adopting an energetic conception of the human body from the second generation of scientific materialists. In this adoption, human force is regarded as an indifferent species of natural force. Marx begins to speak of the economics of the human body as an energy system and the analytics of the human body as divisible into categories such as labor-power or labor-capacity. Consider this passage from the *Grundrisse*: "In the human body, as with capital, the different elements are not exchanged at the same rate of reproduction, blood renews itself more rapidly than muscle, muscle than bone, which in this respect may be regarded as the fixed capital of the human body" (1973, 670; MECW 1987, 29, 51; MEGA[2] II, 2, 1.2, 544–545). Here Marx conceptualizes the human body as a kind of thermodynamic machine, with both the loss and the renewal of energy resources.

In the passage, Marx echoes scientific materialist Ludwig Büchner's notion of a body based on energetic exchange with its environment. In his best-selling *Stoff und Kraft* (originally 1855; English translation 1920), composed two years prior to Marx's *Grundrisse*, Büchner has written,

> With each breath that passes from our lips we exhale part of the food we eat and of the water we drink. The[se] change so quickly that we may well say that in a space of from four to six weeks we are materially quite different and new beings—with the exception of the skeletal organs of the body, which are firmer and therefore less liable to change. (16)

Deriving his metaphors from Büchner, Marx moves beyond these metaphors in order to conceive the human body in the economic terms characteristic of industrial production. Bones are not simply firmer; they are analogous to the enduring factory capital that lasts through multiple production cycles. Like the machines of a factory, bones are the more durable parts of bodily life. Their production and maintenance requires a greater investment of energy than that required by other parts. The body is a mechanized system of production whose parts are replaced at differential rates, a system in full exchange with a natural environment from which it does not qualitatively differ. Thinking about the body in this way is not only uncommon prior to capitalism, it is not possible.

Over the course of his own development, Marx thus moves from what Agnes Heller (1981) calls a "paradigm of work" to what she calls a "paradigm of production" as the foundational scenario in which material wealth is made. In work, wealth is made according to the old model, in which matter is infused with form, usually by a single human craftsman. In production, wealth is made when machines reiterate an already well-established pattern, transforming heat into mechanical energy, replacing on a mass scale the prior human performance of the same actions. In the paradigm of production, the body is reconceived as a productive machine, and, as such, a unit whose contribution to the production process comes in the form of measurable work. If such a portrayal of the human body remains harmless to Marx, this is because his adoption of thermodynamic science did not include a full adoption of the thermodynamic metaphysical leveling between human and machine. For Marx, recognizing some common ground between human and machine does not entail a full assimilation of one to the other.

Ideally, for Marx, the paradigm of production will diminish the need for human energetic labor to an absolute minimum. Humans can merely attend their machines or even step aside entirely while the production process goes on, engaging their faculties in other ways and in other settings. Thus, Marx increasingly portrays human freedom as occurring in spare or leisure time rather than within the labor process itself.

As Postone (1993) argues, this causes Marx to turn away from the bourgeois theme of emancipation *through* labor and toward the theme of emancipation *from* labor.

In his later texts, Marx is increasingly hopeful about the elimination of arduous human labor in favor of the production of material wealth primarily, if not exclusively, by machines. But this hope rests uneasily with his earlier discussion of labor as an ontological principle by which the human being defines himself or herself and spiritualizes nature. For Marx, human objectification is not an historical but an ontological category, although it is described in historically determinate forms under the labels of "labor" and "alienation." But for us, this category *is* a historical mark of the nineteenth-century way of conceptualizing the human being prior to the transformations of thermodynamics, a category derived from the Hegelian schema of the interface between Spirit and Nature. In this humanism, objectification is the foundational moment of human subjectivity, and human beings are set over against nature rather than viewed in continuity with it.[3]

We see this older Hegelian structure retained in the *Grundrisse*, even as the text develops a new vocabulary and means of conceptualizing human beings, labor, and nature. In the passage from the *Grundrisse* considered above, Marx described the machine-like qualities of human bodily renewal, whereas in the following passage he asserts a dualism between the human and the natural in order to describe the wondrous production of machinery as a progressive conquering of Nature by Spirit. He writes,

> Nature builds no machines, no locomotives, railways, electric tele-graphs, self-acting mules etc. These are products of human industry; natural material transformed into organs of the human will over nature, or of human participation in nature. They are *organs of the human brain, created by the human hand*; the power of knowledge, objectified.
>
> (1973, 706; MECW 1987, 29, 92; MEGA^2 II, 1.2, 582,
> emphasis in original)

In this older schema, the spiritualization of nature that occurs when humans objectify their intellects in order to build machines is a necessary moment in the process of human self-making as a species. Marx's critique of political economy never questions the continued development of such productive objectification as the foundational moment of the human species' essence. In these passages, Marx never leaves behind the Hegelian thesis of the progressive spiritualization and rationalization of the natural. Human and nature are different kinds of force rather than articulations of a single fabric of interchangeable energy.

Labor is not the only thing that must be rethought after Marx's contact with thermodynamics. Political revolution, which in Locke is based on labor's protection of the items it has marked with its spirit, must also be rethought. Even as Marx continues to portray revolution as a problem of political will, he also begins to give a structural and systemic account of revolution. If human agency is nothing more than a manifestation of an energetic field, then political happenings must be explained as resulting from imbalances in this field. The modern political discourse of revolution undergoes a crucial modification, making a transition into a theory of crisis. Revolution must be explained in thermodynamic terms rather than political ones: as a restoration of balance necessitated by systemic considerations, rather than as actions resulting from freedom, will, and the self-determination of a laboring subject. Moreover, revolution does not represent an absolute rupture with the past, but is the truth of an already-existing system expressing itself politically.

Such a happening requires little political action or conscious social reorganization, the cornerstones of earlier revolutionary models. Capitalism is not a king or a queen who can be beheaded, nor a rump parliament that can be taunted into withdrawing. Capitalism is a steam engine with a design flaw, a design flaw that will precipitate an explosion, no matter what anyone does or thinks.

I Marx's energeticist turn

While defining communism's specificity as a political strategy in the 1840s, Marx investigated existing European socialisms, Pierre-Joseph Proudhon's among them.[4] It is Proudhon who supplies the impetus for Marx's turn to the study of machines and, more broadly, to science and technology as a terrain in which political and economic questions were increasingly salient.

In 1845, Marx published his *Theses on Feuerbach* and was in the process of writing his critique of German philosophy, *The German Ideology*.[5] In this spate of texts from the 1840s, Marx criticizes Hegel's followers for their abstraction and thus inattentiveness to the real conditions by which human nature is historically produced. Marx gives an epistemological formulation of this critique in *Poverty of Philosophy* (1846), a commentary on Proudhon's adoption of a Hegelian style and language.

This commentary takes the form of a distinction between abstraction and analysis. Abstraction will be the old form of philosophy that Marx wants to overcome in favor of analysis. Marx (1963) writes,

> Is it surprising that everything, in the final abstraction—for here we have an abstraction, and not an analysis—presents itself as a logical category? If we abstract thus from every subject all the alleged accidents, animate or inanimate, men or things, we are right in saying that the only substance left is the logical categories. (105–106)

Marx's hyperbolic self-conception as a materialist during this period is evident from this negative characterization of what the work of philosophy ought not to do.

He will qualify this in later years when he accepts abstraction as inherent to human thought, returns to the method of Hegel's *Logic* as a tool for analyzing capitalism, castigates the scientific materialists for their oversimplifications, and repudiates empirical fact gathering that is not subject to intellectual synthesis. For Marx during these later years, materialism does not retain its classical sense as a metaphysical theory of the composition of the world. According to Marx's own criteria, this would be abstraction, and not analysis. Instead Marx turns to investigating the historical accidents by which the world and nature are built up and transformed through labor. Labor, not atoms, is the material through which the material world is made. Gaston Bachelard describes the resultant philosophy of scientific materialism as "a 'dematerialized materialism': a materialism embodied in the primacy of energy" (quoted in Rabinbach 1990, 48).

In an 1846 letter written just after his completion of *The Poverty of Philosophy*, Marx writes,

> The second evolution is *machinery*. To Mr. Proudhon, the connection between the division of labor and machines is entirely mystical. Each kind of the division of labor had its specific instruments of production. For example, from the middle of the seventeenth to the middle of the eighteenth century, men did not do everything by hand. They possessed instruments, and very complicated instruments, such as looms, ships, levers, etc., etc.
>
> Thus, nothing is more ridiculous than to derive machines from the division of labor in general.
>
> I say to you again in passing that as Mr. Proudhon has not understood the historic origin of machinery, he has still less understood its

development. You can say that up to the year 1825—the period of the first general crisis—the general demands of consumption increased more rapidly than production, and the development of machinery was the necessary consequence of the needs of the market. Since 1825, the invention and application of machinery have been merely the result of the war between employers and workers. And this is only true of England. As for the European nations, they were compelled to adopt machines because of the English competition, both in their home markets and on the world market. Finally, in North America, the introduction of machinery was brought about both by the competition of other countries and by the scarcity of hands, that is to say, by the disproportion between the population and the industrial needs of North America. From these facts, you can conclude with what sagacity Mr. Proudhon develops in conjuring up competition as the third evolution, as the antithesis of machinery.

Finally, in general, it is a real absurdity to make machinery an economic category alongside the division of labor, competition, credit, etc.

Machinery is no more an economic category than the ox that pulls the plow. The actual application of machines is one of the relationships of our current economic regime, but the mode of utilizing the machines is altogether distinct from the machines themselves. Powder remains the same, whether you use it for wounding a man or to dress his wounds.

(28 December 1846; 1979, 48)

In this early characterization of a theme that will become much more pronounced in Marx's later work, machinery comes into being not simply as a product of the division of labor or the related expansion of human knowledge and material wealth but historically, under the influence of market forces. Moreover, it operates in different ways at different stages of capitalist production. There is one overarching characteristic: in the capitalist mode of production, the use or nonuse of machinery is tied to the class struggle. Machinery's use, and its ethical and political status, is epiphenomenal to the economic system and to the class struggle in particular.

Proudhon's confusions about machines were emblematic of those of political economy more generally.[6] The political economists undertook extensive discussions of machinery and the role it played in production. They characterized machines both as a potential source of limitless wealth and as a means of justly extorting greater amounts of labor from workers while minimizing their contribution to the production process, thereby making their labor "easy." In order to challenge these theses, Marx learned a great deal about the operation of machinery of his day. More generally, he turned his attention to the politicized role played by science and technology in production. Marx no doubt absorbed a version of the theses of energy conservation and entropy through the studies of technology, and especially of the steam engine, that formed a portion of his study of political economy during the 1850s.

Marx was also connected directly to the theorists of thermodynamics. Marx's excerpt notebooks from 1851 contain notes on Justus Liebig's vitalist version of the law of energy conservation, presented in *Die organische Chemie in ihrer Anwendung auf Agriculture und Physiology* (1842) (IISG 1851, B49, S. 34–46). Moreover, as we have already noted, Marx was familiar with Büchner's *Stoff und Kraft*, and he drew on the text during the composition of the *Grundrisse*.

Using Rainer Winkelmann's 1982 study, Anson Rabinbach attributes Marx's knowledge of thermodynamics to Pellegrino Rossi, whose texts Marx excerpted in the composition of *Capital* (1990, 79). Although this is correct, Marx's excerpt notebooks reveal, especially in the case of Liebig and Büchner, an earlier, if preliminary, acquaintance with the ideas that he would later review in Rossi. The remarkable prescience of Rabinbach's thesis about the connections between Marx and thermodynamics is thus doubly evident, because Rabinbach derived it with partial information on Marx's excerpt notebooks, in combination with careful reading of Marx's texts.

I will return to the significance of Liebig in Chapter 3. Although Marx often castigated some aspects of Büchner's thinking in private letters to Engels (Gregory 1977, 240), he admired Büchner's work to the extent that he wrote the author directly to ask his aid in procuring a French translator for *Das Kapital*:

> I want the book, after its publication in Germany, to appear also in Paris, in French. I cannot go there without danger, since I have been expelled from France, first under Louis-Philippe and the second time under Louis Bonaparte, and during my exile in London I have constantly attacked [Bonaparte]. Hence I cannot go there personally to look for a translator. I know that your book, *Stoff und Kraft*, has appeared in French, and I assume, therefore, that, directly or indirectly, you could arrange a proper person for me ... I do not have time to undertake the French translation myself.

> (1 May 1867; 1979, 230)

Despite his private protestations to Engels about the process, Marx searched for post-1848 mainstream acceptance among Germany's scientific community. To do so, he appealed to science's revelatory truths of the essence of things, and to chemical metaphors of composition in particular, as the foundation of his political claims. In this, he was like the scientific materialists as a whole.

In Germany, Marx hoped that his reputation as a scientifically motivated economist would supersede the slanderous reputation he had acquired as a political intriguer.[7] Living in poverty in London, Marx was faced with the huge success of Büchner's book, whereas his own writings failed to be profitably received and celebrated by the German scientific community. It is not difficult to detect sour grapes underneath some of Marx's criticisms of Büchner. There were, nonetheless, also real differences between Marx and the scientific materialists, and I will turn to these differences presently.

There is a hidden benefit to contrasting Marx with the scientific materialists. Because Marx gives us so little in his later years in the way of a traditional epistemology or metaphysics, we are left to do some guesswork. One fruitful way to go about this is to outline the differences between his position and those of the German scientific materialists, especially his differences with Büchner and Karl Vogt.

Like all of the scientific materialists, Marx's characterization of his work as science was motivated by the political significance of science in the German context much more than by an empirical method or an unabashed positivism.[8] All of the scientific materialists in Germany began with Liebig's rejection of empiricism and were initially hostile to the English/French methodology and epistemology (Gregory 1977, 151). Empiricism represented a brute collection of facts from which broader general conclusions were disallowed. It insisted on a limited inductive rather than a deductive method of reasoning, not on a broad, symbiotic or dialectical interchange between the two. Such a method would not allow the social and political polemical extensions often employed by the scientific materialists. In the resistance to empirical method, their Hegelian heritage survived its critique.

But although the scientific materialists were initially wary of empiricism's most radical consequences, they were increasingly pushed in its direction. Science came to replace philosophy, not to take instructions from it. Partly in response to a generation of neo-Kantians who argued that the order of being and the order of knowing might not be the same, the scientific materialists came to espouse a naïve epistemological realism. Büchner, the most philosophical of the bunch, argues for "the identity of the laws of thought with the mechanical laws of nature" (quoted in Gregory 1977, 157). Vogt and Moleshcott make claims that rely on this principle: that the brain secretes thought in the way the liver secretes bile, and that someone's political opinions might be manipulated directly by changing his or her diet.

Marx was simply too good a philosopher to agree with these postulates of what he called "vulgar materialism." He returns in the 1850s to the Kantian and Hegelian understanding of science as dependant on the work of the understanding. For Marx, the cognitive faculties must work up an unformed material substrate in order to make any claims about the world. These faculties are dependent upon, but not reducible to, their material operation: if I kill someone, he or she will cease to think, but he or she will not think merely because I continue to feed him or her. The faculties are thus subject to different laws in their operation as thought, if not in their material operation. Marx also objected to the deterministic element in scientific materialist thought, the idea of necessity resulting from material circumstances alone. As early as his dissertation, where he contrasted the swerving Epicurean atom with Democritus's unidirectional atom, Marx had worked to dissociate materialist worldviews from determinism.

II The first law of thermodynamics: *Kraft, Stoff,* and the discourse of energetics

After the defeat of the communist and other democratic revolutions in 1848 and 1849, political radicals in France and Germany were killed, exiled, or forced underground by repressive restoration governments. Marx was doubly exiled: expelled from his Parisian exile first to Belgium, and finally to England. Even moderate liberals remaining in Germany and France had to find a new, less obvious language in which to couch their politics in order to ensure their own survival and also that of their politics. They hit upon the language of science.

This was not a simple transference. The German Enlightenment had already long allied scientific inquiry with republican politics, an alliance exemplified in the early years by Alexander von Humboldt's *Kosmos* (1845–1848) and Feuerbach's writings. However, in the post-1848 period, scientific work became still more explicitly allied with class struggle. The scientific materialists' work was, as we shall see, democratic in content. It was also democratic in form: like Marx's *Capital*, the texts of the scientific materialists were written, at least ostensibly, to appeal to a popular, nonuniversity-educated audience.

As Rabinbach (1990) notes in his account of the changes in nineteenth-century labor,

> Germany was, as the Marxist philosopher Ernst Bloch explained, the classical land of "non-synchronicity," of both extraordinary rapid economic and social progress, and virulent resistance to modernity. If the chorus of antiliberal and antimodern voices from Schopenhauer to Spengler was one familiar pole of that dialectic, the scientific materialists were surely the other, manifesting boundless optimism regarding the potential harmony of nature and industry.... To the extent that liberalism survived the political defeat of 1848, the traditions of German constitutionalism were largely preserved in its scientific, rather than political culture. In the absence of a liberal polity, German science became the most fertile terrain for the antireligious, antiautocratic, and democratic ideals that the post-1848 era extinguished in the public sphere. (49)

Against this backdrop we may understand Marx's appeals to science in his later years, and his increasing insistence that his own work *was* science, as a political move. Although Marx differs from the scientific materialists on crucial epistemological, metaphysical, and political questions, he shares this most general characteristic of their thought.

The scientific thinkers of this generation in Germany were divided into two generations: Feuerbach and Liebig were representative of the first; Ludwig Büchner, Hermann von Helmholtz, Karl Vogt, and Jacob Moleschott were representative of the second.[9] Marx, as we shall see, was influenced by both generations during his lifetime, inheriting the critical energy of the first generation and, by the time he wrote the *Grundrisse* and *Capital*, the conceptual discoveries of the latter.

Feuerbach, as we saw in Chapter 1, was best known for his critique of religion. The second generation of scientific materialists alternatively repeats this critique *ad nauseum* and assumes it, having profited from it in the sense that they no longer invoke supermaterial or other nonhuman vitalist forces in their explanations of the natural world.

Von Helmholtz became famous for his July 1847 lecture to the Physical Society of Berlin on *Die Erhaltung der Kraft* (the conservation of force). This lecture presented a version of the first law of thermodynamics, better known as the conservation of energy. This law insists that energy is at a constant level in the universe, and is neither created nor destroyed. Derived ultimately from the sun, such energy is an inherent property of all matter. Energy is neither created nor destroyed; it merely changes form. According to the new law, heat and motion are convertible, and "work" can be reduced to an amount of heat or motion performed. The conserved energy of which nature is composed operates in a transcendental, though not a metaphysical way, and serves as the basis of all manifestations of both matter and force.

Von Helmholtz was hardly the only nineteenth-century thinker to discover this law. As Thomas Kuhn relates in his essay "Energy Conservation as an Example of Simultaneous Discovery,"[10] "between 1842 and 1847, the hypothesis of energy conservation was publicly announced by four European scientists—J. R. Mayer, James P. Joule, L. A. Colding, and Helmholtz—all but the last working in complete ignorance of the others" (Kuhn 1977, 66). The four scientists Kuhn lists are limited to those who added quantitative proof to a more general theory already espoused in Sadi Carnot, Marc Séguin, Karl Holtsmann, G. A. Hirn, C. F. More, William Grove, Michael Faraday, and Justus Liebig. Kuhn writes, "[t]he history of science offers no more striking instance of the phenomenon known as simultaneous discovery" (69). The simultaneous discovery of the law of energy conservation is the material example from which Kuhn's famous subsequent thesis about paradigm communities began.

As a way of explaining the simultaneity of the discovery of energy conservation, Kuhn points to three cultural and historical resources that the thermodynamic theorists shared. These were (1) work on batteries and the conversion of electric current into heat and light, or the use of electric current to break chemical bonds; (2) engineering and developments in steam and electric engines, which serve as literal explications of the conversion of matter into energy; and (3) German *Naturphilosophie*, especially that of Schelling.

Marx inherited the idea of the conservation of energy both indirectly and directly. Indirectly, Marx belonged to the climate of simultaneous discovery sketched by Kuhn. In particular, he participated in the latter two of Kuhn's exemplary proto-thermodynamic discourses. Marx's critical links, via Hegel, with the *Naturphilosophie* of the German Enlightenment are well known. Far less well known are Marx's studies of French and English engineering, and even his deep understanding of the scientific developments of the steam engine. Likewise unknown is the path by which Marx's immersion in *Naturphilosophie* led him to develop one of the first nuanced philosophies of technology. Marx's familiarity with Büchner's work is also often underemphasized, probably because of the smokescreen Marx threw up to obscure the influence of this work.

Drawing on the work of von Helmholtz, Büchner tirelessly popularized the implications of the scientific doctrines of thermodynamics for the moral sphere, but the implications for the social and political sphere are not difficult to discern beneath his popularization of the new physics. Büchner (1920) writes,

> Credulous spirits or minds who feel unable to manage without some spiritist fealty, may amuse themselves with the fancy that behind the impenetrable veil of phenomena a man stands with a rod in his hands, with which he will one fine day scourge all those who during their lives have not been sufficiently obedient slaves. But thinking and liberty-loving spirits will rather delight in the idea that the universe is in reality a *republic* rather than a *monarchy*, and that it is self-governed in accordance with eternal and immutable laws.
>
> (88, emphasis in original)

Not society but nature demands a kind of radical equality, because ontologically nature is a single substance: energy. Energy becomes the guiding metaphor of the age, a means of explaining the workings of other things during this period: social and political bodies, human bodies, and cosmological bodies.

The political realm is reconceived not as an antiphysis, in opposition to nature, as it was by the contract theorists. Instead, the political realm is woven from nature construed as an energetic system. Political relations are like nature as opposed to countering it and tempering its forces. Marx, who begins with the Hegelian and Aristotelian notion of nature, will be exposed to these ideas. This exposure results in a complex incorporation of their significance into his later political philosophy.

Von Helmholtz and Büchner's new physics required a new metaphysics. From Aristotle onward, until Gassendi resurrects Democritean and Epicurean atomist materialisms, matter and force had been conceived as separable phenomena. But this separation is challenged by the thermodynamic synthesis of matter and force into a unified concept of energy. In Büchner's book, the first nine sections explain the new metaphysics: "No force without matter—no matter without force. One is no more possible, and no more imaginable by itself than the other. Separated from each other, each becomes an empty abstraction or idea.... Force and matter are fundamentally the same thing, contemplated from different standpoints" (3). In the new metaphysics, dignity is conferred upon the material world, which can no longer be conceived of as hostile and resistant to spirit, or as the ground for spiritualization by force.

The convertibility between force and matter and the reduction of both to the term "motion" are key elements of the changing concepts of the thermodynamic metaphysics. All matter is motion of varying degrees, sluggish or fast, and all force is motion as well. Another way this motion expresses itself is heat. The new vocabulary of heat, motion, and energy comes increasingly to supplant that of force and matter. Büchner realized this late in his life, writing that "perhaps it would be better if one allowed [the expression force] to drop completely, and the word motion was put in its place" (quoted in Gregory 1977, 160).[11] Increasingly, Büchner's prediction becomes true. Both matter and force drop out of use as concepts and are replaced by heat, motion, or energy.

According to the older metaphysics, forces began and ended in time. Forces also differed from one another according to type: human force was not the same as natural, divine, or mechanical force; animal, human, and machine forces were subject to different systems of classification, because they participated to differing degrees in spiritualization. Organic and inorganic bodies were thought to be composed of different kinds of elements. Organic matter was distinguished by a vitalist principle that could not be further broken down into chemical or energetic components. Human life and action was the highest and most spiritual expression of this principle.

The new metaphysics binds together these objects under the unifying rubric of energy. Forces do not begin and end in time; rather, they are transformed into one another. For Büchner (1920), both force and matter are "immortal," despite the phenomenal illusions of beginning and end that attend their transformations:

> Matter as such is indestructible, it cannot be annihilated; no grain of dust in the universe can vanish from it, and none can enter it... the phrases "mortal body" and "immortal spirit"...are misnomers altogether. Exact thought might possibly reverse the adjectives. The body in its individual form or shape is indeed mortal, but it is not so in its constituent particles. Not in death only but throughout life it changes unceasingly, as we have seen; but in the wider since it is immortal, since not the smallest particle of it can be annihilated. On the other hand we see that what we call spirit, soul, consciousness, disappears with the cessation of the individual combination of matter; and it must appear to the unprejudiced mind that this action having been brought about by peculiar and very complicated unions, must come to an end with its cause, that is to say, with the cessation of those peculiar combinations. (14–19)

As for the seeming disappearances of force, Büchner writes,

> by combustion or combination of various chemical elements, light and heat are evolved. Heat may further be changed as steam into mechanical force, as for instance by being used in *the steam-engine*; and mechanical energy can again be reconverted into heat by friction, and in the magneto-electric machine it can be retransmuted into Heat, Electricity, Light, and chemical difference.
>
> (24, emphasis added)

In the new metaphysics, human, animal, and machine forces are ontologically indistinct and differ only in the degree of energy they express. Discoveries in chemistry demonstrate that organic and inorganic bodies are composed of the same elements: "[W]e need but refer to chemistry, which was able to place the fact beyond doubt that the chemical elements or fundamental materials are identically the same in the organic and the inorganic world" (Büchner 1920, 339). The notion of a vitalist force that animates organic matter comes to be seen as a superfluous postulate and even to be ridiculed as a theological residue.[12]

In the new metaphysics, all energy is derived ultimately from the sun. Thermodynamics is accompanied by discoveries in cosmology, geology, and anthropology that set the earth in ontological continuity with the surrounding cosmological bodies and set its date of origin in the distant past. In the prethermodynamic picture, these divergent forces and matters could be held to begin and end in time. In the postthermodynamic picture, force/matter, or energy, does not disappear; it is merely converted into different forms.

To characterize this form of energy, the second generation of scientific materialists repeatedly deploys the metaphor of a steam engine; Büchner's use of this metaphor in the passage above is emblematic. A literal explication of the conversion of matter into energy and heat, the steam engine becomes a model for all of nature and for its system of energetic conversion.

This second generation of scientific materialists is therefore working with different symbolism in its descriptions of the operations of the natural world. The metaphorical importance of the clock to an earlier generation of modern thinkers is supplanted by the steam engine. The steam engine acts like all of nature, absorbing energy in one form and spitting it out in another. It is metabolic and self-acting. It produces items of further consumption rather than order, contributing to society's further energetic transformation. Rabinbach (1990) writes,

[T]he metaphor of the machine in 19th century materialism was far more than an extended analogy in which "the machine was a copy of the universe, and the universe itself a machine." It fused the diverse forms of labor in nature, technology, and society into a single image of mechanical work, universalizing and extending the model of energy to a nature conceived of as a vast unbroken system of production. (25)

The problem that plagued the engineers of the era who were constructing steam engines was how to regulate these engines for maximal productivity with minimal loss of heat, but some heat loss was necessary so that the engines would not explode or self-destruct. Design was the key element to this negotiation of force's conservation and loss. Nature, society, and labor are similarly reconceived as transmutations and intensifications of energetic force. Their design must be regulated not only for maximal productivity with minimal loss of heat energy in unproductive expenditure, but also so as not to precipitously wind down, wear out, or self-destruct.

The new physics and metaphysics were perceived by both the scientific materialists and their opponents to have direct political consequences. This politicization goes beyond the stints at the 1848 barricades often served by the scientific materialists themselves. Following such a stint, Rudolf Virchow, a member of Von Helmholtz's lab, writes to his father in 1848: "As a natural scientist I can be but a republican. The republic is the only form in which the claims, derived from the laws of nature and the nature of man can be realized" (quoted in Mendelsohn 1974, 407). But the connections between scientific materialism and radical politics are deeper than the causal links Virchow and others draw between their scientific inquiry and their political republicanism. The connections even go beyond the body of practical work done by these scientists, alongside their theoretical studies, designed explicitly to benefit the working class, especially in the field of nutrition.

More provocatively than Rabinbach, historians Everett Mendelsohn and Frederick Gregory suggest that radical political culture did not simply subside into scientific culture, and did not simply add fervor and vigor to the environment in which these scientists were working. Rather, radical political culture actually shaped the postulates and contents of thermodynamic scientific culture in crucial ways (Gregory 1977; Mendelsohn 1974). Among the most obvious of these ways was the elimination of the political hierarchies in the natural world, especially the opposition between force, as a principle that gives direction, and matter, as a subordinate principle that obeys. If the older master–slave metaphysics underscores a political power differential between force and matter, the new metaphysics eclipses both concepts and replaces them with energetic egalitarianism.

The steam engine metaphor also had an immediate influence on how human embodiment and potential for labor were conceptualized.[13] Büchner (1920) writes,

> Life creates neither new matter nor new force; it only delights in countless changes, which proceed without exception according to the great law of the conservation of energy or the equivalency of all dynamic forces. Each contraction of a muscle, each kind of work performed by an organism, involves the disappearance of a perfectly definite and equivalent amount of heat. (340)

The discipline of physiology is born. In it, human embodiment is analyzed in the same terms as mechanical embodiment.

As Rabinbach argues (1990), this model of thermodynamic human embodiment completely transforms the cultural discourse about labor. In particular, the notion of resistance to labor is transformed by the new model. Workers resist labor not out of laziness, a failure of the spirit or will, but out of a lack of energy, the loss of an inordinate amount of unrecompensed heat. Fatigue rather than willful resistance comes to be seen as the chief enemy of productive labor.

According to Rabinbach, the secularization of the Christian monastic concept of *acedia*, or the prohibition against sloth, characteristic of early modernity, gives way in the 1850s to insuring one's workers against fatigue. In the secularization of *acedia*, lasting "from the 13th century until the middle of nineteenth, Christian writers, ministers, and middle-class moralists all accorded idleness an esteemed place as the nemesis of an orderly life and the discipline of work" (1990, 26). In doing so, Christian writers fought against both the ideals of the aristocracy and against the classical tradition's emphasis on leisure. They strove to discipline a proto-industrial population into the virtue of work. By the end of the nineteenth century, this had been largely successful, but laziness was also in the process of being supplanted by fatigue as the nemesis of productive labor. Rabinbach reminds us that at this point

> [I]dleness began to wane as the predominant mode of conceptualizing resistance to labor. The reasons for this decline can be enumerated: the old Christian prohibition on idleness was losing

its appeal for urban workers and industrialists; the technology of the factory system required more than externally imposed discipline and direction, but rather an internally regulated body ancillary to the machine. Consequently, the ideal of a worker guided by spiritual authority or direct control or surveillance gave way to the image of a body directed by its own internal mechanisms, a human "motor." Almost simultaneously, fatigue and energy emerged as a more modern conceptual framework for expressing the relations between work and the body. Accordingly, the concept of work underwent a crucial transformation: fatigue, not idleness, was the primary discontent of industrial labor ... a more scientific evaluation of work, often materialist in emphasis, gradually replaced the old moral discourse. (35–36)

Rabinbach words the terms of transition too strongly. The new scientific materialist evaluation of labor does not wholly supplant the old moral discourse, which is still prevalent well into the twenty-first century, and especially in the literatures of colonization; rather, the thermodynamic model of labor springs up alongside it. The new model does, however, challenge the older one in crucial respects. Labor is neither a product of the spirit, nor a practice unchallenged by the demands of materiality. Labor must be tempered with periods of rest and repose, not only to preserve the worker, but also in order to ensure the maximal productivity of the labor itself. Fatigued workers are prone to error, not through moral lapse, but through the iron laws of energetic necessity.

Resistance to labor is thereby modulated from the moral to the scientific. But this modulation inaugurates a new "moral" discourse. Objectifying the body and determining its energetic limits becomes a way of defining unfair labor practices, and social responsibilities of employers are invoked in the wake of this form of objectification. As Denis Forest (2001) puts it,

The moment the new science of the living body offers a utilitarian definition of this body, the new science is also given a say in how the corporal machine ought to be used, because the new science claims to show an incompatibility between the given conditions in which the body is placed and the same body's vital demands. "Do no harm" is no longer a medical principle, but a commandment of biochemistry with which the latter discipline will begin to challenge the inconsiderate use of productive forces. From that moment onward, there is a fundamental ambivalence to this mode of modeling the body, since the objective discovery of fatigue depends on the model in which the body is a pure means, understood by the work it produces. At the same time, its productions can only be registered in time, begun again in succeeding efforts where the power of production is either conserved or not. The body will only bring forth what it is permitted to bring forth, according to the care that one either offers or refuses to that which it is, to its needs and to its limits. Use and care are linked. So are the idea of a science of work and the worry of the damages work inflicts. So are the mechanist and medico-social discourses.... It is because the body is given an objective exposition...because work furnished by the body can be appreciated as that of an ordinary motor that, at the same time, the person comes to be protected by law.

(8, 19, my translation here and below)

The worker's comparability to an ordinary engine, the reduction of his or her faculties to the most abstract units of energy, becomes the means of arguing for his or her protection. Paradoxically, the reduction of human labor to the model of the steam engine tends to extend concessions to workers, albeit in energetic rather than spiritual terms. That is, workers must be allowed food and rest *not* because of their humanity or vital spirits, but because all machines require fuel and maintenance in order to work well.

The birth of the discipline of physiology at the end of the nineteenth and the early twentieth centuries also follows upon the changes inaugurated by thermodynamics. The work of Dutch scientific materialist Jacob Moleschott on nutrition showed direct connections between a poor diet and poor performance. Moleschott's work had a practical dimension in which the author advised the underclasses how best to manage their nutrition on a limited budget: he wrote, among other things, a cookbook for the working classes.

The scientific backdrop for this folksy intervention was enabled by the fact that the body was reconceived as a mechanistic engine or motor, and its fatigue profiles were charted. The invention of the ergograph by Angelo Mosso in 1888 showed the effects of muscle fatigue over time on a graphed curve. Mosso's invention demonstrated that a constantly greater quantity of nervous excitement, measured by increasing errors, necessarily accompanied this fatigue. Forest (2001) writes, "as the quantity of work produced diminishes, the quantity of nervous excitement required to produce the work increases. That is to say, fatigue is not only diminishing effectiveness at a task, it is also the increased effort necessary to produce a constant effect" (9). Although ergographic energy profiles were somewhat idiosyncratic to test subjects, they were so only within well-defined limits. Because of this, the physiologists of the period find themselves intervening in the labor struggles, allied on scientific grounds with labor-reform movements of various stripes: reductions in hours, objectively determined responsibility of employers for industrial accidents (19), and other "adjudications of social conflicts mandated by the physiological requirements of work" (20).

Marx is suspicious of these labor reform movements. Marx claims that such reforms merely extend the life of the bourgeois system by putting off crises without changing the fundamental structure of the system: wage labor and, beyond this, the mode of valuation that subordinates exchange-value to use-value. Nonetheless, the later Marx is also concerned with fatigue and from the 1850s onward begins to apply the energeticist notions of work to define surplus value, or what the capitalist gets from the worker without the return of an equivalent. In his mature definition of the concept of surplus value, Marx distinguishes the margin of inequality between what the laborer gives up to capital in the labor process and what he or she receives back in the form of wages. As we shall see, Marx's concept of labor-power [*Arbeitskraft*], as distinct from labor [*Arbeit*], is an energeticist notion.

Though tempered by the new energeticist notions, labor also remains a moral concept for Marx in the old sense. Marx has his doubts about the scientific materialists and what he calls their vulgar materialism. In particular, he does not accept that the first metaphysical consequence of the new science—the postulate of an underlying field of energy—requires the second metaphysical consequence of an ontological leveling of human, animal, and machine. While there may be some common ground between the labors undertaken by human, animal, and machine, because they can all be viewed as representative of an energetic field, Marx's position is that human labor is different from animal or machine labor. Marx refuses to assimilate human labor fully to the model of work done by an animal or machine.

In the *Grundrisse*, Marx calls human labor that "living, form-giving fire" (1973, 361). Even in *Capital*, Marx frequently uses the word "vital" to describe labor. This probably derives from Marx's reliance on Liebig's *Animal Chemistry* in his conception of physiology. Liebig supported the critique of metaphysics but refused to eliminate the notion of a nondivine but also nonmaterial vital force from his accounts of animal life. Because of this, he was a regular target of the second generation of scientific materialists.

Moreover, Marx retains the Christian notion of *acedia*. Marx is horrified by his son-in-law Paul LaFargue's 1880 text *The Right to Be Lazy*, in
which LaFargue bids the proletariat to "return to its natural instincts"
and "trample underfoot the prejudices of Christian ethics [and] economic ethics" (quoted in Rabinbach 1990, 34–35). In the *Grundrisse*,
Marx will sternly remind us that "labor cannot become play, as [French
socialist utopian Charles] Fourier would like" (1973, 712; MECW 1987,
29, 97; MEGA^2 II, 2, 1.2, 589). In Chapter 3, I will return to this passage,
what it demonstrates about Marx's relationship to *acedia*, and what it
reveals about Marx's concept of labor after the revolution.

However, alongside the old moral discourse of labor, the implications
of the notion of energy and its conservation can be seen in the later
Marx, as can the new scientific discourse of preventing worker fatigue. In
Capital, Marx will even discuss human embodiment as a kind of motor-
driven conversion of force, employing the scientific notion of work. As
Rabinbach (1990) writes,

> 19th century thought did not discern as great a distance between
> discoveries in nature and their application to society as contempo-
> rary thought does…thermodynamics permitted an equally broad
> range of interpretations from progressive social reform to the more
> apocalyptic conclusions of Nietzsche's image of history. The most
> important 19th century thinker to absorb the insights of thermo-
> dynamics was Marx, whose later work was influenced and perhaps
> even decisively shaped by the new image of work as "labor power".
> (69–70)[14]

So if, from the 1850s onward, Marx begins to apply a thermodynamic
model of labor, he does this with a great deal of ambivalence about the
reduction of humans to the status of productive machines. Marx therefore cannot fully integrate the new scientific paradigm's metaphysical
presuppositions, even as he integrates certain concepts that derive from
the paradigm, especially the concept of "labor-power."

III   From *Arbeit* to *Arbeitskraft*: Marx's transformation of work from self-actualization to energy expenditure

Marx's acquaintance with thermodynamics shapes and transforms the
ways he talks about the interaction between human beings and the
natural world, subtly altering the meaning of "labor" in his later philosophy, and causing him to generate new categories like "abstract

labor" and "labor-power." Marx's adoption of the concept of *Arbeitskraft* (labor-power or labor-capacity) is one of his major discoveries of the 1850s. Alongside Marx's continued but increasingly ambiguous use of the concept "labor," "labor-power" comes to distinguish the quantifiably measurable units of force added by workers to production, and the quantifiably measurable units of force needed to supply workers with the basic life necessities (e.g. food, sleep). In his later work, Marx also uses the concept of labor-power to distinguish the margin of inequality between what workers give up to capital in the labor process and what they receive back from it in the form of the wage's purchasing power.

Although Marx justly becomes famous for his use of "labor-power," it is not Marx but Von Helmholtz who first introduces the term (Rabinbach 1990, 46). In Von Helmholtz's usage, *Kraft* was extended beyond its original context. Originally, *Kraft* described the forces unleashed by machines that converted chemical or heat energy into mechanical energy. Von Helmholtz expanded the meaning of *Kraft*, using it to describe all of nature, including human labor, in terms of this sort of conversion. Labor, reconceived as a part of the continuous fabric of energy, became *Arbeitskraft* (labor-power).

According to Rabinbach, this extension is crucial for the social and political conceptualization of labor, for through it the concept of labor was distinctively modified:

> Thermodynamics decisively altered the concept of labor, at once modernizing it according to the precepts of industrial technology and naturalizing it in accord with the new laws of physics. The primacy of labor in the theory of property—prominent in the work of seventeenth and eighteenth-century philosophers and economists like [John] Locke and [Adam] Smith—placed human work within a social division of labor that emphasized the identity of human industry and individual autonomy.... This image of work, appropriate to a preindustrial era, still maintained the traditional distinction between labor as the source or property and selfhood, and labor as a burden. But a striking change occurred in the second half of the 19th century as this increasingly anachronistic vision of labor became superseded by the energeticist model of mechanical work. The work performed by any mechanism, from the fingers of the hand, to the gears of the engine, or the motion of the planets, was essentially the same. With this semantic shift in the meaning of "work," all labor was reduced to its physical properties, devoid of content and inherent purpose. Work was universalized.

(1990, 47)

In Marx's system, labor qua labor-power is a degraded and alienated way of describing human activity, even if the concept of labor-power is a useful one for arguing, on scientific grounds, on the workers' behalf.

The new notion of labor as labor-power shifts markedly away from the spiritual or imaginative role that labor plays in the philosophical systems of Locke, Smith, or Hegel. The thermodynamic universalization of work consequent to industrial life transforms the type of force labor represents. The political status and autonomy labor represented to the earlier generation of bourgeois political theorists is similarly altered. Marx's critique of political economy becomes possible because the concept of labor on which Locke, Smith, and Hegel founded, respectively, autonomy, property, and subjectivity is irreparably changed. Instead of dignifying the human being and setting him or her at the apex of the universe, instead of spiritualizing nature via a human force different in kind, labor situates the human in continuity with nature and natural force.

Marx uses *Arbeitskraft* for the first time in the *Grundrisse*.[15] However, the concept of labor-power is not yet fully developed or integrated in the *Grundrisse*, and the text retains much that is characteristic of Marx's earlier texts, including his earlier notion of labor. A much more developed and clearer formulation of the concept of labor-power occurs in Marx's texts from the 1860s, including *Capital*.

A good example of Marx's developed use of the concept occurs in *Wages, Price, and Profit* (1865). Originally a speech to a workers' organization on the concept of the wage, *Wages, Price, and Profit* offers a remarkably clear summary of the main themes of Marx's later work that receive a longer, more methodologically formalized, and therefore less accessible exposition in *Capital*. Marx explains that fluctuations in the wage will accrue no real benefit to workers, and that the source of their struggle should lie elsewhere. He claims, "Instead of the *conservative* motto 'A fair day's wage for a fair day's work!' [workers] ought to inscribe on their banner the *revolutionary* watchword: '*Abolition of the Wages System!*'" (1865, chapter 3, emphases in original).[16]

Marx shows that however widely wages may vary in amount, the capitalist system will always reduce their real value, the value of what they can purchase, to the minimum required by a body at the limits of maintaining and producing itself and its class-specific mode of life. Wages will tend to the absolute minimum required to support the laborer, and subsequent generations of proletarians *as* proletarians, and nothing beyond this. Wages, even those perceived as high, will offer no participation in general social wealth or in forms of activity or enjoyment not immediately relevant to the reconstruction of the capacity to labor again the next day.

Marx employs the concept of labor-power to show this. In this formulation, we see both the conceptual doubling of labor and labor-power and a comparison of the latter to the work done by machines. Marx writes,

> What the working man sells is not directly his *labour*, but his *labouring power*, the temporary disposal of which he makes over to the capitalist.... What then is the *value of labouring power?* Like that of every other commodity, its value is determined by the quantity of labour necessary to produce it. The labouring power of a man exists only in his living individuality. A certain mass of necessaries must be consumed by a man to grow up and maintain his life. But the man, like the machine, will wear out, and must be replaced by another man. Besides the mass of necessaries required for *his own* maintenance, he wants another amount of necessaries to bring up a certain quota of children that are to replace him on the labour market and to perpetuate the race of labourers. Moreover, to develop his labouring power, and acquire a given skill, another amount of values must be spent. For our purpose, it suffices to consider only *average* labour, the costs of whose education and development are vanishing magnitudes.... The cry for an *equality of wages* rests, therefore, upon a mistake, is an insane wish never to be fulfilled. It is an offspring of that false and superficial radicalism that accepts premises and tries to evade conclusions. Upon the basis of the wages system, the value of labouring power is settled like that of every other commodity... To clamour for *equal or even equitable retribution* on the basis of the wages system is the same to clamour for *freedom* on the basis of the slavery system. What you think just or equitable is out of the question. The question is: What is necessary and unavoidable with a given system of production? After what has been said, it will be seen that the *value of labouring power* is determined by the *value of the necessaries* required to produce, develop, and perpetuate the labouring power.
>
> (1865, chapter 2, emphases in original)[17]

All that will be delivered to the laborer in exchange for laboring power is only that which is necessary to perpetuate this power.[18] It will not be enough to perpetuate labor in the older, rich sense the concept had to the earlier generation of bourgeois political theorists, with its implied importance for human development and self-actualization.

Not yet influenced by the industrial transformation of labor in both its literal and its conceptual dimensions, the earlier generation of bourgeois theorists portrayed labor as involving self-cultivation and the establishment of political autonomy and property. A classic example is Hegel's account, in his *Phenomenology of Spirit*, of the inauthenticity of the master's position and his stunted development compared with that of the slave. But these developmental, self-actualizing features of labor are not part of universalized industrialized labor, which involves the barely sufficient remuneration of mere labor-power, and they are not part of the labor process in the capitalist system. Such developmentally rich labor would require resources in excess of those necessary only to "[replace] a definite quantity of human muscle, nerve, brain, etc.," resources that exceed the "value of [the] definite quantity of the means of subsistence" into which the value of labor-power, unlike that of labor, can be resolved.[19]

Nor, in a related limitation, will workers be allotted enough general wealth to develop human activity beyond that which is required for capitalist production. Particularly, the artistic, intellectual, and scientific activities Marx takes to be proper to the human species as such, activities only ambiguously characterized as labor, are annulled for the class whose mere labor-power is to be maintained. Marx's critique is a moral critique of the reduction of a part of the human species to the maintenance of its mere labor-power. Because to be a laborer is to have barely enough to replace one's labor-power, laborers are absorbed by the capitalist system in the way of other means of production.

Entire modes of life are generated out of the limitation of the laborer to his or her labor-power. Workers' sense of entitlement and range of pleasures are bounded. Workers' political imaginations are hindered, limited to thinking about wage increases that will be compensated elsewhere in the capitalist calculus. Marx develops this insight in *Capital* with the observation that many unhealthy and short-lived generations will suffice so long as they supplant one another's labor-power with sufficient continuity and rapidity.[20]

In his later work, Marx uses the concept of labor-power to illustrate the gap between the value needed to maintain the worker's labor-power and that which is set free by this labor-power. The surplus created in this gap accrues to the capitalist as surplus value. As commodities needed to maintain the laborer's labor-power are cheapened, in part due to machines, this surplus is increased. It is also increased by longer and more intense working hours, which, although they wear out an individual laborer's labor-power more quickly, do this only to the threshold of his or her immediate replacement by a member of his or her own class.

For the Marx who investigates this, the concepts of "alienation" and "exploitation" lose the value-neutrality they possessed for the earlier generation of bourgeois political theorists. Prior to the transformation of labor in industry, exploitation simply meant *use*; it did not carry with it a moral indictment of the type of use involved. Likewise, alienation simply meant exchange, not the totalizing reduction of a human being's importance to the maintenance of his or her labor-power. As Greg Godels (1997) points out, "Before [the appearance of the word 'exploitation'] in the cauldron of 19th-century working-class politics, exploitation was used in a general, nonmoral nonjudgmental manner, as in, for example, 'the exploitation of the farmland' or 'the exploitation of raw materials" (510).

After Marx's application of the concept of labor-power to industrial life, the terms "alienation" and "exploitation" are transformed to carry moral indictment within their very meaning. Moreover, exploitation and alienation are not simply concepts that critique inequality or the social prominence of the wealthy over the poor; rather, they are new ways of judging the social relations peculiar to the industrial system and the peculiarities of its transformation of labor (Godels 1997, 510). The new concepts alienation and exploitation even relate poverty and wealth and show their interaction; for Marx, labor-power will allow the calculation of the precise amount of surplus value added by the worker to the capitalist accumulation. Poor and rich are not simply labels of hereditary good or bad luck, nor are they character traits; their relationship to one another is causal, and it can be charted scientifically.[21]

Marx is suspicious of the reduction of human beings to their labor-power. At the same time, he uses the concept of labor-power as an analytical tool in order to explain the workings of capital and to designate what the worker sells in the capitalist wage system. So reduced, labor cannot be a source of property and selfhood. It becomes only a burden, an even exchange with the world in which none of the inner capacities of the worker are developed. This is why general wealth is increasingly conceived by Marx not as meaningful labor but as free time. It is also why Marx describes the projects one will undertake during this free time not as "labor" but as "higher activity" or "development."

Among Marx's most undertheorized ideas is his notion that human activity is not reducible to labor. This idea is barely conceivable in the advanced capitalist environments of today, where the tendency is rather to describe every valuable human undertaking as labor or as supporting labor. In Chapter 5, I will return to the rising importance of free time to Marx's conceptualizations of human entitlement. Here I will note briefly that the empty bracket of free time has, in Marx, absorbed some of the content of the richer, spiritualized notion of "labor" we find among the earlier bourgeois political theorists.

Thus, one underexplored way to understand the much contested early/late Marx split is not simply to view Marx's work as increasingly scientific, but also to understand the related changes in his concept of labor consequent upon his scientific studies and subsequent adoption of energeticist terms. Following Rabinbach, I suggest that greater attention be paid to the transformation of labor as both a process and a concept, a transformation inaugurated by industrialization and the related conceptual apparatus of thermodynamics. As Rabinbach (1990) puts it,

> After 1859 Marx gradually redefined labor from a metabolic exchange of substances between man and nature to a conversion of force...where the human being "confronts nature as a force of nature."...Labor is no longer a creative or singularly human act...the distinction between social labor and nature is all but obliterated. Marx's phenomenology of labor power is not only contemporary with the Helmoholtzian revolution in scientific perception; it is a direct consequence of it. By placing the weight of transformation on the "objective" expansion of the productive forces, Marx argues that the full development and unfolding of the productive potential of nature and technology is the organizing principle of society... [and] the distinction between the natural forces of production and the productive forces of society is no longer decisive. (77–81)

In Marx's accounts written after this redefinition, machines themselves are reconceived as forms of natural force, just as both natural force and human labor have been reconceptualized by contact with thermodynamic machines.

IV   The second law of thermodynamics: entropy, the heat death of the universe, and revolution

We have seen how the human body, reconceived as a thermodynamic engine, is vulnerable to the crisis of fatigue. Both society and nature as a whole are also vulnerable to improper regulations of energy—and perhaps also to its inevitable loss. Catastrophic events are a pronounced theme in nineteenth-century scientific thought. In debates with clear political overtones, physical scientists argue over whether the geological and developmental history of the earth moved in slow increments or in violent climactic leaps. Marx's concept of labor, then, is not the only thing that is transformed by his contact with thermodynamic discourses. So is his concept of revolution.

The thermodynamic law of energy conservation was accompanied by a second discovery and a second law: entropy. During the conversion between heat and mechanical force, a certain amount of heat is unproductively lost to the environment. Individual systems tend to lose energy as an inescapable consequence of transforming it. Because of this, nineteenth-century physicists debate the question of whether the Earth as a whole is losing heat. In this debate, the prospect of an irreversible energy flow tending toward inertia and exhaustion was raised. The ultimate culmination of such a flow was apocalyptic: an ice age that would not sustain life.

This so-called "heat death of the universe" postulated the apocalyptic demise of the world's energy forces. The heat death could be either temporary or permanent, depending on the variant of the theory. In a modified version of the claim, the Earth might only temporarily become uninhabitable. Given sufficient time, perhaps millions of years, the small, unusable quantities into which energy had dissipated (e.g. that dissipated heat continually lost to friction, or the low-level heat of the earth's oceans) might again recombine into usable degrees of intensity and again give rise to life.

A final apocalyptic teleology was initially countered by optimists like Von Helmholtz, who early in his life argued that although any particular system may run down, the universe as a whole maintains constant energy: what is lost by one system is recouped by another. That is, there is no such thing as pure loss. But even the late Von Helmholtz acknowledged that although the universe's energy as a whole may remain constant, the Earth may be dissipating its energy and tending, slowly, toward a state not of temporary but of eternal rest (Rabinbach 1990, 62).

The debate was ultimately solved only in the twentieth century, with the discovery of radiation and its constant small additions of heat to the universe, a discovery that explained how heat needed for life on Earth was replaced.[22] What is important for us is not the scientific outcome of this debate, but the significance of its metaphor for nineteenth-century thought, because the connections between this discovery and its metaphysical, social, and historical implications were immediate in the minds of the age's thinkers.

Even the adoption of a moderate view of entropy, in which the loss of one system was recouped by another system, had profound effects on the thought of the period. As an example of the effects of the moderate view of entropy on natural philosophy, Rabinbach (1990) points to Herbert Spencer's postulate of the decay of civilizations as a positive step in the evolutionary generation of new forms of life (62). Rabinbach (1990) points also to Nietzsche's idea of eternal recurrence as, among other things, a response to the postulate of the heat death of the universe (62). He concludes that the "paradoxical relationship between energy and entropy is at the core of the 19th-century revolution in modernity: on the one side [the universe] is a stable and productivist universe of original and indestructible force, on the other an irreversible system of decline and deterioration" (63).

One immediate consequence of the discovery of thermodynamics' second law is the postulate of an absolute temporal direction of the universe, the effects of which cannot be reversed mechanically. Even if the processes that brought about a particular effect were reversed and work of a particular sort undone, the effect of heat loss cannot be recouped; rather, it is doubled or trebled. This counters the mechanistic Newtonian universe with its unconsidered effects of irreversible temporality. As Brush (1977) writes, "by introducing the notion of irreversible heat flow to explain why real engines cannot attain the maximum efficiency, thermodynamics makes a statement about the direction of time in our world" (11). The importance of history in nineteenth-century thought has a relationship to this scientific discourse of time's direction.

The powerful new metaphors of entropy invest the discourses of social and political change with new urgency. In order to understand Marx's discussion of revolution, and especially the shifts in this discussion that occur in the 1850s, the properties of apocalyptic systemic change must be considered. There is some distance between the *Communist Manifesto*'s appeal for the working men of the world to unite and the diagnosis, already begun in the same *Manifesto*, but more pronounced in later texts, of a system in crisis. In *Capital*, regarded as a long argument explaining why the system is in crisis, there are only a handful of mentions of revolution. These discussions of revolution are always connected with specific historical events of the past, particularly the revolutions of 1848–1849 and their failures and the bourgeois revolutions of seventeenth-century England. They are not suggestions for coalitional working-class politics to bring about a future society.[23]

The diagnosis of inevitable decline is limited to a theoretical gesture that is at once simple and enormously complex: the analysis of the capitalist mode of production not as hegemonic but as self-contradictory. Marx must point to the crisis of capital as a system of production whose amplification and extension comes with increasing losses, whose means of production are in tension with the mode that has developed them, as a system that tends, therefore, to disorder. Rabinbach (1990) writes,

> Marx also discovered the principle of entropy at work in capitalism: the unidirectional time flow of history produces the inevitable tendency of capitalism to decline as the productivity of labor power increases. By transforming labor into capital, capital amplifies its force: conversion of force is a conversion of magnitudes.... But because of the well-known tendency of capital to require greater and greater intensity to increase the profitability of labor in a competitive atmosphere, the conversion process yields proportionately less "value" for the capitalist, or, as Marx expressed it, the rate of profit declines. (80)

The declining rate of profit means that the very thing on which the capitalist system is founded—profit—becomes a diminishing quantity for it. The tendency of the profit rate to decline expresses the irreparable entropic loss of the capitalist system, a loss which undermines its conditions of possibility. Capitalism is like a poorly designed steam engine that must be run at top speed, despite the fact that this speed contributes to a greater overall loss of heat. This increased overall heat can be neither transformed into productive work nor released in adequate quantities. Instead it threatens to blow up the engine itself.

For Marx, capital will, of course, only have its energies recouped in a different, more evolved system. This situates him, oddly enough, among his age's great optimists. The declining rate of profit that is emblematic of the loss to the capitalist system will be recouped in the coming system as the need for less labor-power. More technological infrastructure, and the concomitant transfer of labor into capital, will mean that less labor-power will need be added to an increasingly automated production process. This will not have dire consequences for a system that is not founded on the value produced by labor-power, but on the material wealth mass-produced, with the minimal addition of labor-power, by machines.

Marx's theory of agent-based, political revolution is therefore increasingly supplanted by a theory of crises into which the capitalist system must inevitably fall, and out of which the communist mode of production must, equally inevitably, emerge. In this way, the postulated communist revolution is as far away from the bourgeois revolution and its foundation in the dignity, primacy, and political sovereignty of the laboring human being as it could possibly be. Instead, Marx appeals to the politics of human agents only as temporary way-stations on the path to structural crises asserting themselves. Finally, Marx's appeal is not so much to political action, the false forms of which he often warns against. It is simply an observation that the capitalist way of life is unsustainable, and that it squanders the very energy it should struggle to preserve.

Revolution is the site in which the earlier and later scientific paradigms with which Marx is working are most incompatible, and in which this incompatibility is most obvious. From the perspective of the earlier paradigm, human beings shape nature and their own destinies, spiritualizing their environment and rewriting the natural as well as the social laws that must be obeyed. From the perspective of the later paradigm, there is no such degree of human control. Human political organization is also denatured, because the prospect of human extinction trivializes the importance of the political order.

There is also no way to evaluate capitalism morally: it decays like any other complex system according to the iron laws of energy exchange. One can only forecast the trajectory of the system and wait for it to fulfill this projection. A call to conscious political action to combat such a system is absurd. It is like the call to row faster in the same direction as a current so strong that it does not register human force working either with it or against it. The laws of thermodynamics will themselves prepare and bring about any necessary social and political transformation, largely as epiphenomena to energy movements.

In a theory of such systems, there is also no final resting place, because ensuing systems will be subject to similar laws. Our state after the revolution is a temporary one, one that will be subject in turn to dissolution and renegotiation of energetic motion. The Marx who realizes this looks increasingly less like the Marx who, in the *Communist Manifesto*, encourages solidarity among the workers as a vehicle for change.

3
Machines in the Communist Future

I Technology and the boundaries of nature

Because Marx's philosophy is absolutely unique, it is not always easy to situate it properly in the history of philosophy. When treating the issue of technology in Marx's texts, one must remember not only the legacies of Feuerbach and Hegel, of the socialist utopians and the political economists, but also the contest between Enlightenment and Romantic attitudes toward nature and technology. These can be linked back still further to a reversal of values that, if incomplete, is nonetheless traceable to the transition between the classical and the modern world. Hans Blumenberg (1983) addresses this reversal of values in his *Legitimacy of the Modern Age*.

Specifically, Blumenberg explores the moral value of curiosity about nature. To be curious about nature and whether its received limits can be overcome: is this hubris? Or is it the proper posture of the human toward the natural world? As an attitude, curiosity implies that relations between human beings and nature could be transformed. In ancient moralities, curiosity was censured for this very reason. In the related themes of early Christian moralities, curiosity was accused of speculatively tampering with the received miracle of the world given, benevolently or otherwise, by God. But in modernity, the moral cachet of curiosity is transformed. Beginning with Giordano Bruno and culminating in Francis Bacon, the meaning of curiosity undergoes an evaluative reversal.

When this reversal is complete, curiosity is no longer loaded down with moral prohibition, nor is it simply a morally indifferent attitude, one among many. Instead, it is the proper and morally positive attitude toward nature. At its apex in the seventeenth century, before the return to a version of the classical wariness in Romanticism, curiosity becomes the defining feature of what is appropriate to human knowledge. Finally, curiosity becomes the appropriate existential comportment of the scientific and technological attitude.[1] Scientists and philosophers gradually extend the purview of curiosity not only to the known contents of the natural world but to the perceived limits of this world—and to the task of determining whether these limits might be overcome.

At the same time as curiosity defines a scientific attitude increasingly dissatisfied with the received limits of the natural world, modernity's new discourses of scarcity and overpopulation forcefully reinstate such limits. Though thinkers as late as Montesquieu can still echo the traditional view that the total population has declined since antiquity (Blumenberg 1983, 222), Thomas More, Francis Bacon, and Thomas Hobbes all work on the assumption that population is on the increase. They discuss the rational management of a burgeoning population, including, in the case of More, the spatial displacement of this population to uninhabited lands (Blumenberg 1983, 221; see also More 1989). In Hobbes, the theme of overpopulation is one of the ultimate threats to peace: scarce resources can trump good laws, bringing disorder to even the most carefully managed political body.

By the turn of the nineteenth century, overpopulation scenarios have become apocalyptic in tandem with the thermodynamic discourses of crisis discussed in Chapter 2. Thomas Malthus sets a geometrical progression of population increase against an arithmetic progression of food production, and declares the modern population increase unsustainable. Malthus then draws social, political, and theological consequences from this immutable boundary of nature. Malthus argues that such a boundary is the will of God, that it will ultimately assert itself, and that it therefore ought to be protected from any human interference that might delay its inevitable consequence.[2] Malthus thereby makes a bizarre hybrid of the premodern classical limits and the modern discourse of manipulating these limits. In Malthus, human beings both can and cannot influence the ultimate immutable boundaries posited by God or nature. Scarcity will have its way regardless, but it is best not to retard its progress. This suggests simultaneously both the efficacy of human agency and its failure.

Even a thinker as late as Darwin uses a concept of nature composed of such immutable boundaries, and, in particular, Darwin uses the postulate of scarce natural resources as an element in his system. In this scenario, a world of scarce resources supports a fixed amount of food production. This ensures a mathematically fixed boundary of survival through which the weak are eliminated. As Blumenberg writes,

Malthus and Darwin had both made their theories culminate in the advice that man should *obey the law of nature* by clearing away the social hindrances to its unmediated and unadulterated operation. The greatness of the much reviled 19th century lay in the fact that, at least in the greater part of what it actualized historically, it opposed this advice. The opposition was in the breakthrough of technicization . . . . Even Hegel . . . still expresses his opposition to the public and private "poor relief" illustrated by the English example by arguing from the irreducible difference between needs and means of subsistence . . . technical progress made it evident that the scope available for life was not a natural constant and did not stand in a necessarily ultimate disproportion to the growth of population.

> (Blumenberg 1983, 225, emphasis added)

In its vast production of wealth, and especially the advances in food production resulting from the discoveries of agricultural chemistry, nineteenth-century technicization challenged the received limits of the natural world. Nature is not composed of immutable boundaries that must be respected; rather, nature managed by human technology has the potential to push back these boundaries, an act which is concretized in increasing quantities of food production. The scarce resources appealed to in the discourses of overpopulation are, from the perspective of technicization, ideological. Blumenberg continues,

The foundation of agricultural chemistry—that is, the theory of artificial fertilizing—by Justus Liebig in 1840 revealed that Malthus's dual progressions could not only be disputed as a "law" but could also be conceived as a reality alterable by improved technique. Technique is a product of human impatience with nature. The long periods of time that Darwin required for the tiniest steps of evolution may indeed have made the great waste of nature, its huge expenditure of individuals, suffering, and death, appear in a new light of significance; but as human security, as justification of man's historical status, they were empty of comfort . . . man as an individual now had to perceive himself as impotent vis-à-vis time, the omnicompetent. The position of transcendence was reoccupied by the element of postponement . . . the lack of temporal congruity between the natural process and the acute historical situation in which man finds himself emerge[s] with extreme sharpness.

> (Blumenberg 1983, 224)

Against this backdrop, the idea of scarce natural resources appears to Marx as a mere social norm masquerading, ideologically, as an immutable natural law. Marx's materialism, from its beginnings in his doctoral dissertation on the swerving paths of atoms, appealed to the possibility of a nature not marked by a fixed determinism. Marx also read and made extensive notes on Liebig in 1851.[3] In his manuscripts of the decade that followed, including the *Grundrisse*, the idea of technology takes on an enhanced significance. A new world, founded on the advances of technological production, makes possible undreamt material wealth.

To designate this new world, Marx uses the Hegelian language of "objectification" [*Vergegenständlichung*].[4] Marx always employs "objectification" to designate the general, collective production of the human species as a whole, rather than the production of any individual. The chief objectification with which he is concerned is science. Applied to nature, science combats the scarcity of the received natural world and contests its boundaries. The "objects" in question produced by this science, especially machines and agricultural fertilizer, come to benefit their human creators as a species, not simply to benefit individual humans or social classes. The historical accumulation of such science drives the potential productivity of nature exponentially upward. The degree of immediate human control and management of the natural world is high, and the degree of immediate human control and management of the social world is high in consequence.

Liebig was, as we recall from Chapter 2, one of the few remaining vitalists among the scientific materialists. And just this vitalist view, in which humans are separated from the natural world by a qualitatively different kind of animating force, may be a prerequisite for the postulate of a technology that qualitatively transforms nature according to its own requirements. For in this postulate, humans act on and transform nature for the better through the application of intellect. These intellects do not merely circulate as an intrinsic part of a nature subject to fixed laws. Caught between the two views of the human interaction with nature—designated as "vitalist" and "energeticist" in Chapter 2—Marx's later work shows how technology is a social product of such views and of the modes of production that work, symbiotically, to generate such views. For Marx, technology will differ according to the mode of production in which its structures are concretized, a process that philosopher of technology Andrew Feenberg (1999, 2000) calls technology's essential ambivalence.

In Marx's late work *Capital*, the Enlightenment ideal in which nature's fixed boundaries can be driven back in order to improve the human lot is less pronounced than in his earlier texts. This is because capitalism progressively supplants this ideal with two others: on the one hand, a technophilic embrace of progress that loses sight of human beneficence; on the other hand, a corresponding Romantic and conservative demonization of technicization. Both capitalist discourses lose technology's relationship to the mode of production, and instead treat technology as having a fixed, nonhistorical essence.

In a parallel move, Marx's accounts of human activity in *Capital* progressively eliminate the vocabulary of vitalism. The Liebigian Enlightenment ideal requires the vitalist vocabulary, a vocabulary that is still common in Marx's *Grundrisse*: "[W]ealth ... draws new *vital spirits* into itself" from the worker's body (1973, 453, emphasis added). Finally, Marx's sociopolitical diagnostics in his late work *Capital* become subject to the problem of postponement outlined by Blumenberg in the previous passage. Although political revolution was a tangible reality in 1848, it was far less so by the time *Capital* was published in 1867. Instead, the waiting had begun.

In his analysis of the capitalist mode of production in *Capital*, an analysis that reveals the norms of capitalist thinking in addition to the norms of capitalist making, Marx empties his own "acute historical situation" of the comforts of either immediate revolution or the struggle for better wages. Instead, Marx postulates an inevitable, though temporarily deferred, totalizing transformation. For Marx, society rather than nature enforces the operation of scarcity: the law of scarcity that appears in the works of Smith, Hegel, Malthus, and Darwin is a bourgeois rather than a natural postulate. But this view still commits Marx to scarcity as a socially regulatory principle. In his postulate of revolutionary transformation, the nineteenth century's amalgamation and analogy between the social and the natural has been reversed, but it has not been left behind. The logic of postponement so characteristic of nineteenth-century scientific description, the invisible hand at work over large stretches of time, continues to determine the prospects of social and political revolution. This element of postponement not only leaves Marx powerless to address the question of immediate human comfort, but actually obscures this question in the giant units of political time that intervene before such comfort could be realized.

Oddly, this means that Marx is intellectually conservative at precisely the moment when he is politically most radical. At this moment, Marx transcribes the structure of the natural law of scarcity he has inherited from Smith, Hegel, Malthus, and Darwin into capital's operation and eventual overcoming. Marx's prediction of crisis is also nature's revenge. In the refusal to ameliorate the immediate human situation (through, for example, better real wages) in favor of the deferred but inevitable political revolution that will end all wage labor, Marx calls on the scarce resources of a natural human body at its limits as the driving motor of history. Refusing the claims of labor unions to more material wealth within the capitalist system for fear of pushing back the revolutionary apocalypse, Marx reinstates the structure of scarcity and its inevitable operation, as well as the invisible hand of economics. In such a view of society, the degree of immediate human control and management of both the natural and the social worlds is, once again, low rather than high. All we need do is await the inevitable.

In this chapter, I describe Marx's positive account of technicization from the 1850s and early 1860s, an account that unfolded prior to these darker themes of Marx's later work. In the earlier texts, the overcoming of the supposed boundaries of nature result in the production of material wealth that creates the possibility of a form of human association not based on scarcity as either a natural or a social postulate. The question of immediate human comfort is very much alive. But already there are also inklings of the technological skepticism that will be increasingly characteristic of Marx's later years as his view of technology becomes increasingly circumscribed by the form technology takes in the capitalist mode of production. In Chapter 4, I will describe Marx's largely negative account of technology in *Capital*.

II   Material wealth and value: the *Grundrisse's* "Fragment on Machines"

Marx's excerpt notebooks on science and technology from the 1850s, including the passages from Liebig, are a part of his preparation for the manuscripts collectively known as the *Grundrisse*. In the London autumn and winter of 1857–1958, the *Grundrisse* emerged from Marx's studies and criticism of political economy and utopian socialism, work that he had begun in the late 1840s. The texts that compose the *Grundrisse* are unpolished compared to what we will find in *Capital*, though polished compared to some of the excerpt notebooks on science and technology from which they are derived. Traditionally, the *Grundrisse* has been considered a working outline for *Capital*; however, here and in Chapter 4, I have emphasized the differences rather than the continuities between the two texts.

Marx scholars came to know about the manuscripts making up the *Grundrisse* only in the mid-twentieth century. Though a few Russian scholars had access to the notebooks in the 1930s, they were published in German only after Stalin's death in 1953. Thus the work of decoding these texts and linking them to the studies Marx was undertaking in the British Museum has only really just begun. Some of the most current work in Marxist philosophy is based on the *Grundrisse*, particularly that of Antonio Negri and Moishe Postone. Both Negri and Postone justify their choice of the *Grundrisse* as the foundation for their interpretation of Marx with the claim that the *Grundrisse* still contains possibilities and suggestions foreclosed by *Capital*'s difficult structure. My work on the excerpt notebooks confirms and deepens this line of argument.

In particular, the first volume of *Capital* presents challenges for interpreters because it isolates the logical substructures of the capitalist mode of production rather than its historical realties. Methodologically, Marx has modeled *Capital* on Hegel's *Logic*, a strategy he hit on and made obvious during the composition of the *Grundrisse*, but this strategy is not again discussed so much as it is performed by *Capital*.

Hegel's *Logic* is followed by a *Nature* and a *History*. Likewise, Marx's work is meant to open onto empirical reality in volumes II and III, having first disclosed the inescapable logical substructures of this reality—and its logical inconsistencies—in volume I. Many early economic critiques of the first volume of *Capital* make empirical criticisms of its content, emphasizing Marx's exclusion of the service industry or his failure to relate profit to value. Unsurprisingly, these come largely from French and English pens, whose authors have foundered on *Capital*'s structural indebtedness to idealist German philosophy.

Capital rarely gestures outside of the capitalist mode of production to other possible modes. Marx has largely eliminated explicit historicism from the account. The claims in *Capital* are, for this reason, always bracketed by the understanding of the alienated mode of production he has situated historically in his earlier works. Marx has bracketed off the capitalist mode of production, and he makes claims that fit only in the capitalist worldview.

By contrast, the *Grundrisse* begins with the broadly historical, even ontological categories of "production/consumption/distribution/ exchange" that characterize human objectification. In *Capital*, Marx replaces this opening discussion with the narrower category of the commodity and the commodity form. This category characterizes production/consumption/distribution/exchange in the alienated capitalist world. Both Negri and Postone return to the less formalized *Grundrisse* in order to reveal the conceptual and philosophical framework on which *Capital* rests. Without explaining this framework, *Capital* assumes the reader understands that the universal category of objectification—production—has been wholly colonized by an alienated partial form, commodity production (see Negri 1984; Postone 1993, 21–22).

Likewise, the *Grundrisse* offers possibilities for technology that do not conform to technology's deployment in the alienated mode of production. Rather, in continuity with the excerpt notebooks and the Liebigian attitude toward nature (discussed earlier), the *Grundrisse* emphasizes the potential for technology to produce material wealth that will be available to the human species as a whole, and that will assist in pushing back the limiting boundaries of the natural and social worlds, the very boundaries that create and enforce scarcity.

Within the *Grundrisse*, the longest sustained section of texts on technology or, to speak more precisely, on machines is split between the end of Notebook VI and the beginning of Notebook VII, deep within the section entitled "Capital." Following Negri, I am calling this section "The Fragment on Machines." Sections III–VI of this chapter offer a commentary on the "Fragment on Machines," slightly enlarging the excerpt treated by Negri to include the distinction between fixed and circulating capital that Marx outlines immediately prior to turning to machines explicitly.[5]

Production in the alienated capitalist mode drives the intensification of labor and the wearing out of the worker, phenomena that machines are used to exacerbate. The human–machine interaction within the factory scene is a parasitism rather than a symbiosis. But the parasitism inheres in the mode of production in which the worker and machine are placed rather than in the means of production themselves or the human relationship with machines *per se*. Beneath the surface of the antagonistic relationship between human and machine is a deep class kinship that mirrors the class kinship of proletarians amongst themselves, and that suggests a different mode of production would enable better relationships between humans and machines.

For Marx, the transition to this different mode of production is accomplished through a redistribution of the means of production spawned by the capitalist mode itself. Capitalist production marks a necessary transitional phase and is itself productive of the material wealth that will bring about its dissolution. After this dissolution, workers need not to smash but to own machines, for in doing so they reclaim the accumulated wealth of their class.

The redistribution not of wealth but of the means of producing it undoes the real subsumption[6] of labor by capital, though it does not necessarily need to eliminate communal forms of production.

The technical distinction Marx makes in the *Grundrisse* between alienation and objectification, which we looked at in Chapter 1 in the context of the Marx/Hegel relationship, helps to explain the simultaneous dissonance and potential of the human–machine interface. It also explains how the shape of this interface depends on the mode of production in which humans and machines are born and in which they take shape. For Marx, a just redistribution of the means of production will cause technological alienation to become simple objectification. The story of how this will come about is hardly a simple one, and it is not one Marx tells so much as glimpses. However, the redistribution of the means of production is the crucial starting point. After this redistribution is accomplished, the means themselves, like the humans conditioned with them, will not be the same. Both technology and humanity will be subject to a different social form, and have a different *telos*.

This call for the redistribution of the means of production does not alter the fact that Marx's fundamental critique is of the mode of capitalist production, and not simply of capitalist distribution. Redistribution of capital's spoils rather than its means would not rectify the inequalities of the system, which not only fails to reward labor with its own immediate product, but also requires a mortification of human physical and intellectual capacities—labor becomes a form of activity that is not rewarding in itself, and which is tainted by the notions of pain, suffering, and undergoing. Marx uses the term 'labor' in many ways, and, importantly, he uses it to describe the alien form activity takes in the capitalist mode of production.

The call for the redistribution of the means of production does, however, indicate the continued importance of technologically enhanced material making to Marx's account of postrevolutionary communist life. In the "Fragment on Machines," Marx uncritically copies Lauderdale's claim that "One of the traits that characterizes and distinguishes the human *species* is thus to supplement its work with a capital transformed by machines" (MEGA^2 II, 1.2, 569; French in original, my translation). Though Marx is working through the texts of the political economists critically, his thought retains some of this definition of the human essence as supplementing its work via machinery—or, anthropologically, the definition of tool use. For Marx, the purpose of this supplement will be the increased production of material wealth and the ability to drive back conservative estimates of natural boundaries.

If we recall that in Marx's original formulation of alienation, alienation from one's species was a concern, here we find that the human species is defined by its use and ownership of tools. The proletarian alienation from tool use accomplished in the real subsumption of labor by capital is part of the alienation of this class from the capacities of the human species. Workers must own the means of production in order to have their species-being restored. And not any means of production will do. The workers are entitled to have access to the most developed means of production, which is defined as that capable of producing the most material wealth.

Marx's emphasis on the continued importance of material making means that he is neither an ascetic nor a primitivist. He recognizes the importance of material wealth to human culture and human flourishing. In the *Grundrisse*, he even defines this wealth as the expansion of human needs: "The greater the extent to which historic needs—needs which are themselves the offspring of social production and intercourse, are posited as *necessary*, the higher the level to which real wealth has developed. Regarded *materially*, wealth consists only in the manifold variety of needs" (1973, 527, emphases in original). These needs will, of course, be intellectual or social as well as material, but Marx thinks material plenitude is a necessary condition for the development of higher needs.[7]

Marx distinguishes between "material wealth" and the notion of "value" characteristic of the capitalist mode of production. As a category, wealth is not reducible to value except in the limited capitalist imaginary. Again in the *Grundrisse*, Marx writes that "the aim of capital is not served merely by obtaining more 'wealth' in the Ricardian sense, but because it wants more *value*, to command more objectified labour" (1973, 353, emphasis in original). Postone cites another section from the *Grundrisse* to explain the difference Marx outlines here:

> Marx does not deal with value as a category of wealth in general, or in terms of a quasi-automatic self-regulating market, but as the essence of a mode of production whose "presupposition is—*and remains*— the mass of direct labour time, the quantity of labour employed, as the determinant factor in the production of wealth." With the development of industrial capitalism and the rapid growth of productivity, material wealth increasingly becomes a function of the general state of science and its application to production, rather than of the amount of labor time, and hence, direct human labor employed. The difference between material wealth and value becomes an increasingly acute opposition, according to Marx, because value remains the essential determination of wealth in capitalism even though

material wealth becomes ever less dependent on the expenditure of direct human labor. Hence, direct human labor is retained as the basis of production and becomes ever more fragmented, although it has become "superfluous" in terms of the potential of the forces of production that have come into being. The enormous increase in productivity under capitalism, then, does not result in a corresponding reduction of labor time and a positive transformation of the nature of work. The basic contradiction in capitalism, seen thus, is grounded in the fact that the form of social relations and wealth, as well as the concrete form of the mode of production, remained determined by value even as they become anachronistic from the point of view of the material wealth-creating potential of the system.

(1993, 232, emphasis in original)

For Marx, material wealth is the net productivity of a system of machine-enhanced production, and is not dependent on human labor for its measure. "Value" is an antiquated system, peculiar to capital and desperate to maintain itself, that measures all material wealth by the standard of human labor. Such human labor could virtually disappear if technology and science were maximized. In the *Grundrisse*, Marx links real wealth explicitly to science. Marx writes, "The *development of science alone*—i.e. the most solid form of wealth, both its product and its producer—was sufficient to dissolve [feudal] communities" (1973, 540, emphasis in original). Here we see yet another definition of wealth in addition to the needs definition: wealth is science. In addition, Marx shows that science is a key political force in the modern world. Marx thus links science to political change, offering one of the first syntheses of the technical and the political.[8]

Capital's self-preservation and profitability as a system rests on the maintenance of human labor—and the exploitation of this labor—as a standard for the production of value. Capital is therefore inimical to a standard of material wealth outside of the notion of value, and, with this, actually inimical to the very science and technology it develops. Nonetheless, capital is unable to avoid the introduction of science and technology into production in order to increase the production of surplus value. Capital thus progressively undermines the system of value on which it is based, a theme I explore further in Section III.

Marx investigates this hybrid environment, rife with contradictions, in the "Fragment on Machines." Here Marx's distinction between use-value and exchange-value with respect to the commodity finds its counterpart in his distinction between labor and labor-power with respect to the worker. Any given commodity's value can be seen either from the perspective of use or from the perspective of exchange: for enjoyment consumption or for productive consumption. Likewise, any given worker can be seen as capable of concrete labor or abstract labor-power. Labor is a qualitative relation, labor-power its quantitative counterpart. In capitalism, human labor becomes progressively interchangeable with mechanized forces, and it becomes increasingly conceptualized in these terms. Thus, labor is increasingly seen as mere labor-power, the units of force to which the motions of human work can be analytically reduced. In capitalism, machines have labor-power but do no labor in the sense of value-creating activity.

Moreover, human labor-power suffers by comparison with machine labor-power in almost every respect. As Radovan Richta writes, "simple human labor power is incapable of competing with the technical component of production; the average physical capacity of human labor power barely reaches 20 watts, the speed of sense reaction is of the order of 1/10 a second and mechanical memory is limited and unreliable" (Richta 1969, 27). Richta's comment illustrates the thermodynamic mechanization inherent to nineteenth- and twentieth-century conceptualizations of the human being, shows the way the human being has been made calculable in mechanical terms, and demonstrates the massive human inferiority to mechanical devices according to the standards of labor-power.

Humans, however, can be hired to do arduously what a machine can do quickly. In the capitalist mode of production, humans are often hired because more human labor-power is still cheaper than less machine labor-power. The householder makes a similar decision when he or she washes dishes by hand rather than using the dishwasher in order to save on the electric bill. Such an action includes the normative judgment that the householder's time is worth less than the money it would take to replace it with a faster and more efficient means of production. In a less innocuous example, female workers assembling television sets in the *maquilladora* are not replaced by robots that could do their jobs faster and more accurately. Rather, female workers are habituated to embody the minimal amount of mechanical movement necessary to perform the labor required, a process that results in repetitive stress injuries, insufficient bathroom breaks, and a host of other terrors (Wright 1997, 1998, 2001).

Such anachronistic labors occur when the worker's value falls far below that of the machines that could replace him or her. Capitalism forces this anachronism: workers do what could be done by machines.

Hiring the slow labor of workers rather than replacing it with the fast and accurate labor of machines is both cheaper and ultimately produces more surplus value. In the communist future, when scientific and technological advance will be truly maximized in order to expand the general wealth of society without dividing it into classes, this sort of anachronistic labor must necessarily cease. For the Marx of the *Grundrisse*, the communist future simply realizes the amplification of material wealth that is already potent within capitalist society—and suppressed by the regime of value. Just as wealth cannot be reduced to capitalist value, the potential of machine production cannot be reduced to the form it takes historically in the capitalist mode of production. Far from criticizing technology, the Marx of the *Grundrisse* actually argues that capitalist production is not mechanized enough!

III The strife between technology and capital: the fall in the rate of profit

The "Fragment on Machines" begins with the distinction between fixed and circulating capital. Though Marx uses the German *Flüßigen und Fixem Capital* to designate this distinction, he also uses the French *capitale fixe* and the English "circulating capital." The terms originate in the Francophone and Anglophone literatures of political economy, not in German philosophy or German scientific materialism. During these years, Marx's transition among these languages offers a clue to the etiology of a particular concept.

Marx defines fixed capital as "the character in which capital has lost its fluidity and become identified with a *specific* use-value, which robs it of its ability to transform itself" (1973, 679; MECW 1987, 29, 69; MEGA² II, 1.2, 560, emphasis in original). Fixed capital remains in the capitalist's hands, where it is a use-value for production. Circulating capital, by contrast, leaves the capitalist's hands, realizing its value in exchange. Circulating capital is also fluid, a medium of exchange. Its exemplar is money (see Section IV).

The exemplar of fixed capital is not money but machines. Marx defines machines as fixed capital *par excellence*. In a machine, a specific use-value appears in a particular product that has been formed with a particular technology and the market, materials, and infrastructure mandated by this product and the technology that produces it. This is the case whether machines are instantiated as instruments of production (e.g. the steam engine) or as independent infrastructure to support the capitalist system of production (e.g. railways). Marx writes, "[F]ixed capital appears not as a mere instrument of production within the production process, but as an independent form of capital, e.g., in the form of railways, canals, road, waterworks, as capital wedded to the soil, etc" (1973, 686; MECW 1987, 29, 76–77; MEGA^2 II, 1.2, 566).[9] Marx then highlights the key characteristic of fixed capital: its tendency to return its value piecemeal rather than all at once. Consequently, fixed capital requires a considerable initial outlay of resources, resources that are not immediately recompensed. Fixed capital is a risk.

Fixed capital's lack of flexibility means that once it is instantiated as such, fixed capital can only be used in a single way. It is frozen into a particular functionality. Because fixed capital can return the value invested in it only part by part, it can also do so only as long as the conditions for its functionality are maintained. After it has been purchased, a machine is dependent on a fixed power source and raw material, on the demand of a market, and on available transport to this market. Such machines are often designed with technologies certain to be surpassed in productivity prior to the wearing out of the machine itself. This will sometimes occur prior to the machine's return of the initial investment made in it.

Industrial machines are not the only technologies subject to such exigencies—so is infrastructure. Railways, however laboriously put into place, lose their functionality in an environment where goods and persons begin to be moved by internal combustion engines along roads. A given machine instantiates a certain level of science and technology, both in its energy source and in its mechanics. The social productivity of science and technology is frozen into an object at a particular historical and developmental juncture. And in becoming frozen in this way, fixed capital loses its flexibility.

Once instantiated, fixed capital has no *intrinsic* value. It can only pass "as value into the product…its total value is completely reproduced, i.e. is fully returned via circulation only when it has been completely consumed as use-value in the production process" (MECW 1987, 29, 71; 1973, 681; MEGA^2 II, 1.2, 561–562). Use-value ends for fixed capital in only one way: the fixed capital wears out, more or less quickly, more or less profitably, with more or less of its promised value reclaimed. Fixed capital works by dying out, piecemeal.

The capitalist turns a greater profit if the machine can be worn out as quickly as possible. Constant additions of the social labor of scientific and technological knowledge are appropriated, in Marx's narrative, "free of charge" from the society as a whole. In a society that operates according to these constantly increasing normative standards of productivity, the capitalist will have to invest in a more productive machine before the old one is worn out.

The introduction of new machinery initially raises the profitability of an industrial operation. The capitalist can, with a new machine, produce articles more quickly than the rest of society. The individual value of these articles (i.e. the cost at which they can be sold) is still determined by the labor time required by the old system of production, which has not generally introduced the new technology. But this time of profit is limited to the period before the new technology comes into general use, or before it is supplanted by a still-more productive technology.

The more accumulated resources work to expand this scientific and technological infrastructure, the faster the capitalist's machine becomes a dinosaur. In this mode of production, speed is thus of the essence if the capitalist is to redeem as much use-value as possible from machines that have been purchased. Speed will be the key element to the maximization of profit. The products of a new technology are most valuable before the benefits of the new technology (i.e. its increased production of material wealth) become generally applied to the production of a commodity, and employed by competitors in addition to the initial innovator. This results in the tendency to guard the secrets of technology rather than to generalize its benefits to humanity as a whole. It bears repeating: capital is interested in the increase of value, not in the expansion of material wealth.

The capitalist also has some interest in fettering scientific and technological productivity as a whole, trapping it at particular stages that support the regime of value. The capitalist's profit comes not from the excess wealth produced by machinery, but from the value this is able to capture in a market where the commodity in question is still generally produced by slow, human labor (or, in later stages, by slower machines than those owned by the innovating capitalist). Capitalism seeks to innovate in its use of science and technology, but not to maximize its productivity beyond what is profitable in a regime of value. Indeed, once capitalism has invested in a particular technology and its mandatory infrastructure, it is hesitant to let it to be replaced by the cutting edge of science and technology. One contemporary example is our continued, increasingly volatile dependence on fossil fuels for both power and transportation.

In later stages of capitalist development, the impulse to fetter scientific and technological productivity is compounded by yet another problem for the capitalist, a problem brought on by successive continual increases in the productivity of real wealth. This problem has a technical name in Marxism, where it is known as "the fall in the rate of profit." Although profits as a whole may rise through the introduction of new machinery, the rate of profit (i.e. the percentage gained with any increase) gets smaller and smaller. A system designed to enhance not only profitability but also the rate at which profitability can be extorted is instead forced to accept falling rates of profit.[10] Notebook III of the *Grundrisse* meditates on this problem and its effects. Marx writes,

> [Capital's] surplus value rises, but in an ever smaller relation to the development of the productive force. Thus the more developed capital already is, the more surplus labour it has created, the more terribly it must develop the productive force in order to realize itself in only smaller proportion, i.e. to add surplus value ... The self-realization of capital becomes more difficult to the extent that it has already been realized.
>
> (1973, 340–341)

Scientific and technological advances reduce the necessary contribution of living labor to a vanishing point in the production of basic commodities. Thus, they limit the main source of the capitalist's profit: the exploitation of the worker. This shapes capitalist use of science and technology, which is a use that is politicized to accommodate this paradox. In this usage, the introduction of new machinery has two effects. First, the machine displaces some workers whose functions it supplants. Second, the machine heralds a step up in the exploitation of the remaining workers. The intensity and length of their working days are increased. In addition, as machinery is introduced, capital must both produce and sell on an increasingly massive scale. Losses from living labor are recompensed by the multiplication of the small quantities of remaining labor from which value can be extorted.

In all of these ways, capitalism and technological advancement, far from going hand in hand, are actually inimical to one another, and drive the system into crisis. In this respect, a straightforward identification of constantly increasing technicization with capitalism misses the crucial dissonance between the two forces. We find a clear recognition of this dissonance in Marx's *Grundrisse*.

IV Enjoyment not value: challenging the capitalist logic of exhaustion

The identification of a machine with a specific use-value, as fixed capital, is how Marx contrasts it with money. Money is Marx's example of circulating capital; having no fixed form, money is fluid and can be converted into anything. The concept of fixed capital is concretized in machinery, that of circulating capital in money. Marx considers both machinery and money to be "destructive forces" not in or of themselves, but they operate as such when employed in the capitalist mode of production.

In the "Fragment on Machines," Marx's clarification of circulating capital (i.e. money) takes the form of a discussion of wages. He illustrates the distinction between fixed and circulating capital by contrasting machines with wages. The wage paid to the laborer circulates, is not crystallized into any fixed form, and is therefore transferable into any type of use-value within a certain limited economy. The wage never enters production, but merely cycles from the worker to the bank—or company store—and back again. In the hands of the worker, the wage is never an instrument of further independent production, nor is it designed to be. The wage merely circulates in cycles of productive consumption that benefit the capitalist: the worker consumes in order to perform alienating work again the next day, and consumes only so much as this performance requires.

Just as wages do not become independently productive, so too machines never circulate independently.[11] More precisely, the machine enters circulation only as the metal and elements of design that compose it wear out and pass piecemeal into commodities. The wage enters production only in the marginal sense in which it serves to wear out the worker whose bare existence it subtends. The worker oscillates between factory and bare subsistence for the duration of capital's extraction of surplus value, a process in which the wage operates only as a sign, if a highly fetishized one. On the level of exchange-value, or value as determined externally by how much a society will give for a certain unit of undifferentiated labor-power, a similarity appears between the worker and the machine. Each can be measured only by wearing out.

For the factory owner, workers fit the definition of fixed capital, or are conceived of as forces similar to machines. This is very explicit in Robert Owen, who refers to his workers as happy machines, though Owen was fairly unique in his concern for worker-machine happiness. In this construction, workers are units of labor-power, instrumental in production. They have a specific exchange-value invested in their accumulated habits of labor, which the capitalist system of undifferentiated (or abstract) labor seeks to minimize as much as possible. And, as with their mechanical coproducers, the goal is wearing these workers out as speedily as possible. Several short-lived generations are suitable for capital's purposes, so long as bodies are present to replace those that have become obsolete. The triumph of value over wealth, as Marx defines it, is the narrow sphere of needs the worker's life expresses in the face of the massive resources capital creates.

In a system that runs on what I call the "logic of exhaustion," the circulation and exchange characteristic of productive consumption will always be privileged over the fixed forms and use characteristic of enjoyment consumption. For Marx, productive consumption is that type of consumption that occurs during the process of further production and that has this production as its aim. The exchange-value of productive consumption is further production. Productive exchange is valued above all in the capitalist mode of production, and use or consumption is eclipsed, seen, and valued only insofar as it becomes instrumental, productive consumption, and therefore part of productive exchange.

Enjoyment consumption, dependant on a specific use-value that forever exits economic life because it is not available for further exchange, is negligible or devalued in the productivist metaphysic of the capitalist economy. One consumes only to produce; future work and future productivity become the justification of all forms of consumption. The discouragement of enjoyment consumption may even cause any form of consumption outside of productive consumption to disappear or become unthinkable. For this reason, as Max Weber's work illustrates (1992), enjoyment consumption is denigrated not only by capitalist metaphysics, but also by capitalist ethics.

Moreover, enjoyment consumption is eclipsed not only for the worker, who struggles to survive only to work another day, but also for the capitalist. The capitalist hoards and saves in a miserly fashion not only in order to feel virtuous, but also because the individual capitalist's position is motivated by the consciousness of its tenuousness: by the fear that he or she will be reduced to the status of the worker. This fear is not without cause, because capitalism retains a respect for purchasers but is no general respecter of persons. Successful workers in the early bourgeois period became capitalists, and the two figures share a common genus that neither shares with the aristocracy. The capitalist is unable to forget that he or she has no noble blood, and therefore no "natural" marker that separates him or her from the working class.[12]

In order to understand the fear that motivates both worker and capitalist, we will have to chart its historical terrain. In the eighteenth and nineteenth centuries, the historical transition of types of available labor is fast and furious, supplanting the generations of unchanged agricultural labor that characterized feudalism with rapid changes in occupation and class position. For the worker, there are rapid changes in the skills required by labor within a single generation. *Pace* Marx's account of labor's deskilling, there is no such thing as unskilled labor. However, particular skills do become obsolescent, and new ones develop. These new skills are often not immediately culturally recognizable as such: for example, patience with or facility for machines is a skill, even if it is not the skill of wielding a tool or the ability to exert more units of force than your neighbor. The technique of managing interactions among people is a skill, even if it is not the technique of a given handicraft.

The pressure on workers to develop new skills rapidly in order to have work and stay alive is what Marx's idea of deskilling really encompasses. Even faster than new machines, but like them in kind, workers become obsolete at an astonishing rate. In such an environment, the worker's accumulated habits of labor, skill, and strength become liabilities. Limitless self-transformation is not only a goal of capitalist personhood, it is a requirement. Because "wearing out" is the only possible calculation of value for fixed capital, the worker must struggle to use his or her skills before they are threatened by obsolescence. The intensification of labor thereby receives its foundation and impetus not only from the capitalist, but also from the worker, to whom these features of the capitalist mode of production appear as inexorable natural laws.

For the capitalist, labor's intensification goes through three stages: the introduction of machinery, an increase in labor's extensive magnitude, and an increase in labor's intensive magnitude. First, there is the introduction of machinery itself: the machine replaces a skilled craftsperson or system of persons. In the nineteenth century, new, less socially valuable—and therefore cheaper—workers (generally women and children) replaced male members of their class. Usually a fewer number of cheaper workers plus some kind of mechanical ensemble replace a human skilled in a handicraft and his[13] tools.

In this environment, one's relationship to ownership and one's understanding of the most current means of production determines one's position on the social ladder (IISG B 91A, 193). To take Marx's favorite example from the nineteenth century, first women, then children, working with newer, faster looms, began to do the carding and weaving work once done by men, and for a cheaper rate. Younger men, not the same ones who were put out of work in the old system, were set to work constructing the frames and engines required for this. One's male sex determined whether one could construct the machines themselves, a practice that developed a significant, socially valuable skill. One's female sex or one's youth relegated one to the operation of the machines, and advanced age relegated one to the sidelines altogether. Thus, with the introduction of machinery, gender divisions of labor assumed new configurations and also new importance, a topic I explore at greater length in Chapter 4.

Intermediate, transitional labor configurations, which seem odd to those accustomed to a wage system, also occurred as a part of the development of labor with machines. In the sharecropping of the nascent factory world, steam engines were set up in long buildings, and workers could rent as much time as they could afford on these engines in order to complete their projects. The ability to operate these engines, and to rent more time with them, resulted in a greater amount of sellable commodities. These were then sold to a middleman, which allowed each worker to retain the illusion of individual proprietorship in his or her interactions.

Second, there is an increase in labor's extensive magnitude—the length of hours of labor spent by the human beings superintending the machines. Idle machinery is of no value. For reasons we have explored, from the moment of the machine's purchase, the clock is running on the marketability of its products. Machines make value only by being used up or wearing out, and the faster the fixed capital can be recompensed, the greater the surplus value.

Third, there is an increase in labor's intensive magnitude—the rate of production of goods. Time itself is no longer an adequate measure of labor. Even when legislative attempts to limit labor time (e.g. the Ten-Hour Bill) were adequately enforced, labor's intensification (i.e. the increase in the rate of work) remained unregulated. Indeed, labor's intensification was probably stepped up in order to compensate for the losses to surplus value brought on by legislative enactments on the length of the working day. Workers first had to produce twice as much as before in a single hour or be fired, then three times as much, in order to keep pace with mechanical improvements and to ensure profitability. The effect was new forms of nervous fatigue, exhaustion, and illness among working populations. A more subtle effect occurs because time is no longer an adequate measure of labor's magnitude.

The two ways of increasing worker productivity were (a) increasing the number of hours spent doing work and (b) increasing the intensity of work performed during a given unit of time. In *Capital* Marx will use the distinctions of absolute and relative surplus value to designate the two methods of increasing worker productivity. He calls the increases deriving from the increasing number of hours "absolute surplus value" and those deriving from the intensity of work performed "relative surplus value." Under capitalism's constantly falling profit margins, both forms of labor's intensification occur simultaneously. It is only with communist production that the intensity of work performed will lay the foundation for free time, as we will see in Chapter 5.

All three types of intensification work to cheapen labor and render machinery valuable, not because the worker is paid low wages, but because the worker's labor-power—subsistence commodities, the stuff of which this labor-power is made—is produced with less expenditure of energy. The worker buys subsistence products produced cheaply and gains limited material sustenance from them. The capitalist buys less when buying this sort of power. Conversely, machinery is expensive and has a precise and constantly increasing cost for its maintenance. The effect is a devaluation of human beings and a hypervaluation of scientific and technological advance, so long as the latter remains private property.

Note also that in all three types of intensification, it is the symbiotic pairing of workers and machines, rather than their antagonism and strife, that becomes a requirement for the day-to-day production of commodities. This symbiosis, a habituation to the human–machine interaction, becomes a matter of life and death as the speed at which machines operate increases. The symbiosis is conditioned by the interchangeability of human and machine in the factory, a stage prepared by the historical era of manufacture's division of human labor into detail functions. Human labor, a habituated quantity of force, is acculturated to work symbiotically with machines for maximum productivity, and new configurations of this hybrid human–machine embodiment are the result.

The need for labor's intensification is not merely the result of competition from other capitals. Indeed, labor's intensification is required independently of competition. Although competition may drive and escalate the accumulation of capital, it is only a symptom of the fundamental logic of capital. Referring to the first form of intensification, the large-scale introduction of machinery, Marx writes,

> It is easy to develop the introduction of machinery out of competition and out of the law of the reduction of production costs which is triggered by competition. We are concerned here with developing it out of the relation of capital to living labor [*lebendigen Arbeit*], without reference to other capitals.
>
> (1973, 776; MECW 1987, 29, 160; MEGA^2 II, 2, 1.2, 647)

Intensification is inherent in the way both machines and the workers have value only through being used up as quickly as possible. Marx's major critical target is capital's inability to understand and deploy real wealth outside of this system of value, and the accompanying reduction of all use-value to instrumentality, to productive consumption, and thus to exchange-value.

From the perspective of capitalist production, value is calculated solely by the amount the machine is able to produce before wearing out. If a well-made machine wears out rapidly, it means it has produced well, or been used up with the maximum amount of efficiency. Here too the machine and the worker are similar: they fulfill their function only in working themselves to exhaustion as quickly as possible. And the most can be gotten from them when they are at the height of their energy, before fatigue or obsolescence sets in. Pliable workers are also prized, workers whose other life options are slim or nonexistent.

Exhaustion in its various manifestations—Marx's "wearing-out," Anson Rabinbach's nineteenth-century "fatigue" (1990, 19–44), and Donna Haraway's twentieth-century "stress" (1991, 63)—only becomes a category of such importance against a backdrop in which a productivist metaphysic has become the unquestioned norm. When production is such a norm, exhaustion itself becomes the goal of all processes. The enjoyment or use of any process is obscured in favor of this exhaustion. When the goal in view is the obsolescence of all processes through wearing-out or death, then enjoyment, or use unaccountable to future production, becomes impossible in both thought and action.

With the distinction between fixed and circulating capital stated at the beginning of the "Fragment on Machines," Marx lays the groundwork for the analysis of surplus value he will give in *Capital*: the explanation of how exchange-value is extracted from the worker and accumulated by the capitalist. Near the end of the "Fragment on Machines," Marx makes this connection explicit:

> [T]he labour time employed in the production of fixed capital relates to that employed in the production of circulating capital, within the production process of capital itself, as does *surplus labour time to necessary* labour time. To the degree that production aimed at the satisfaction of immediate need becomes more productive, a greater part of production can be directed towards the need of production itself or the production of the means of production.
> (1973, 709–710; MECW 1987, 29, 95; MEGA^2 II, 2, 1.2, 585, emphasis in original)

The cheapened sustenance of workers means the production of vast surplus wealth. Capital is not a problem of scarcity so much as a problem of maintaining profitability in the face of constantly accumulating super-fluous wealth, a point developed best by Georges Bataille.[14] Marx reveals that at its root all fixed capital is a product of surplus production—production far beyond any satisfaction of immediate need that has resulted, first, in an accumulated stockpile of resources and, later, in the creation of advanced means of production. Science and technology are themselves historicized as the products of societies with already devel-oped stockpiles of real wealth, and are themselves accruals of additional real wealth.

Machines, as fixed-capital *par excellence*, reflect a concentration and accumulation of surplus material, intellectual, and social resources. It is hard to remember this surplus in light of the scarcity and poverty in which the worker of the Industrial Revolution lives. Marx shows how overproduction, and its foundation in the exhaustive logic of constant exchange-value, leads to poverty. Poverty is a natural companion to hoarding and accumulation of the means of production, because the resources being stockpiled have to come from somewhere.

This will not mean that Marx advocates a simple Luddism as a solution for wealth's redistribution. The scientific and technological resources accumulated during the capitalist period need not be reaccu-mulated. The foundation for Modern Industry in its communist form, for what Feenberg calls an alternative modernity (1999, 183), has already been laid. Continued machine production in the communist mode of production should result not only in continued but in increasing mate-rial wealth, because the capitalist fetters on scientific and technological progress will be removed. Consequently, real wealth will be free to develop as the extension of needs other than material needs: especially the development of the artistic, social, political, and scientific capacities of human societies.

In the "Fragment on Machines," Marx suggests that capitalism's model of valuation, which remains a globally significant model, must be addressed at its root. In order to address it, a means for calculating value other than a productivity based on "wearing out" must be sketched, and a different *telos* for fixed capital must be posed. A use-value outside of exchange economies should attach to fixed capital itself. Likewise, a qualitative notion of human activity should replace the degraded notion of labor that reigns in all capitalist conceptions of such activity.

Machines should be valued for what they add to our lives, includ-ing the extension of material wealth and the aesthetic possibilities they make possible. Furthermore, we ought to be able to conceptualize a mode of human activity without pain, the doing of which is its own reward, a mode of activity that requires not simply the renunciation of our instinctual drives but also their amplification and enjoyment. Effectively conceptualized, such a notion might eliminate the concepts of "work" and "labor." The need for such activity will be the first development based in real wealth.

Many thinkers working in the Marxian tradition have suggested visions of noninstrumental use-value that honor this vision, and have redeployed broader notions of the practical activity of the human being than "labor" alone can encompass. This is especially true of thinkers in socialist utopian traditions, phenomenology, and critical theory. Following Donna Haraway (1991, 1997), Georges Bataille (1976 1988), and Herbert Marcuse (1966), my suggestion is that use-value be conceived as enjoyment or pleasure, here in the complex sense argued for by ethicists such as John Stuart Mill and Aristotle. Such enjoyment ought not to be ethically suspect as an impediment to work, but ethically desirable as an incitement to life.

By enjoyment, I mean something different from simple hedonism, which in modernity is itself often driven by the logic of exhaustion. If I recreate, or "blow off steam" like an engine, in order to work more productively the following day, then my leisure activity is as commodified by the logic of exhaustion as my labor. Forms of recreation dependent upon self-obliteration often follow this structure.

Forms of enjoyment dominant within the unchallenged capitalist productivist metaphysic are usually not enjoyment at all, but rather coercions to further production or enforcement of the norms of the system of production. So it is with the parties I must attend to socialize for work in order to endear myself to the boss. So it is with the drinking I am required to do as a social accompaniment to work. (It is telling that adolescents in the most repressive environments are initiated into drinking as an unadulterated pleasure: a pleasure so fulfilling that it merits considerable prohibitions. Although no one really respects these, they serve to highlight the activity itself.) So it is with a sexuality fully repressed into only genital expression with a member of the opposite sex: a sexuality that has at least a marginal chance of making subsequent generations of workers to follow the same rules.[15] (Recent assaults, economic and otherwise, on forms of birth control, including abortion, suggest that it is in someone's interest to increase these margins.) So it is with an instinct for cruelty that is not repressed enough, but rather encouraged as a means of reinforcing human domination.

By enjoyment, I do mean the sort of cultivation that is eclipsed for all, including the most privileged, in capitalist structures. Enjoyment must especially include the cultivation of the mind, body, and emotions as nonmutually exclusive ways of life, as systems that work together. It must include the simultaneous cultivation of sociality and solitude, and a relationship between the public and the private spheres that is neither coercively integrated nor dichotomized. Such enjoyment will require the removal of socially punitive measures for forms of perceived and actual nonproductivity. Current results of these measures include the devaluation of the work of caring for children or other dependent or independent folks out of love; hostility to some forms of religious practice; prohibitions on nonreproductive sex; the end of the education of the mind, body, and spirit at the age of 22, if not earlier; the neglect of proper rest and time for reflection; and the risibility of the practice of philosophy.

V   Man himself as fixed capital: the symbiosis of human and machine in the production of material wealth

In the "Fragment on Machines," Marx shows how the symbiosis of human and machine forms the volatile alchemy for the production of real wealth. In the communist mode of production, human and machine are to be paired in a happy, rather than an antagonistic collaboration. This is an unusual image, as French phenomenologist and philosopher of technology Gilbert Simondon observes in his study *Du mode d'existence des objets techniques* (1958). The possibility of human–machine symbiosis is usually neglected in favor of setting human and machine in some form of opposition. In the typical portrayal, one of the figures is analyzed and explained by using the other as a contrasting and boundary-drawing definitional term. The human is that which exceeds the machine in some mystic capacity; the machine is a soulless or spiritless system. The pairing of the one figure with the other, and the potential of this coupling for embodiment and the production of wealth, is far less common. At the same time, such a coupling is a basic component of actual modern reality (Haraway 1991). Simondon (1958) writes, "There is a inter-individual coupling between man and machine when the very functions of self-regulation are accomplished better and more subtly by the man–machine couple than by man alone or by the machine alone" (120, my translation).

This tells us a lot about the conditions of human embodiment in Modern Industry: humans have come to live with and among machines, and have come to be conceptualized as machines themselves. Marx is critical of what he perceives as a devaluation of human activity, but insofar as his work adopts the energeticist model I described in Chapter 2, he will struggle not to invest this human activity with a spiritual status in order to separate it from the machines with which it operates. Marx will want to portray the human being as a material thing, not as a spiritual one, and to make a case for the worth of its materiality. This means human beings will have to remain envisioned as the complicated material-like structures of nineteenth-century science, a science which portrays human beings as machine-like, and also be worthy. The human being will have to be materially honorable without recourse to God or the divine within. Moreover, human activity can retain none of the occult qualities that inhere in the vitalist explanations of the creative act of labor.

For the Marx who has been influenced by energeticism, humans and machines are continuous forces. They are alike in their material substance and in the kinds of functions they perform; this feature also permits their interaction and their ability to regulate and substitute for one another. In the historical and genealogical account Marx gives of machines, he shows that they are the frozen labor of the past, and thus human and very political in content. Conversely, humans, when portrayed in energetic terms, are machine-like. In production, humans and machines working together can produce massive material wealth, eliminating scarcity, and providing time for the free development of the individual beyond his or her laboring capacity.

This continuity and symbiosis between humans and machines is especially acute at the end of Marx's "Fragment on Machines." Here Marx suggests taking "man himself as fixed capital" (1973, 712; MECW 1987, 29, 97; MEGA^2 II, 2, 1.2, 589) as the principle of his humanism. This is to turn capital's mode of valuation against itself in an attempt to restore the lost use-value of the human being, and to serve as a way of glimpsing the reinstatement, in a worldly way, of human priority.

Recall that Marx was witnessing an age in which machines became for a time more valuable, because they were more calculable, than their operators, whose value was "below all calculation" (I.IV.XV.2; MECW 1996, 35, 397; MEGA^2 II, 9, 343; MEGA^2 II, 8, 385). Marx seeks to remind us that fixed capital, an investment of energy and resources, ought not to be limited to the productive machines of the factories. Above all, *human beings* ought to be regarded as sites for the investment of energy and resources. A society that followed this principle would express itself in the richness of the kinds of human being that it produced and in the types of machines it would make. This richness would express itself in the new modes of activity these human beings exhibit, in the use of science and technology they deploy, and the forms of social and political organization they found.

The elision of the single purpose of fixed capital is also glimpsed in Marx's demand that humans be treated as fixed capital. What might the human become were as much energy invested in him or her as is currently being invested in machines? The brilliance of Marx's suggestion here is that he does not have recourse to categories of the human spirit to amplify his vision, but to material well-being. As a regulative ideal, humans do not seek to become more like their gods, but more like their machines: the worldly products of invested energy and resources, of design and accumulation. Surplus wealth finally makes good on its promises for human development.

The freedom for which Marx hopes in this closing passage in the "Fragment on Machines" is "the capability as well as the means of consumption" (1973, 712; MECW 1987, 29, 97; MEGA^2 II, 2, 1.2, 589) for these human beings. He hopes "in no way for the renunciation of enjoyment [*Genuß*], but the development of power, of the capacity to produce and hence of both the capacity for and the means of enjoyment." Power's development and enjoyment are not opposed in this text; rather, they are complementary. This depiction of the relationship between power and enjoyment calls into question the bourgeois portrayal of power as renunciation. The bourgeois view of power requires the renunciation of enjoyment as a condition for the accumulation of wealth and its concomitants, including political power.

A lesson may be drawn from the hoarding that characterizes bourgeois life. The lesson is that objects with use-values of enjoyment and pleasure are not enough: human beings must also be able to live in social and political environments that permit the enjoyment of such objects. Human beings must be capable of consuming well, of treating themselves as an investment. They must be acculturated to enjoy, not simply exhausting themselves and others according to the dictates of the capitalist productivist metaphysics. Objects, bodies, persons, and pleasures must have inherent as well as instrumental worth.

At the end of the "Fragment on Machines," Marx wants free time in the sense of "time for full development of the individual" (1973, 712; MECW 1987, 29, 97; MEGA^2 II, 2, 1.2, 589). This must take place outside of an exchange economy within which such development would be calculated. Though he cannot yet answer it, Marx dares to ask the question of what it is to be capable of consuming well. Because technology has made social wealth a reality, what would it mean for *all* human beings to have the means and the capabilities of consumption, the development of power, and the enjoyment of use-value? In this ideal state, the human being is both producer and consumer. But he or she perceives neither sort of activity as labor. The fully developed individual's activity, liberated from the coercion of need, becomes play, without for that reason undermining material and intellectual culture. Instead, like power, culture is amplified rather than canceled by enjoyment.

But at the end of the "Fragment on Machines," Marx pulls back from these radical conclusions, and reinstates labor as the normative mode of human activity. Marx has adopted the economic function of the human being (i.e. labor) as an ontology, even as he criticizes all such ontologies as historical and imposed. Marx ultimately conceptualizes human beings as laboring, within the context of a productive system. Consumption is justified "as itself the greatest productive power" (1973, 712; MECW 1987, 29, 97; MEGA² II, 2, 1.2, 589) or is justified as productive consumption. Marx's account folds back into the *telos* of productivity and the necessity of labor.

Marx's continuation of the productivist metaphysics is the way he distinguishes himself from his contemporary socialists, the utopians. In particular, Marx's insistence on labor's necessity is a response to Charles Fourier. Fourier crafted elaborate social and political systems called *phalansteries*: 810 types of human character are analyzed and their permutations explored. In Fourier's system, every table has freshly cut flowers every day, the relations between the sexes are fully egalitarian, and the children take out the garbage because they like to be dirty.[16] In the "Fragment on Machines," Marx writes, "labour cannot become play, as Fourier would like, although it remains his great contribution to have expressed the suspension not of distribution, but of the mode of production itself, in a higher form, as the ultimate object" (1973, 712; MECW 1987, 29, 97; MEGA² II, 2, 1.2, 589). Fourier's prescription for a better world involves changed relations to production and the suspension of production as labor. Labor, a notion of human activity necessarily identified with suffering, is replaced by a pleasant notion of activity that nonetheless remains adequate to social tasks.

Though Marx recognizes undifferentiated, alienated labor as a historical category peculiar to capitalism, perhaps destined to end, he is at least ambivalent about the obsolescence of labor. In some passages, production and labor are universal, anthropological constants. When this occurs, the concept of labor is being used by Marx, as it was by Hegel, to describe the primordial interface between the human being and nature. Painful work on nature and the self is the cost of their transformation, and power over the world is based on enjoyment's renunciation. Marx's hesitation before the radical consequences on his own analysis retains the traces of a condemnation of *acedia*.

Moishe Postone argues that labor, as a category of human activity, is delimited to the era of capital, and with this that Marx does not retain a productivist metaphysic, ontologize labor, or repeat the political economists' labor theory of value. Postone is right to note that the end of labor is the radical conclusion of Marx's analysis. However, in failing to recognize Marx's own limitations before these consequences, Postone also pushes Marx a bit too close to the utopian socialists from whom Marx sought to dissociate himself. Labor *could* become play if, as Postone argues, the *Grundrisse* only supplied evidence that Marx was committed to the end of labor (Postone 1993, 28). In fact, when Marx envisions a changed mode of production, this vision sometimes retains obsolete features of the old mode: labor and the productivist metaphysic recur in the brief sketches we get of the communist future. This shortcoming also can help us understand why communism's historical life took the form of labor's glorification and fetishization rather than its critique and abolition.[17]

VI Class kinship and the redistribution of the means of production

In *Capital*, the importance of labor is retained. The force of Marx's mature political critique may be seen in his emphasis on the *redistribution* of the means of production. It is no longer as focused, as the *Grundrisse* still is, on the obsolescence of labor in the free development of individuals, the redistribution of resources of consumption and enjoyment, or the form of human activity that is to supplant labor. In both the capitalist era and the communist one to follow, the means of production are machines, and power is having access to them. Thus, the "Fragment on Machines" concludes not with the image of humans developing themselves in abundant free time, but with the image of workers who now own and direct the machinery of production. As we will see, the image is justified by the extension of the bourgeois notion of private property to the working class. In this notion, one ought to own the things that one's labor has created. Marx extends the domain of ownership to those things created, historically, by the members of one's own class.

This is a huge change from the capitalist mode of valuation. Capital's domination of wage labor relies on the separation of the worker from the means of production. Perhaps Marx even knows that the worker's ownership of machines would be an intermediary step, and one that must be accomplished prior to speculation about the communist individual and his or her forms of life. Workers first became wholly dependant on wage labor when they ceased to own the means of production; that is, when the tools, instruments, and machines of production become incorporated into the capitalist's rather than the worker's body. This form of body-snatching characterized the era of manufacture.

Thus, Marx is right to define socioeconomic class as more than simple access to monetary resources. One's class is determined by one's relationship to the means of production, of which the access to money is only one expression. Communism, in its first stages, reclaims the lost embodiment that occurred when the worker was first separated from his or her tools. What is reinstated in communism is the right to work and to retain the ownership of the surplus resources one creates, including these tools.

When Marx turns to class kinship and issues of just redistribution of the accumulated wealth of capitalism, it is not the enjoyment of consumption he has in mind, but the just redistribution of the means of production. Marx's political critique of distribution follows the familiar structure of illuminating relations between part and whole, and in this instance requires a class-based analysis for us to be able to see true relations. I get the fruits of my labor, but "I" and "my" are reconceived not individually, but rather as the conglomerate accumulations of the proletarian class. My kinship with the members of my class and the fruits of its labor mean that I should inherit the wealth of the production of my class in accordance with this alternative kinship structure, and not in accordance with the rights of birth.

Let us see how Marx's critique of distribution operates around the issue of machines. The material continuity between human and machine is the precondition for a kinship between the two. If humans and machines are set against one another as contrasting terms, this kinship is less visible. In the manner of all capital, both humans and the machines with which they work can be reduced analytically to a frozen form of past labor: that is, dead or objectified labor, as Marx calls it. Laboring humans are the product of the (often-limited) surplus energy of worker parents. Machines are the product of the surplus labor of generations of workers and technicians channeled into scientific innovations.

Here production and reproduction reveal their common historicity, and as the living stuff of the world they carry the mark of this historicity. Genealogies can be given for things as well as persons: here the work of the historian of technology has its parallel with that of the anthropologist (Appardurai 1986). Let me sketch an example that pertains to human–machine class kinship, and that illustrates the worker's class-based entitlement to the machine.

A female worker operates a machine in the factory. She is the offspring of generations of workers; the machine is the offspring of generations of surplus value workers have created. In the machine, the worker confronts labor extorted from those of her own class, converted into surplus wealth and then back into fixed capital. The initial conversion supported not only the owner of the factory and his or her familiars, but also a new and growing class of experts in science and technology. Studying advances in mechanics, chemistry, availability of materials, and the resultant new forms of thermodynamic energy production, these experts infuse new machinery with elements that contribute to the further intensification of its productivity.

All these forces come together in the machine this worker operates. A new machine is put in her place, which takes over her function and renders her jobless. It is as though her mother and grandmother's exhaustion are driving her out of work—as though they themselves had come to stand over against her. The very powers that created her, the powers of her class, powers that should be her own powers, are undermining her. Instead of machine–worker class kinship, strife appears between the worker and the machine.

An analysis based on class illuminates this kinship. This sort of analysis understands the proletariat as a kind of conglomerate body, with machines and human beings in continuity, and it substitutes class for familial kinship. Class kinship reveals the following false ideologies: conceptions of workers as carved up into individual units stopping at the skin, conceptions of workers in traditional family networks, and conceptions of an entirely unbridgeable discontinuity between the human and the mechanical. These ideologies are not merely illusory fictions, but deliberate, politically consequential ways of obscuring the truth of lived relations that do not correspond to these conceptions. Effective as ideologies, they hide the truth that workers are haunted by their own historically accumulated forces, purloined and reified in the disguise of a mechanical enemy. Only workers conceptualized in the new models of a class-based kinship can show how working-class labor has been unjustly distributed to benefit those outside the "family."

Just distribution in accordance with class would make the workers the owners of machines, and, more broadly, of science and technology.

But in the bourgeois era, the ideal of individual achievement is upheld. This ideal is married with old aristocratic notions of inheritance, and the result is the patriarchal transmission of property that one's father worked to accumulate. This differs from the aristocratic notion of inheritance, which is based entirely on bloodlines, family name, and position, rather than on work as the source of entitlement.

Thus, the class-kinship systems Marx envisions still build upon the bourgeois notion of inheritance merited through work. However, instead of being benefited by one's family, one would be benefited by the members of one's class. This would eliminate the last vestiges of the bloodline from the concept of inheritance. Workers would be made wealthy as owners of machines and other accumulated capital that their forbearers suffered to produce. This would eliminate the strife between workers and machines, which workers would own rather than smash. And when workers own machines, alienation becomes simple objectification, for the worker's body and labor is returned to him or her. In the Hegelian sense, the reunification and return consequent to objectification affords the opportunity for self-recognition and with it greater self-consciousness. In this way, the worker receives the "family inheritance" of the laboring class in accordance with a just redistribution of the means of production.

Historically, such class kinships have, notoriously, been superseded by other identifications, especially identifications with oppressive familial or quasi-familial structures. Marxist feminists have struggled to sketch and maintain a class kinship among women that is stronger than the affinities established by women to the men with whom they live.[18] Critics of first-wave feminism have claimed that women's racial affiliations supersede their identifications with other women: that first-generation feminism is marked more by its whiteness and concerns over the problems of whiteness than by any cross-racial identification between women (hooks 1981; Echols 1989). In communism's historical life, the moment when the working classes of the various European nations went to battle against one another during World War I is generally regarded as the moment of communism's political defeat. Here nationalism overcame class kinship. Thus, the doctrine of class kinship—and its failures—forms the basis for subsequent, unsolved developments in false consciousness.

In these three examples, the family, the race, and the nation retain the *symbolics of blood* and of the bloodline over against forms of class-based identification.[19] Even if class identification is more significant in shaping one's experience, it does not automatically wield more social power, act as a magnet for self-identification, or function as a kinship structure. Instead, class is often supplanted by more dominant, if historically anachronistic, forms of identification, even if these do not define one's experience as readily or as accurately as one's social class.

The aristocratic notion of the bloodline, as it became manifest in the bourgeois notions of family, race, and nation, has retained this sort of attraction. The bloodline retains this power even in an environment in which the class that relied on its privileges has been surpassed, and in which other, more salient, identifications like class are possible. The bloodline thus fits the definition of what some Marx scholars and historians of technology have called a "survival."[20] A survival is an object out of the past that carries with it the mark of its historicity, and yet continues to produce power effects even though they are anachronistic. A survival brings the past into the present.[21] We live out social relations that have survived from a different era, that do not necessarily describe our situations, and that fetter our possibilities of affiliation, action, and self-definition.

Conclusion

I turn now to Marx's fully developed account of machinery from volume I of *Capital*. In *Capital*, Marx's conceptual framework is much more polished, and his sentences are finished. But despite these clear advantages, the text is not necessarily easier to interpret. *Capital*'s theme is no longer tied to the specters of nonalienated human activity and material wealth also haunting Europe. As we have seen, these Hegelian political ideas are indebted to a vitalist, humanist scientific paradigm that Marx thinks has been overcome by the capitalist mode of production.

In *Capital*, Marx's adoption of the energeticist paradigm is much more complete than it was in the *Grundrisse*. Labor is no longer described in vitalist terms, and thus its status as the source of all value and wealth becomes ambiguous. In *Capital*, Marx documents the contradictions of the capitalist world in a discussion bracketed by the context of the capitalist mode of production, with little reference to any other potential modes of production. In the capitalist mode of production, machines are not optimally employed and even become ways of intensifying worker exploitation. This bracketing of machines to their use in the capitalist mode can produce misunderstandings about the ultimately positive notion of technicization that characterizes Marx's work as a whole.

Thus, the continued development and deployment of the technicization that begins in the capitalist period is a necessary condition for the communist notion of production. Technicization founds the most important characteristic of this mode of production: the plenitude of real wealth, produced with minimal labor, is the foundation of free time. Properly developed, technicization alone is even a sufficient condition for the communist mode of production, because the constant accruals of real wealth eliminate both the labor and the motivations of scarcity that, according to Marx, found relations of domination. Political revolution alone, without this accumulation, will not be sufficient for the inauguration of a new mode of production. In various letters written between 1877 and his death in 1883, Marx expresses his reservations about a communist revolution in feudal Russia, a country that simply did not have the technological infrastructure necessary to bolster this political shift.[22]

Marx's narrative of developmental continuity rests uneasily with his narrative of absolute revolutionary rupture. Here we see the energeticist paradigm in direct conflict with the vitalist, because the former supports a physics of continuity, whereas the latter supports its opposite: discontinuity and absolute variation in types. Marx's philosophy of history insists that development and revolutionary rupture cannot become uncoupled from one another. The communist revolution should occur in environments that are already prepared with a developed technological basis. However, this uncoupling is exactly what occurred historically, in feudal Russia and later China. Political revolutions, to paraphrase the words of Georges Bataille, may be inseparably linked to the breakdown of feudal orders (1970, 321; 1988, 279). If so, revolutions appear to combat either feudalism or its survivals, and are not so much a name for violent political change generally as they are a historically specific name for the kinds of political changes that occurred in the modern world.

On this reading, the communist revolution simply completes the work of the preceding bourgeois revolutions. Such revolutions end the symbolics of blood and extend the entitlements of labor. But historically, these revolutions also founded the kinship relationships of the bourgeois family rather than fundamentally transforming these relationships. They also amplify and glorify labor rather than working toward its elimination.

Moreover, revolutions are indebted to the vitalist metaphysics of the prethermodynamic era: they reassert human priority over the natural world. The world of blood and nature becomes the world of work, technology, and human industry. In revolution, human political life is shaped by design rather than by material or structural exigencies.

But we have seen, in the *Grundrisse*'s glimpse of a different mode of human activity, that Marx is able to envision in communism something beyond these perfections or even radicalizations of the bourgeois revolutions. Sadly, this is material *Capital* does not re-explore. In *Capital*, the contrast between a will-based revolutionary project and the structural crisis of capitalist society is more complete. Insofar as these are incommensurable, the revolutionary project is the loser.

As a part of his progressive erasure of Hegelian vitalist metaphysics in *Capital*, Marx does not restate the distinction between objectification and alienation, a distinction that ties Marx's early work to his later work. In the *Grundrisse*, the concept of objectification [*Vergegenständlichung*] is used to describe the general features of the nonalienated production of the human species taken as a whole. In objectification, human beings infuse nature with their own separate and more orderly natures, working up the world in the image of the human species.

Emblematic of this form of production, science and technology are too precious to be treated as private property. For Marx, human culture ought to regard science and technology less as commodities and more in the way we regard great art. According to Marx, if science and technology are appropriated free of charge from the storehouse of human knowledge, they ultimately can have nothing but positive consequences for humanity as a whole. Insofar as he maintains his vitalism, Marx's romantic critique of technology's momentary historical evils remains encircled by his enlightenment belief in the ultimate good of scientific and technological practice for the human species.

4
Machines in the Capitalist Reality

I Between thermodynamics and humanism: approaching *Capital*

Marx's work *Capital* is more a performance of thought than a straightforward treatise. In this performance, Marx adopts the characteristics and concepts peculiar to capitalist thought. In other words, he speaks in a variety of voices in the text, but rarely his own. When he does speak in his own voice, it is reined in by the norms of capitalist reasoning. Although *Capital* tells us a lot about capitalism and its functioning, it tells us little about Marx, who does not speak straightforwardly in the text. Thus, we must decode the text with some care.[1]

Marx's method in *Capital* is deeply informed by Hegel's *Logic*. Logical categories are used to determine empirical capitalist reality: "use-value," "exchange-value," and "commodity" replace the *Grundrisse*'s more universal and transhistorical "production," "consumption," "distribution," and "exchange." Unlike Hegel's categories, Marx's are increasingly circumscribed by history, and delimited to the logical substructures of capitalist thinking and capitalist reality. When Marx claims in the afterword to the second German edition to have liberated the Hegelian methodology from its mystified encasement, he is referring to this substitution, in which he has historicized the categories of Hegel's logic.[2]

Marx has indeed replaced Hegel's categories with historicized versions, but he has not eliminated the structure of organizing categories that determine empirical reality. The categories generate the presentation of the event being described as much if not more than the event determines which categories will be used.

Marx claims to have found the guiding logical substructure of the mode of capitalism in the data he assembles in the first three books of *Capital* under the concepts of living labor, use-value and exchange-value, and commodity. In the first three books of *Capital*, Marx has distilled the empirical data to its meaning for these categories. It is only in the fourth book that Marx turns to what he calls the "historical-literary" recapitulation of his insights. This recapitulation will be framed, he hopes, by the logical categories he outlined in the early chapters. He described his method to Engels in various letters from the mid-1860s:

> [T]he method of presentation in [the first part of the work] was very unpopular. This was due to the abstract nature of the subject, the limited space at my disposal, and the purpose of the work. [The later part] is more easily understood because it treats more concrete relationships. *Scientific* efforts to revolutionize a science can never be really popularized.
>
>   (28 December 1862; Marx 1979, 162; emphasis in original)

> There are still three chapters to be written in order to complete the theoretical part (the first three books). Then there is still the fourth book, the historical-literary one, to write, which is for me relatively the easiest part, since all of the problems have been solved in the first three books, and this last one, therefore, is more of a repetition in historical form.
>
>   (31 July 1865; Marx 1979, 198)

Marx's descriptions of his method tell us a lot about the meaning of the "science" with which he is operating, a science that he links explicitly to the Hegelian work of the category in determining what realities become possible and thinkable in a given historical environment: a science that Marx in his own early work has characterized, negatively, as abstraction. Marx also explicitly invokes science's self-critique: his own Hegelian method is applied as a revolutionary force on the domain of bourgeois economic science. Science in the narrow sense will be revolutionized by science in the enlarged sense.

Thus, in *Capital* Marx is not trying to get at all aspects of empirical reality. Instead, he means to display the conceptual essence of the reigning mode of production, and to explicate the historical as a consequence of this conceptual essence. Marx's historical account in *Capital* is tightly enclosed by the key categories of the capitalist mode of production, and logically circumscribed by the essence of this mode.

In *Capital*, Marx is always implicitly operating in the context of alienation. He is documenting the norms of the capitalist world according to its logical essence, not the norms of any possible world. Marx's choice to sketch the alienated capitalist world is not only conceptual, it was also precipitated by historical events. Rebellion after rebellion against the capitalist mode of production and its bourgeois political instantiation failed. Expelled from the continent and living in England, Marx was witness to the first generation of unregulated capitalism, its attendant miseries, and the first wave of sociological data emerging from this mode of production. Concluding, at the end of *The Eighteenth Brumaire of Louis Bonaparte* of 1851, that the Revolution was in its purgatory (1996, 115; MECW 1979, 11,185; MEGA^2 I, 11, 178), Marx has turned his attention to documenting this purgation by the 1860s. In other words, he has gone to work explaining the details of alienation as it exists in economic life (i.e. in the world of exchange-value). Alienation is treated as a "fact" of bourgeois existence.

Marx's prognostications about the good life to come are infrequent in *Capital*. The revolutionary prescriptions and hopeful visions that still run alongside the economic analysis in the *Grundrisse* are often not selected for a second presentation in the later work. Gone too are Marx's philosophical anthropology and the possible positive changes in human status brought about by symbiosis with machines. The Enlightenment's promises of objectification are eclipsed by the reality of alienation. The human–machine symbiosis produces only monstrous and deformed ways of life for the working class, rather than wealth, enjoyment, or free time.

In *Capital*, especially when it is read in isolation from Marx's other texts, the immediacy of a revolutionary future brought about by political will has become murkier. The role of human agency in bringing about revolution is deferred or eclipsed by other, more structural considerations, like the development of technology itself. An occasional remark asserts the necessity of capital's own systemic self-overcoming; indeed, this overcoming is the always implicit and usually explicit conclusion of the analysis itself. These features of the text allow Engels and later Lenin to interpret Marx as an economic and technological determinist. The inevitability of revolution is based not in class consciousness but in systemic crisis and collapse. But this is an error of interpretation. For it is not Marx that requires a fatalistic crisis rather than will-based revolution; rather, it is capitalist thought that cancels this form of human agency.

It is unsurprising, then, that when the human being appears in *Capital*, he or she appears as little other than an archetype: a puppet pulled by commodity relations, a pathetic wretch, an occluded and trapped exploiter, or a cog that is part of a factory.[3] In the fulfillment of the thermodynamic picture, humans are indifferent parts of the systems of energy exchange. They retain no particular feature that marks them out for special consideration, no feature that distinguishes them from animals or machines, no feature, at least, other than Marx's bare moral insistence that they ought to be considered as such.

Thus, in *Capital*, unlike in the *Grundrisse*, the energeticist picture of human embodiment is presented as accomplished. At the same time, romantic capitalist thought reacts to his accomplishment as a denigration of the human being. A peculiar oppositional humanism is unleashed within the bracket of capitalist thought, a humanism that Marx's thought performs within *Capital*, a humanism that I will call "capitalist humanism." The key characteristic of this oppositional humanism is that it is crafted as a reactionary response to the tenets of scientific materialism. Although it appears to be a species of the older Hegelian humanism—and it certainly has a relationship to this humanism—it is actually not the same kind of humanism. Rather, capitalist humanism is a backlash to changes in modern industrial life that threaten to cancel the traditional privileges accorded to human priority. These include the patriarchal privileges of the manufacturing classes, the male sex; and the sex-specific use of tools in guild labor. As such, capitalist humanism unleashes particularly virulent misogyny, anti-Semitism, racism and technophobia.

Thus, *Capital* is not a straightforward political work in the manner of the *Communist Manifesto*. It is, nonetheless, a political work, and a political work that seeks to reveal the capitalist mode of production and its effects on human thought, presenting readers with both the logical structure and the material realities of the society in which we are participants. Marx hopes to show that capitalist society sets up both a scientific illusion and a humanist illusion. In the scientific illusion, the human being is reduced to his or her function as a productive animal-machine. In the humanist illusion, a romantic longing for precapitalist forms of labor and political life is expressed.

Capitalist society has undergone the necessary conversion to the thermodynamic, energeticist notion of labor-power. It has eliminated vitalist language as a tool for describing labor. Humans, animals, and machines are functionally interchangeable in the actions they perform. But despite these eliminations, a variety of counterdiscourses have sprung up, including romantic, capitalist humanism. Capitalism unfolds not simply according to the norms of thermodynamics, but also as a reaction to these norms. Thus, capitalism is the product of the intersection of thermodynamics and humanism, reflecting the crisis of human demotion in the new scientific paradigm.

Marx shows this in *Capital*. As a system of production, capitalism maintains undercurrents that are neither empirical nor scientific in accordance with the mandates of the new paradigm, but humanist and vitalist in accordance with the reactionary paradigm. The most important of these is the distinction between human labor-power and other types of labor-power, particularly those performed by animals and machines. In order to reemphasize human priority, capitalism refers to human labor, and human labor-power, as a special entity. In doing so, it produces a counterdiscourse to the scientific materialism that would eliminate the humanist and vitalist markings of this form of energy.

This occurs because capitalist profit is based on human labor, not on the production of material wealth that occurs when this cheap form of labor is replaced by machines. Hence, capitalism cannot do without a robust and fetishized notion of human labor as distinct and irreplaceable, much as it also wants to constantly threaten human labor with replacement in order to keep it in check.

To be sure, Marx diagnoses this capitalist humanism. But in *Capital* Marx also works to clarify his own description of human labor (derived from Hegel and Ricardo), and to integrate this description with the new idea of labor-power. He writes that "[t]ailoring and weaving, though qualitatively different productive activities, are each a productive expenditure of human brains, nerves, and muscles, and in this sense are human labor [*Arbeit*]. They are but two different modes of expending human labor-power [*Arbeitskraft*]" (I.I.I.1; 1887, 51). In this statement, we see Marx's suspension between labor, which has qualitative characteristics, and labor-power, which can have only quantitative ones. In his insistence on the qualitative difference of human types of labor, Marx also insists on investigating labor from a human perspective, a perspective that cannot be reduced to the productive expenditure of human brains, nerves, and muscles. In this search to restore the qualitative dimensions of labor, Marx flirts with the very capitalist humanism his own work diagnoses.

For example, Marx offers a criticism of the concept of living human labor as mystical and occult. In *Capital*, Marx has become aware of the problem, among certain political economists, of mystical accounts of human labor. He therefore warns that value and wealth "in no case ... arise from some occult quality inherent in human labour" (I.V.XVI; 1887, 483). Instead, human labor should be subject to the same materialist account given of any other energetic phenomenon. At the same time, Marx continually appeals to the occult qualities of human labor: "[T]hat this same labor is, on the other hand, the universal value-creating element, and thus possesses a property by which it differs from all other commodities, is beyond the cognizance of the ordinary mind" (I.V.XIX; 1887, 506). Far from canceling the vitalist vocabulary, Marx also refers to the "animal spirits" of human labor, using language he has drawn directly from Liebig's account of animal physiology.[4]

As a materialist, Marx knows that certain descriptions of human labor's uniqueness are an occultism. At the same time, he seems to insist on this uniqueness in order to show how capitalism relies on human labor as the source of all value and wealth. This is not simply confusion on Marx's part. Rather, it is capitalism's anachronistic reliance on antiquated forms of human labor. In the accompanying capitalist humanism, human labor must somehow differ in kind from the activity expressed by machines and animals, and from the dead labor expressed by prior generations of workers.[5] To distinguish human labor from the labor-power machines produce, capitalism deploys a residual and operative humanism and vitalism that, although disavowed, persists.

In his performance of capitalist humanism in *Capital*, Marx deploys the particularity, priority, and importance of human force. To distinguish human labor from the unconscious (though purposive) actions of animals and machines, he requires that the human producer be the giver of form to unformed nature. The human producer's work is therefore distinguished on the grounds of German Idealism's appropriation of the Aristotelian account of work. Marx writes,

> We suppose labour in a form that stamps it as exclusively human. A spider conducts operations that resemble those of a weaver, and a bee puts to shame many an architect in the construction of her cells. But what distinguishes the worst architect from the best of bees is this, that the architect raises his structure in imagination before he erects it in reality.
>
> (I.III.VII.1; 1887, 174)

This model of production falls back on the human spiritualization and rationalization of the natural world characteristic of the older Hegelian paradigm. As such, it is a version of the new capitalist humanism, constructed in conscious mindfulness of the imminent threats to the specificity of human labor. Machines did not threaten the specificity of human labor in Aristotle's or Hegel's accounts, but they are prominent threats in *Capital*. There, living human labor is under continual threat of assimilation to the actions of animals and machines.

Marx's account of work's collectivist nature in both communist and capitalist modes of Modern Industry seems, however, to thwart this description of imaginative individual scientific production. So does his materialist account of making, in which the structure of the imagination cannot be wholly divorced from materiality, and in which matter and form are not able to be neatly separated. At the very least, the architect's imagination must be involved with the materials out of which the building will be made, particularly if the building is to be constructed in reality as well as in the imagination. But according to thermodynamics, the architect's imagination is already an energetic constellation: an amalgamation of matter and form that must be accounted for in energeticist terms rather than a form-giver exempt from the pulls of materiality.

Moreover, this account of human intellectual design and dominance over reality is the exact opposite of the features that Marx, following Smith and Hegel, seems to attribute to the political life of capitalism. In political life (as described by the later Marx), revolutionary crises occur because humans work more like spiders and bees, collectively bringing about a design of which they have no imaginary forecast (see Chapter 2). That is, human will has been eliminated from the revolutionary equation. But should this happen, humans are not acting qua human in the way Marx outlined, but rather qua animal or machine.

Marx thinks that at a certain stage of development, albeit one now relegated to an uncertain future, humans will again plan and construct their societies consciously. Contrasting the unconscious spontaneity of the political products of the present generation with the conscious planning of those of future generations, Marx writes,

The life-process of society, which is based on the process of material production, does not strip off its mystical veil until it is treated as a production by freely associated men, and is *consciously regulated* by them in accordance with a settled plan. This, however, demands for society a certain material ground-work or set of conditions of existence which in their turn are the *spontaneous* product of a long and painful product of development.

(I.I.III.4; 1887, 84, emphasis added)

There is a key reversal here. Human agency does not do the groundwork for a better society; instead, society lays the groundwork for future human agency behind the backs of the human agents. Marx has spotted the changed material environment, but not the fact that this environment will require models of human agency and change that differ from those of the modern period. The contract theorist's notion of free association and the utopian socialist's top-down strategies of imaginative social design will have to be replaced by figures of political agency working within material strictures. Rather than sketch such agency, Marx appeals to the return of these older fictions. Humans will once again be able to imagine societies and impose these imaginings on a malleable reality.

In *Capital*, Marx often deploys monstrosity as an accompaniment and sign of the new capitalist humanism. When the human being is too closely assimilated to his or her animal or mechanical functions without imagination or will, or when living labor is set into continuity with past labor (what Marx calls "dead labor"), the result is a monstrosity. Monsters mark the boundaries where capitalism is unwilling or unable to fully assimilate the thermodynamic paradigm that would treat human beings in full continuity with both animals and machines, and the living in continuity with the dead, considering all of these forces as forms of energy. The use of monster figures as an indictment of capitalist production is especially pronounced, as we shall see, in Marx's account of technologically mediated labor in *Capital*.

As with the *Grundrisse*, *Capital* reveals the research to which Marx's condensed and rhetorical polemical works of the late 1840s and early 1850s led him. We have seen that a key part of this research was in the area of science, technology, and society—particularly machine technology and its relationship to the class struggle. We have also seen that this research gives rise to changes in the way Marx conceptualizes labor and labor-power. The transformation of these concepts continues throughout *Capital*. However, Marx's account of machines in *Capital* differs from that in the *Grundrisse*.

On the one hand, the account given in *Capital* is simply more complete. By the time *Capital* was written, Marx had largely completed his studies on technology (begun in the 1840s), and he draws on this material in its most polished form. *Capital* contains Marx's fullest and most historically detailed account of machinery, the lengthy chapter XV.[6] But the tone of this chapter is radically different from that of the fragmentary *Grundrisse*. Marx limits his description of the role of technology to the role played by technology in the capitalist mode of production. This leaves him less and less optimistic about technology's ultimate good for the human species. Because of capitalism's reliance on human labor for profit, technology is only deployed within capitalism to mortify and discipline human labor, never to eliminate it.

Below, I have pulled three things out of Marx's account of machines as it appears in *Capital*. Each of these discussions emphasizes the role played by machines in the context of an alienating mode of production. In each of the discussions, I have also sought to display the effects of capitalism's suspension between the thermodynamic/energeticist paradigm of production and the reactionary capitalist humanism that seeks to reinstate the priority of human labor.

First, I describe what a machine is for Marx and how historical eras are delineated by the use they make of technology. Second, I show how *Capital*'s overarching framework of alienation undercuts the possibility of a positive account of technologically mediated labor. To do this, I develop the theme of Marx's vocabulary of monstrosity in relation to machinery. Third, I explore two monstrosities targeted by capitalist humanism: the laboring female body and the racially othered body. In conclusion, I turn to the few comments in *Capital* where Marx *does* sketch a path between current, alienating employment of machines, and their employment in the revolutionary future. I emphasize his increasing bewilderment at how to explain, rather than merely assert, this transition.

II Machinery as an historical category of production

In *Capital* Marx writes, "It is not the articles made, but how they are made, *and by what instruments*, that enables us to distinguish different economic epochs" (I.III.VII.1; MECW 1996, 35, 190; MEGA^2 II, 9, 156; MEGA^2 II, 8, 194, emphasis added). Marx calls machines "instruments of production" and "means of production." The latter term has a merit that the former does not: its greater generality allows it to encompass a wider array of objects, and it is less limited to a given economic epoch. This is important because, as we will see, the machine has features that cause it to exceed its status as an instrument in the narrow sense of the term.

Marx defines a means/instrument of production in order to delineate an economic epoch. The economic epoch becomes his principle for delineating historical epochs. At the most general level of analysis, the "articles made" (i.e. the products of human consumption) are largely the same in kind: food, clothing, shelter. Taken at a more individual level, the articles will bear the marks of the instruments, or means, by which they have been produced. For example, an aluminum soda container imparts a metallic taste to its product. Text scanned using word-recognition software is marked with typographical errors. These features particularize the experience of consumption in accordance with a particular means of production.

Just as the tool was the means of production emblematic of the era of manufacture and the hand the means of production emblematic of Marx and Hegel's so-called "prehistory,"[7] the machine is the means of production emblematic of Modern Industry. Machine use separates the era of Modern Industry from that of manufacture, the era immediately preceding it in Marx's history.

In *Capital*, Marx is concerned with describing the realities and instruments of production that lead to capitalism and that develop and function within the mode of capitalism. In his early work, and even in *Capital* up until chapter XV, Marx discusses the effects of machinery without defining what machines—the nineteenth-century means of production *par excellence*—are for him. This gap is filled in the first section of the chapter. Marx writes,

All fully developed machinery consists of three essentially different parts, the motor mechanism, the transmitting mechanism, and finally the tool or working machine. The motor mechanism is that which puts the whole in motion. It either generates its own motive power, like the steam-engine, the caloric engine, the electromagnetic machine, &c., or it receives its impulse from some already existing natural force, like the water-wheel from the head of water, the wind-mill from wind, &c. The transmitting mechanism, composed of fly-wheels, shafting, toothed wheels, pulleys, straps, ropes, bands, pinions, and gearing of the most varied kinds, regulates the motion...and divides and distributes it among the working machines. These two first parts of the whole mechanism are there, solely, for putting the working machines in motion, by means of which motion the subject of labor is seized upon and modified as desired. The tool or working machine is that part of the machinery with which the industrial revolution of the 18th century started. And to this day it constantly serves as such a starting point, whenever a handicraft, or a manufacture, is turned into an industry carried on by machinery.

(I.IV.XV.1; MECW 1996, 35, 376; MEGA² II, 9, 325; MEGA² II, 8, 365)

Like an organism, the machine's parts work in symbiosis, and changes in one part result in changes in the others.

The first part of the distinction Marx draws here derives from Charles Babbage. In his excerpts from Babbage's *On the Economy of Machinery and Manufactures*, Marx highlights the division between those parts of the machinery "employed to produce power" and those "installed merely to transmit force and execute work" (IISG B 91A, 182–183). Recognizing the key element of the nineteenth-century's Industrial Revolution, Marx underlined the passages in Babbage that emphasize machines that produce power directly, unlike those that merely transmit the power of wind and water. The distinction Marx takes from Babbage is the distinction between the gaining of force and its mere transmission.[8] The Industrial Revolutions of the seventeenth and early eighteenth centuries innovated the transmitting mechanisms. Machines were constructed to step in for the detailed functions of hierarchically divided guild labor. The Industrial Revolutions of the late eighteenth and nineteenth centuries produced power in the form of self-acting motors, especially steam engines, and applied this power industrially.

Anticipating the debates over the periodization of the Industrial Revolution among twentieth-century philosophers of technology, Marx even worked on a theory of technological development during the composition of chapter XV.[9] Marx writes in a letter to Engels that "the [first] industrial revolution does not spring from the *motive forces* but from the part of the mechanical equipment that the Englishman calls a working machine ... following this first great industrial revolution, the employment of the steam engine as a machine producing movement, was the second" (quoted in Richta 1969, 25, fns 1 and 2). For most of chapter XV, Marx is concerned with the development and application of this second revolutionary element: the steam engine and its amplification of force.

In nineteenth-century science and technology, no changes are as frequent as changes in available energy sources. The motor mechanism becomes the most revolutionary element of production. Chemical and thermodynamic science is applied to the already revolutionized mechanics and to untransformed, although multiplied, hand tools. Changes of design in the types of engines used cause reverberations through the physical bodies of the working machines, which must be accommodated to these forces, leading to new discoveries in metallurgy and the standardization of hardware.

In his notebooks, Marx studies machine construction in order to understand the technical workings of the new motors (see Cover Illustration). The motor either introduces or transmits extant force into the operation. It is "that which puts the whole in motion," and it replicates all of the logical problems of causation that attach to any prime mover. The first English edition of *Capital* even uses the philosophically loaded term "self-acting prime mover" for *"einem sich selbst bewegenden erste Motor"* (I.IV.XV; MECW 1996, 35, 384–389; MEGA² II, 9, 332–336; MEGA² II, 8, 372–375).

The sections from Hegel's *Lectures on the History of Philosophy* that address Aristotle's *Metaphysics* use different locutions for this force: *Das Unbewegte, was bewegte* and *die erste Ursache* (Hegel 1995, I, 161). This suggests that Marx is not explicitly invoking a link between the machine and God, or between the machine and the metaphysical paradoxes associated with the unmoved mover. Nevertheless, the steam engine must have appeared like a magic source of energy to its first generation of users, especially when compared with wind and water power, whose mechanics were more readily visible and whose power was dependent upon the blessings of nature. This leads to social confusion about how the machine works as well as whence it derives its energy and value, along with considerable fetishization of machines as objects.

In Marx's account, the motor is therefore either *causa sui* or caused by nature—either a thermodynamic engine or an apparatus for harnessing wind or water power. The steam engine is the new means of production in Marx's time, replacing the old means of production, the mill or the wheel. The seemingly self-causing thermodynamic engine is a more proper motor. If caused by nature, a motor is actually a transmitting mechanism for natural forces. Moreover, it can work only when such forces are amiable, that is, when the wind blows or the water churns. Yet Marx's machine has three parts, not two, which would suggest that it is the late eighteenth- and nineteenth-century developments in thermodynamic engines that he really has in mind in this account of the motor as the source of factory motion.[10]

Though it may have seemed magical to the first generation of producers using it, the nineteenth-century motor gets its power from precise sources. It gets its power from applied thermodynamic science, technology's discovery, and from the amplification of "natural" force. This changes the meaning of nature and fundamentally alters the relationship between the human being and nature. Human faculties could not witness the full-scale operation of these natural forces in the old sense, as the full scope of wind or water power was beyond the limits of human perception. Nor could these forces be controlled, except in the small measure of harnessing what can only appear, in these conditions, as a gratuitous power. Thus, the operations of natural forces were largely out of the reach of the human mind and will and necessitated an explanatory concept like God. But the steam engine appeared to the natural philosophers of the age as a power source entirely subject to the human will, an instantiation of Baconian nature doing human bidding.

This is confirmed when Marx writes that with machinery the human being "for the first time succeeds in making the product of his past labour work gratuitously, *like the forces of nature*" (I.IV.XV.2; MECW 1996, 35, 391; MEGA^2 II, 9, 338; MEGA^2 II, 8, 379, emphasis added). The point paraphrases Bacon's seventeenth-century notion of the function of inventions to improve the human species and subdue nature by following her laws (Bacon 2000, 85). Past labor is "like" nature in that it offers force gratuitously, that is, without additional human labor. Again, Marx has the steam engine in mind. The human labor accumulated in this technological device is able to supplant natural force. The steam engine is superior to natural force not only because of its greater power, but also because it is able to be controlled, that is, turned on and off at will. Force's self-causation, at the bid of the human intellect that designed the machine and the human will that turns it on or off, is a godly power.[11]

For Marx, machine use also affects human embodiment. The integration of a set of instruments into the human corporeal schema defines the human species as such. In chapter XV, Marx uses the bodily integration of tools to set off human beings from animals and to elevate them above nature. He writes,

> Thus Nature becomes one of the organs of his activity, one that he annexes to his own bodily organs, adding stature to himself in spite of the bible... [T]he use and fabrication of instruments of labour, although existing in germ among certain species of animals, is specifically characteristic of the human labour-process, and [Benjamin] Franklin therefore defines man as a tool-making animal.
> (I.III.VII.1; MECW 1996, 35, 189; MEGA^2 II, 9, 155; MEGA^2 II, 8, 193–194)

Here Marx identifies humans and machines, with the "human being" always as a primary term, as a way of setting both apart from animal life. Because of the traditional notion of human beings deployed in this passage, Marx does not extend this philosophical anthropology to its historical consequences: that the embodiment of different forms of tools produces different types of human being just as the use of different instruments produces different types of society.[12]

In addition, the changes brought about by hybrid human–machine embodiment are not all Promethean victories over the gods. Marx quickly shifts emphasis, stressing the negative aspects of this form of embodiment in capitalism. For although the human species as a whole may have annexed some powerful organs, working-class humans suffer direct damage to their bodies as a result of the interaction of these bodies with machines.

Marx claims that when employed by capital, machines work like vampires, co-opting the skill and strength of human laborers that work upon them. When a motor mechanism substitutes for human power, it steps in for accumulated strength: the human analogue of the mechanical term "force." I emphasize the motor-mechanism's co-optation of strength, or its force, because in Marx's analysis of the effects of machine production on labor, the category of strength/force threatens to disappear in the face of the emphasis placed on the skill co-opted by the transmitting mechanism.

Throughout his work, Marx speaks of labor's deskilling; he repeatedly notes labor's destrengthening as well. In the formulation of alienation in the *Economic and Philosophical Manuscripts of 1844*, Marx writes that the laborer is miserable because he does not develop his mental *and physical* energies freely (MECW 1975, 3, 275–276; MEGA^2 I, 2, 368–369, emphasis added). In a passage about the employment of machines in capitalism in the "Fragment on Machines," Marx writes, "it is the machine which possesses skill *and strength* [*Kraft*] in the place of the worker, is itself the virtuoso" (1973, 693; MECW 1987, 29, 82; MEGA^2 II, 1.2, 572; emphasis added). In chapter XV of *Capital*, Marx will even call light labor a torture (I.IV.XV.4; MECW 1996, 35, 426; MEGA^2 II, 9, 369; MEGA^2 II, 8, 411), because not only intellectual but also all bodily interest in work is annulled.

But Marx subsequently overemphasizes the issue of the deskilling of labor, paying less critical attention to the importance of strength. By the end of the "Fragment on Machines," Marx has dropped strength from his account of alienated labor and substituted the intellect. He writes, "In machinery, *knowledge* appears as alien, external to [the worker]" (1973, 695; MECW 1987, 29, 84; MEGA^2 II, 1.2, 574; emphasis added).

Strength can be viewed as a type of skill. It would be unclear how to classify, for example, a body's accumulated habit or knowledge. To take an example from Aristotelian habituation, the potter develops the muscles needed to kick his or her wheel through the practice of kicking itself. But Marx rarely if ever makes the Aristotelian connection between skill and strength explicit in his published works.

Marx analyzes the machine's possession of knowledge or intellectual skill in his account of its second part, the transmitting mechanism. Marx lists the devices of mechanical science whose job it is to regulate and transmit the motion (i.e. force) of the motor mechanism to the working machines. The "improvements" that will allow greater mechanical productivity in the nineteenth century largely consist of more powerful motor mechanisms and changes of design in transmitting mechanisms. Working machines are largely unchanged.

The working machine evolves from the tool wielded in the manufacturer's workshop under human power. For use with machines, this tool is modified in two crucial ways. First, it must be set into motion not by the human body but by the motor and transmitting mechanisms. Hence, the tool is modified to fit into these new mechanisms as sources of power and direction. This means that where the transmitting mechanism leaves off and the working machine begins is ambiguous. As the working machine comes to fit the transmitting mechanism, some features of the transmitting mechanism are built into the working machine, or tool.

Second, the working machine is a tool quantitatively multiplied. There are not one but many tools operating simultaneously. Each subsequent part of the machine reflects a numerical increase: one motor mechanism may direct thousands of working machines through an intermediary number of transmitting mechanisms. The tendency is a proliferation of parts, but centralization of power.

The interrelation among the machine's three parts is important for distinguishing Marx's notion of technology from its classical and early modern predecessors. The nineteenth-century machine proper is neither a tool nor a mechanical device powered by wind or water. The nineteenth-century machine implies an entire context, technological as well as cultural: the full factory scene. A heat-producing engine runs the scene. Machine tools transmit its force through the bodies of nascent commodities and their worker attendants. This occurs at maximum speed and intensity in an economy in which the principle of greatest possible productivity is an unquestioned norm.

Marx writes of this abstractly in the *Grundrisse*'s "Fragment on Machines":

[O]nce adopted into the production process of capital, the means of labour passes through different metamorphoses, whose culmination is the *machine*, or rather, an *automatic system of machinery* ... set in motion by an automaton, a moving power that moves itself; this automaton consisting of numerous mechanical and intellectual organs, so that the workers themselves are cast merely as its conscious linkages.

(1973, 692; MECW 1987, 29, 82; MEGA^2 II, 1.2, 571, emphases in original)

In *Capital*, Marx's picture of machinery is much more concrete. Marx fills in the abstraction "machine" that had hitherto been the object of his discussion with the content of the motor, transmitting mechanism, and working machines, and further specifies the relation among the three parts. His emphasis is no longer on the consciousness of the worker, but on the consciousness embodied in the machine.

In alienation, it is no longer clear that the worker is conscious. For that matter, he or she neither retains nor is required to retain other traditionally "human" attributes. In capitalism, the machine is animate via the motor mechanism, conscious of its intent via the transmitting mechanism. According to Marx, its human operator is "reduced" to the role of "watchman and regulator" (1973, 705; MECW 1987, 29, 91; MEGA^2 II, 1.2, 581). The repetitive and boring action of such a task is an offense to the human worker's "animal spirits," which naturally crave variation. But what is a human operator reduced from, if not from the model of feudal labor in which an individual craftsman wields a tool? Marx makes a problem for himself here that he probably does not solve. After the revolution, human beings are not restored to feudal labor. Rather they continue work with machines in this "reduced" capacity, a seeming contradiction that I will explore further in Chapter 5.

The quantitative multiplication of the working machine has analogues in the qualitative multiplications characteristic of all three parts of the machine. The motor mechanism quantitatively multiplies strength; the transmitting mechanism quantitatively multiplies skill; the working machine quantitatively multiplies subsistence commodity production. This quantitative multiplication results in qualitative shifts that demarcate the features and character of machine production in capitalism. One such shift is the negligible cost at which human workers can be maintained in comparison to the value they are producing.

The nineteenth-century machine body has heart, head, and hands: motor, transmitting, and working machines, respectively. In his account of the effects of machinery on worker embodiment, Marx no longer accounts for the machine body with its technological lineage in mind, but with a focus on the worker the machine replaces. An implicit analogy is therefore always in play between the worker's functioning and the machine's functioning. The resemblance between worker and machine is Marx's fundamental assumption in this account. He repeats the science and technology of his time while he criticizes it. The assumption of a homology between worker and machine repeats the scientific materialist insistence on the similarity of the two. Simultaneously, the Marxist critique of alienated labor challenges the notion that workers ought to be treated merely as functional machines or labor-power. Even as Marx's own analysis shows how workers and machines are functionally interchangeable, he shows how viewing them as interchangeable may itself be a product of capitalist science.

The vision of human machines is explicit in *Capital* because it was explicit in the economic literature of Marx's time. At the end of volume I, in the sections on accumulation, Marx paraphrases a text from Edmund Potter, whom he calls the "chosen mouthpiece of the manufacturers" (I.VII.XXIII; MECW 1996, 35, 575; MEGA^2 II, 9, 503; MEGA^2 II, 8, 542–543). Potter analyzes "two sorts of 'machinery,' each of which belongs to the capitalist, and of which one stands in his factory, the other at night-time and on Sundays is housed outside the factory, in cottages" (ibid.). That is, from the perspective of the political economists, the workers are nothing but machines themselves, fixed capital to be maintained alongside other forms of fixed capital, though cheaper to use than other forms of fixed capital. Marx indicts Potter for this assimilation on what can only be described as moral grounds. For Marx in *Capital*, as for many other humanist thinkers of the period, humans are to be protected because they are human beings, not because doing so will result in more productive work.

The interchangeability of humans and machines has one additional dastardly consequence in capitalism. Machines are employed in counterrevolutionary ways. The functional interchange of human and machine means that capitalists retain the upper hand in constantly sinking the value of human labor-power. Capitalism selectively develops technologies in order to deprive the working class of its demands for better conditions, because its labor-power can always be replaced by machinery. Marx writes that "it would be possible to write quite a history of inventions, made since 1830, for the sole purpose of supplying capital with weapons against the working-class" (I.IV.XV.5; 1887, 411). With the organization of the new motor mechanism and the transmitting mechanism, the machine becomes, for the first time, a direct competitor with human labor for tasks that produce material wealth. In capitalism, the effect is to produce strife and competition between the worker and the machine that drives him or her out of work. Marx writes,

The instrument of labour, when it takes the form of a machine, immediately becomes a competitor of the workman himself.... So soon as the handling of this tool becomes the work of the machine, then, with the use-value, the exchange-value too, of the workman's labour-power vanishes.... Therefore, it is with the advent of machinery that the workman for the first time brutally revolts against the instruments of labour.

(I.IV.XV.5; 1887, 405–407)

By contrast, in the later forms of communist production Marx sketched in the *Grundrisse*, it is this interchangeability between human and machine that will leave humans free to pursue other forms of activity apart from labor. The entitlement will be freedom from labor altogether, not the right to undertake it in anachronistic forms. But in capitalist production the revolutionary employment of machines is nowhere in sight, for the worker, for the capitalist, or for Marx himself, who has limited his descriptions to those befitting the capitalist mode of production.

III   Machines, trains, and other capitalist monsters

Too often when treating Marx's political theory in isolation from its historical context, we forget that we have inherited capitalism in a much more legislatively regulated form than that sketched by Marx in his magnum opus. When people defend capitalism, it is usually not the capitalism sketched by Marx. In Western countries, massive legislation that regulated and transformed capitalist production intervened between Marx's understanding of capitalism and our own. At his most cynical, Marx would argue that these modifications in capitalist production occurred only out of bourgeois self-interest, and not for humanitarian reasons. Faced with falls in the rate of profit and the vulnerability of individual capitalists to competition, the original Factory Acts of England were supported by far-sighted members of the bourgeois class who were not simply acting altruistically, but also responding to the realization that their long-term business interests were at stake. This cynicism is perhaps too strong, as this legislation was at least in part motivated by progressive empathy. But whatever the reasons, in most Western nations we are no longer faced with the consequences of unregulated capitalism. If these spectacles still exist, they are at least safely out of sight, and usually relegated to places beyond our borders.

Marx faced the spectacle of *unregulated* capitalism. Documenting the horrors of factory life, he gives a moral argument about human decency and its failures, about the incremental and systematic murder of a class of persons for profit, about a system of slavery in which the life of the slave is not even worth preserving beyond the most minimal functionality. Against this backdrop, we can understand why Marx's analytic and scientific pretensions drift to the background, and why he falls back on inflamed rhetoric when sketching this appalling system. Nonetheless, some of these descriptions can appear to endorse a technophobia that Marx's philosophy of technology, taken as a whole, does not espouse.

Marx gives the following description of the changed scene of production once the factory, run by alienated labor, has replaced the workshop:

> As soon as the machine executes, without man's help, all the movements requisite to elaborate the raw material, needing only attendance from him, we have an automatic system of machinery, and one that is susceptible of constant improvement in all of its details.... a mechanical monster [*Ungeheuer*] whose body fills whole factories, and whose demon power, at first veiled under the slow and measured motions of his giant limbs [*versteckt durch die fast feierlich gemessene bewegung seiner Riesenglieder*], at length breaks into the fast and furious whirl of his countless [*zahllosen*] organs.
>
> (I.IV.XV.1; MECW 1996, 35, 384; MEGA^2 II, 9, 332; MEGA^2 II, 8, 372–373)

The infinity of hands, hands beyond all measure, the gigantism of an automated system of machinery: these are demonic. For Marx they represent forces of past, or dead, human labor solidified and standing over against living labor. The living, as Derrida (1994) explained, are haunted by the undead dead.

What is fascinating in Marx's description of the monstrous factory scene is the way in which machinery itself is described as a body with a central power source (or heart) in the motor mechanism, a brain in the transmitting mechanism, and an infinity of hands in the working machines. In the face of such a system, the "natural" limits of human power no longer have any meaning: the machine can work around the clock at any pace. The worker is not limited to day labor, or to a pace set by the human capabilities of wielding a hand tool. Conversely, the monstrosity of machines has no meaning without the contrast with "natural" human power—a contrast Marx draws several times in this section. In this image of the capitalist employment of machines, technology is not annexed by the human body, adding to its stature. Instead, machines dwarf and humiliate human power, coming to appear as its foes and adversaries.

In the nineteenth century, machines play not only a material, but also a highly symbolic role, standing in for capitalist modernity as a whole. Marx often uses the vocabulary of monstrosity to describe machines within the factory scene, and, via this vocabulary, criticizes capitalist modernity. Machines, monstrosity, and alienation become allied in his rhetoric. Marx can then extend the vocabulary of machinery to describe the monstrous features of capitalist production and capitalist political life as a whole. He describes capitalism as a "social *mechanism*... of which [human beings are] but one of the wheels" (I.VII.XXIV.4; 1887, 555, emphasis added).

These technophobic rhetorical effects do not begin in *Capital*, nor are they limited to *Capital*. When Marx turns to describing Bonaparte's police state in the final sections of the *Eighteenth Brumaire of Louis Bonaparte*, he describes Bonaparte's regime as a *Staatsmaschinerie* [state machine] (Section VII; MECW 1976, 11; MEGA[2] I, 11).[13] This reflects the Hobbesian tradition in political philosophy in which the state itself begins to be regarded as a machine that exemplifies and exacerbates political alienation: forces that have gone beyond the human subject whose interests they should be serving.

Such a state is monstrous, impersonal, and applies its laws mechanically and indifferently to its subjects. Marx uses the rhetoric of machinery to describe this political state. This connects to the Marxist conception of the state as solely a vehicle for capitalists and other opportunists, and therefore as never anything more than an instrument of class warfare. The state thus conceived is identical with capitalist civil society and the bourgeois class whose interests it protects. Such a state is a machine to be smashed, overthrown with violence, because parliamentary measures at redressing wrongs have proven ineffective.

Through the rhetorical alliance of machines, monstrosity, and alienated life in capitalist cultures, machines become a synonym for the alienation we experience at work, in political life, and in our own bodies, a fact that has come to be written into our language. In the *Communist Manifesto* Marx writes, "That culture, the loss of which [the bourgeois] laments, is, for the enormous majority, a mere training to act as a machine" (MECW 1976, 6, 501; MEW 1959, 4, 477). But this claim, although made from the best of motivations, also exemplifies the technophobia that characterized Marx's age and its capitalist humanism. This technophobia is a politically fraught attitude, most emblematic of a feudal aristocracy resistant to industrialization and the shifts in political power it mandates, including the railroads that were carving up feudal estates. Technophobia shows feudal society reacting to one symptom of its own elimination. Technophobia will hardly be the ideal attitude for the rising working class Marx envisions.

Nonetheless, in some passages from Marx, machinery itself appears as a participatory agent of oppression, and of the impoverishment of human activity in labor. Marx characterizes Modern Industry as a "giant": a mythological figure exceeding natural bounds. The vocabulary of monstrosity Marx uses to characterize machinery derives from Engels's book *History of the Working-class in England.* David Pollack writes,

> Engels's striking description of the lives of the textile-mill laborers are considerably amplified by Marx in his extended observations in the first volume of *Capital* on the "monstrous" [*ungeheuerlich*] and "demonic" [*dämonisch*] aspects of automated factory life and their effect on the human spirit. Marx's use of the term "cyclopean" no fewer than six times in six pages to describe machinery illustrates the sort of irrational response machinery can incite in man.
>
> (1988, 7)

In the *Communist Manifesto*, Marx writes of the disastrous effects of machinery and the division of labor: "owing to the extensive use of machinery and to division of labour, the work of the proletarians has lost all individual character, and consequently all charm for the workman. He becomes an appendage of the machine" (MECW 1976, 6, 490–491; MEW 1959, 4, 470), and he reminds readers that "Not only [are masses of laborers slaves] of the bourgeois class, and of the bourgeois state; they are daily and hourly enslaved by the machine" (ibid., section 1). Machinery and division of labor appear as culpable agents, and premodern labor is charming by contrast. Marx is closer, in such passages, to the negative Romantic rather than the positive Enlightenment valuation of science and technology.[14]

Granted, Marx is at his most polemical in the *Communist Manifesto*. The text does not exhibit the care with distinctions Marx is able to achieve in his lengthier works. But because Marxism was popularized in the nineteenth and early twentieth centuries almost exclusively through only two works, the *Communist Manifesto* and Engels's essay "Socialism: Utopian and Scientific," each of which was polemical in intent, these careful distinctions did not enter the communist movements.[15] This extremely narrow access to Marx's ideas as a whole helps to explain the limited knowledge of Marx with which so many scholars, activists, politicians, and revolutionaries were working in the early years.

The technophobic rhetoric of the *Communist Manifesto* also helps us to understand the rhetorical form in which technophobia was passed on to nearly all subsequent forms of Marxism, and with it, a conservatism that Marx scarcely would have recognized and certainly would not have condoned. Marx's positive accounts of technology and scientific life, limited as they are to the manuscript material external to *Capital* and to certain detailed passages in the central chapters of *Capital,* are often eclipsed by the indictments of technology in his famous works.

Even for Marx, the distinction between the means and the mode of production is difficult to maintain in a context in which nearly all machine use exacerbates labor's alienation. If machines never work in a way that produces wealth and minimizes labor, it is hard to argue that this is their ultimate purpose or goal. The rational distinction that Marx draws is not always really operative in such a setting, or it requires an act of imagination to see how the means by which labor's alienation is exacerbated could themselves be the means of labor's liberation. That liberation is not, however, a restoration of labor's self-determination in agrarian or bourgeois forms; rather, it is the introduction of the free time I sketched above. That is, it is a liberation that is itself conditioned by capitalist industrial life's accumulation of scientific and technological resources for the production of wealth.

In an alienated mode of production, the worker's temptation to smash machinery is at least understandable. Machines themselves appear as the sign of the introduction of labor's more barbarous forms, not the progressive elimination of labor.

In order to sketch the resulting nineteenth-century technophobia, let me turn to the Victorian context in which Marx was writing. To historicize Marx in 1848 is different from historicizing him in 1867, after his emigration and almost 20 years in London. In Victorian London, the factory was not the only venue in which the monstrous steam engine made its appearance. There was also the railway.

Charles Dickens survived a terrible railway accident, only to suffer for the rest of his life from what we might today recognize as posttraumatic stress disorder. But although the term "accident" implies aberrant circumstances, railway accidents and their horrors were a regular feature of Victorian life, much as automobile accidents are a regular feature of our own. In the first generation of railway use, the "kinks" had not been worked out of the technology. A system of rules that would later include the standardization of time in English towns had not yet been formulated. In *The Railway Journey: The Industrialization of Time and Space in the 19th Century*, Wolfgang Schivelbusch writes that the railway

> transformed the nation, dramatically reshaping the landscape, blurring the lines between rural and urban, facilitating the growth of the major cities, sweeping away local times, and introducing its own standard time—in effect, "annihilating" an older perception of time and space.... What the industrial worker learnt on the factory floor, [the middle classes] learnt on the station platform.
>
> (quoted in Daly 2004, 20)

The railway informed not only the material circumstances of the Victorian period, but also the artistic reflection of these circumstances in the theatre.

Nicholas Daly (2004) analyzes a new genre of theatre that appeared in 1860s London: the sensation drama. The railway was a staple character in the sensation drama, and human escape from an oncoming train was a staple narrative. According to Daly, the sensation drama worked as a form of industrial education, training the senses to absorb a thousand small shocks (e.g. flashing lights and loud noises) while still directing their attention to a task of monitoring and watching. The sensation drama thus prepared its watchers for industrial life and industrial tasks; it modernized the senses. Daly writes,

> [A] discourse of attention, dealing with the topic of creating attentive subjects, of measuring attention, and of guarding against distraction and fatigue, emerges from almost complete silence in the 1850s to scientific respectability from the 1870s on ... it is tempting to see the emergence of the popular "sensation drama," with its mesmerizing sensation scenes, as also taking place against this grander backdrop of the problems generated by the collision of modernization with the (resistant but presumably expandable) limits of the human sensorium. What we see at [the theatre] is an audience seeking escape from the wear and tear of industrial culture with its demands for attentiveness, alertness, and concentration, only to find that attentiveness is also the price to be paid for the pleasures of the popular theatre.
>
> (2004, 25)

In Dion Boucicault's famous 1868 play *After Dark*, "A man is lying unconscious on the track of the London Underground; an express train is hurtling towards him, its lights cutting through the gloom; a second man makes a heroic dash, seizes the prostrate figure and rolls with him to safety as the train rushes past" (Daly 2004, 1). Here we have, in the most literal sense, the human confrontation with the monstrous machine, representing the onslaught of modernity and its changed forms of life. Within the narrative, the human overcomes the machine against impossible odds. Daly writes that "[m]odernity is made visible—it is embodied on stage in the express train—and thus made beatable, and the pastoral is reaffirmed" (25). The irony is that the spectacle that retrains the senses to adapt to modernity contains, as its conceit, an indictment of this modernity.

Making its debut the year after *Capital* was first published in German, *After Dark* gathered together the elements of railway dramas that had found their way to the stage as early as 1863. But Boucicault's play reveals an additional and troubling dimension of the technophobia that was sweeping industrializing London. Technophobia often appears paired with other attitudes: the demonization of machines is accompanied by a more general demonization of modernity. Boucicault's play demonizes not only machines, but also Jewish people, industrialists, and other central characters of industrial modernity. Boucicault's villains are the central characters of this modernity, and its heroes come from the old military and aristocratic institutions.

The main villain in *After Dark* is an industrialist. He colludes with a Jewish gambling-house proprietor. The captive prisoner comes to be tied to the railway tracks via the intrigues of these two dark characters of modernity. Conversely, the hero of the drama is a young aristocrat who will remain penniless until he marries the daughter of the other hero, a retired officer. In the drama, the heroes are played by the old institutions of the aristocracy and the military, and the villains by the new representatives of modernity: Jewishness and industrialization. The two latter figures are paired in the Victorian imagination and identified with the onslaught of mechanization. Daly writes,

"[T]he Jew" becomes a crucial figure for the imagining of modern British identity. Matthew Arnold's *Culture and Anarchy* (1869), with its analysis of the "Hebraic" and "Hellenic" strains of British life, is a well-known example, in which Arnold ultimately associates the bad, uncultured modernity of the Victorian bourgeoisie with the "Hebraic." But long before this, occupational restrictions in pre-Emancipation Britain meant that Jews tended to be over-represented in business and finance, and this in turn shaped the image of British Jews as "the personification of capitalism" (2004, 27).

Anti-Semitic elements in Marx's *Capital* are complex, well-known, and much debated, but we have hardly paid enough attention to the subtle and sublimated forms anti-Semitism takes in capitalist humanism. In addition to machinery like the railway and the automated factory system, common monster figures in *Capital* include the vampire and the werewolf (I.III.X; MECW 1996, 35, 241, 263; MEGA^2 II, 9, 201, 222).[16] From a contemporary perspective, the narrowness of capitalist humanism is evident in the norms by which these concepts of monstrosity are necessarily regulated: in them the age partakes not only of the scientific vitalism of the time, but also of its racism and anti-Semitism.

The vampire figure in particular is nearly always anti-Semitic: a bloodsucker with Semitic features draining away the lifeblood of good, Gentile Europeans.[17] In *Capital* Marx writes, "Capital is dead labour that, vampire-like, only lives by sucking living labour, and lives the more, the more labour it sucks" (I.III.X; MECW 1996, 35, 241; MEGA^2 II, 9, 201; MEGA^2 II, 8, 239). The werewolf is similarly employed: Marx speaks of capital's "were-wolf hunger for surplus-labour" (I.III.X; 1887, 252).

Links between the anti-economism implicit in this discussion of surplus value and its anti-Semitic metaphors are visible since Marx's early work, especially his consideration of the political relations between a particular group and the universal state in *On the Jewish Question*. Robert Tucker (1978) writes in the introductory essay to the text:

> In the second part, Marx proceeds to the criticism of economics or commerce, which he equates with "Judaism." His concluding call for "the emancipation of society from Judaism" (which has been seen on occasion as a manifesto of anti-Semitism) is in fact a call for the emancipation of society from what he here calls "huckstering" or from what he was to subsequently to call "capitalism" (26).

The relationship in Marx between rhetoric mobilized against commerce and anti-Semitism deserves further consideration. In the figure of the vampire, a subtle anti-Semitism is expressed not only in Marx's early works, but also throughout his later works. More importantly, we must ask whether a non–anti-Semitic critique of economic life was possible in the nineteenth century, and whether Marx's indictment of economic motivations and his demonization of commercial life can be lifted from these origins. Finally, we must be wary of the cluster of ideas that accompany technophobia, whose ugly pedigree has historically served as a license to violence against people perceived as threats to a pastoral norm.

Marx's deployment of monstrosity in *Capital* is not limited to modern monsters like the machine, the vampire, and the werewolf. In numerous passages, Marx also uses the cyclops (I.III.X; MECW 1996, 35, 260; MEGA^2 II, 9, 219), a classical monster. The Cyclopes were a race of one-eyed giants who, in Hesiod, crafted thunderbolts. Below we see that only such monsters would be fit to deal with running a railway for the length of time mandated by capitalism. Once again, the Hellenistic combats the industrial. Marx writes,

> A tremendous railway accident has hurried hundreds of passengers into another world. The negligence of the employees is the cause of the misfortune. They declare with one voice that... [their labour has been screwed up to 14, 18, and 20 hours, and under a specially severe pressure of holiday makers... it often lasted for 40 or 50 hours without a break. These were ordinary men, not Cyclops. At a certain point their labour-power failed].
>
> (I.III.X.3; 1887, 242)

Monster figures like the machine, the vampire, the werewolf, and the Cyclops have access, albeit an unnatural access, to excessive energies and powers. No one can fault Marx for drawing attention to the abuses of labor that occur when machines are introduced in the capitalist mode of production, and when workers' working hours are absurdly lengthened. But the effect of his discussion in *Capital* is to highlight human limitation rather than human malleability and amplification in the face of technological means of production.

In *Capital*, Marx often impugns the monster figures of modernity. He repeatedly stresses the limitations of the "natural" human body. In this way, he performs his age's pastoralism and technophobia and participates in capitalist humanism. He also fails to restate the positive aspects of capitalist production and machinery about which he writes, so forcefully, in the *Grundrisse*. Finally, Marx does not suggest that the human body as he portrays it might be rather narrowly determined by already-surpassed feudal norms, including traditional gender roles, the ideal of a single craftsperson wielding a tool, and other forms of embodiment not yet subject to qualification by contact with the steam engine, commerce, and other aspects of industrial life and its sociological consequences.

If capitalist humanism is dangerous, it is in part because this humanism longs for the return of the norms of an unequal society that protected only a limited number of subjects, and often protected these subjects at the expense of others. These subjects were overwhelmingly male, noncolonial craftspersons. But the forms of embodiment and skill that regulated this form of subjectivity are increasingly erased in the industrial-technological synthesis.

In capitalist humanism, the role of technology in amplifying human capacities, creating great wealth, loosing the grip of the patriarchal family with positive effect, and inaugurating other positive changes in social life is not emphasized. The monster figures from *Capital* do often, however, appear as *symptoms* of these positive aspects or their potential—inverted and demonized images of positive social changes. In this sense, the monster figure in Marx assumes its original etymological function of showing or revealing something else, appearing as a warning, or portent. The Cyclops to whom Marx appeals above will be replaced, historically, by the synchronization of clocks in various English villages, eliminating the necessity for a lookout. This will eliminate the margin of human error and the need for constant human monitoring, minimizing railway accidents. Ultimately an automated system will leave the laborers free to be elsewhere.

In Marx's discussion, monster figures also appear at the shifting boundaries between human/machine, human/animal, and living/dead. The factory scene is one place where such boundaries are called into question. The disappearance of these boundaries characterizes an energeticist worldview, where those possessing a true human essence are no longer marked out by special signs. By setting up monster figures to police these borders, Marx continues to demonstrate capitalist humanism's reaction to the new paradigm.

If we do not take such monstrosity at face value, we find that those whose bodies are monstrous according to the narrow limits of capitalist humanism are hardly monstrous today. Below I look at two particular examples of this: the laboring female body and the racially othered body. The nineteenth-century characterization of these bodies as monstrous is well documented among feminists (Braidotti 1997; Gunnarson and Trojer 1994; Haraway 1985, 1991, 1997; Wajcman 1991, 2004) and among critical race theorists. Capitalist humanism, responding to the widespread entrance of women into waged, productive labor, to changes in the slave system of production in the American South, and to the colonial system of production that is part of capitalism's global unfolding, reacts to these changes by viewing laboring women's and racially othered bodies as monstrosities.

IV Rough, foul-mouthed boys: women's monstrous laboring bodies

In *Capital*, Marx cites some factory statistics from 1866:

> The greatest evil of the system that employs young girls on this sort of work consists in this, that, as a rule, it chains them fast from childhood for the whole of their after-life to the most abandoned rabble. They become rough, foul-mouthed boys before Nature has taught them that they are women. Clothed in a few dirty rags, the legs naked far above the knees, hair and face besmeared with dirt, they learn to treat all feelings of decency and shame with contempt. During mealtimes they lie at full length in the fields, or watch the boys bathing in a neighbouring canal. Their heavy day's work at length completed, they put on better clothes, and accompany men to the public houses.
>
> (1887, 437)

Here Marx invokes the end of Victorian femininity as one of the monstrous products of capitalist industrialization. The female laborers described above are monstrous in two ways. First, they exhibit aberrations of form, especially the adoption of the characteristics of the other sex. They are boys, not girls. Second, they are dirty, not clean. It is not difficult to discern that the major concern here is not with dirt itself, but rather with women's sexuality. We are told, *sotto voce*, that working-class females have the habit of expressing, and perhaps even acting upon, sexual desires. They are capable of the indiscretions of voyeurism and the perversions of scopophilia. They are no doubt prone to the various displays of loose or even aggressive sexuality that characteristically accompany drunkenness. And what else might they be doing while lying full length in those fields?

The text occurs within Marx's most substantial published account of female labor and women's history. It is no accident that it is located in *Capital*'s chapter XV, the chapter devoted to machinery. According to Marx, Modern Industry, just like any other system of production, has sociological consequences. In particular, the introduction of machines into production affects traditional divisions of labor, and especially those distributed by sex, age, and race.

First, the introduction of machines eliminates the need to hire a worker with the specialized knowledge of a craftsperson. This knowledge has become a property of the machine itself rather than the worker. The machine requires someone to monitor and stoke it, that is, someone to perform abstract labor. Abstract labor is not measured by the useable products it produces but by the duration of time in which it occurs. Abstract labor is remunerated with another abstraction, a wage, rather than with the product it has made.

The requirement for abstract, undifferentiated labor can be fulfilled by anyone, regardless of age, sex, or race. Machines lessen both the actual physical strength and the skills required by previous systems of production. Thus, capital can employ workers who, according to previous natural categories, had been classified as weak or unskilled. Because it can also employ such workers more cheaply, factory work quickly spreads throughout the entire populace.

Moreover, in the capitalist mode of production, "strength," "weakness," and "skill" become social rather than natural categories. The small, dexterous fingers of a woman or child become strengths, whereas heft and bulk may be regarded as weaknesses where the introduction of machinery into labor has rendered them superfluous. Various weaknesses, such as the tedium and minuteness of traditional women's work under guild conditions, also become strengths. This shift shows the essential malleability of the categories of strength and weakness, which change according to the dominant means of production. It also shows the essential malleability of the category "skill," as I discussed in Chapter 3. Women were less likely than men to have acquired the liabilities of particularized strength and skill, because guild restrictions did not allow them to become apprentices to a profession. As such, women were optimal subjects for abstract capitalist labor, and capitalists would indeed often choose malleable female over recalcitrant male employees if such a choice was possible.

The widespread entrance of women into the wage labor force occasioned a wide variety of backlashes. Working-class men resented the women that swelled the ranks of available human labor-power. Such women, available at low cost, were not competitors; rather, they appeared as agents of obsolescence for the skilled male labor market. Among the bourgeoisie, the visible spectacle of female labor caused an oppositional and ideological reinforcement of women's natural weakness. One viewed women as unfit for work, and high social status was demonstrated through leisure. But this weakness was countermanded, at every turn, by the realities of working-class female labor.

The working-class women of Victorian London could be seen performing not only the abstract labor of monitoring industrial machines, but also many arduous tasks without mechanical assistance, including work in coal mines. A worker was not replaced by a machine simply because a new machine supplanted the worker's function. Human labor in general was often less expensive than the mechanical labor that would have been required to replace it. This was even truer of female labor, which was cheaper than male labor. So women were hired to do arduously what a machine could have done quickly. Labor that, technologically speaking, was anachronistic occurred in many branches of industry. It was not in the capitalist's interest to buy an expensive machine when human labor, and especially female labor, could be had so cheaply.

The discourse of women's natural weakness must have been difficult to maintain in an environment where working-class females were visibly performing hard labor.[18] For this reason labor and femininity had to be dissociated. Among the bourgeoisie, the discourse and performance of women's natural weakness and unfitness for work becomes all the more insistently pronounced and enacted. As the women of the nineteenth-century's working classes headed toward the factories, canals, and mines, bourgeois women's activity became increasingly circumscribed. A bourgeois woman, to mark both her class and her femininity, must always give the appearance of being leisured.

Anne McClintock points out, however, that the bourgeois woman's mythology was quite different from her reality. McClintock (1995) writes,

> Apart from the tiny, truly leisured elite, idleness was less a regime of inertia imposed on wilting middle-class wives and daughters than a laborious and time consuming *character role* performed by women who wanted membership in the "respectable class." For most women whose husbands or fathers could not afford enough servants for genuine idleness, domestic work had to be accompanied by the historically unprecedented labor of rendering invisible every sign of that work...idleness was less the absence of work than a conspicuous labor of leisure (162, emphasis in original).

For such bourgeois women, domestic labors were both nonremunerated and had to be made to disappear. This means that a large portion of women's labor was necessarily rendered culturally unrecognizable as labor, because such a recognition would also have entailed an identification with the repudiated features of the working classes.

The exclusive disjunction between the concept of femininity and the performance of labor forced the progressive reformers of the Victorian era into the gender binary we saw in the above extract about the boyishness of working-class girls. If the definition of femininity excludes the performance of wage labor, and, at its apex, mandates the performance of absolute idleness, then working-class girls are not girls, but boys. The concept of femininity itself is marked by class, and limited to a narrow range of subjects who either possess or can simulate the leisure required by the concept.

Some working-class women of the period were conscious of this. An anecdote that appears in McClintock (1995) tells of a love affair between members of two different Victorian classes. Domestic servant Hannah Cullwick becomes the lover of her upper-class employer Arthur Munby. Munby, himself unmarried and horrified by his sexual contact with Cullwick outside of the confines of bourgeois marriage, besieges her with marriage proposals. Stubbornly, and continually, she refuses these. In 1864, she wrote of the prospect of submitting to this marriage and thereby joining the ranks of the bourgeois: "It is too much like being a *woman!*" (177, emphasis added).[19]

When Cullwick finally agrees to the marriage, it is on her terms, not Munby's, that the marriage will progress. Cullwick marries Munby in a secret ceremony and consents to appear, from time to time, in public as his wife. But she never fully becomes a woman according to the standards of her time. In fact, she only resides with Munby for four years. More pertinently, during the whole of their marriage, Cullwick both continues to perform her assigned domestic tasks and insists that Munby continue to pay her wages for doing so. Her diary reflects that this allows her to maintain her financial and psychological independence.

This brings me to a problem with Marx's account of the alienation inherent in all wage labor. By their own accounts, women did not always experience wage labor as alienating. In fact, the wage involves a powerful recognition of the working subject's activity. Because of the wage, the activity is recognized as meaningful, and the person performing it is given an unmistakable social acknowledgement. Within patriarchal strictures, women's activity is not considered to be independent. Wages involve the recognition that the activity possesses a certain independence. Wage labor, with or without machines, was a way for women to gain substantial independence from patriarchy, and to begin the economic independence that would later result in the political independence extended, in waves, by liberal twentieth-century feminist movements.

Under patriarchal systems, women were for the most part excluded from apprenticeship in guilds and from the development of guild-related skills. Historically women have also been excluded from owning property, however much labor they had mixed with it, and thus from this form of bourgeois political subjectivity. To put it bluntly, one cannot lose what one does not have. From this perspective, the alienation inherent in wage labor can only appear as a masculine lament.

I wish to tread lightly here. I am not suggesting that the unqualified labor of women and children struggling for mere survival in the first generations of the Industrial Revolution was an equally unqualified liberation. That moment, like many historical moments, was full of ambiguity. It should be borne in mind that working-class women were allowed into the labor market only as a way of further exploiting the working class, of spreading out a family wage in order to maximize surplus value, and of dividing the working class amongst itself. We should also not lose sight of the fact that women were desirable as industrial wage workers because they could be paid less, ordered about more effectively, and were of lower social value. In isolation from kinship structures that could support them, women workers also had much to lose if they did not keep their jobs.[20] In addition, they had less experience than men in moderating the demands for intense labor through various kinds of subterfuge. Factory owners were quick to exploit this. As Marx (1887) relates in a chilling assessment of female workers' vulnerability, "women and children, once set going, impetuously spend their life-force ... while the adult male laborer is shrewd enough to economise his as much as he can" (650).

However, the entry of women into wage labor also marks a site of liberation. In this site, women's contact with technology conditions liberation from bourgeois strictures on femininity and from older structures of patriarchal oppression, including limitations on female skill development. The liberation is twofold. First, technology explodes the naturalistic functioning of categories like strength and skill. Second, the prospect of earning wages within the new industrial economies conditions the liberation of women from economic dependence on *familial* patriarchy. Women's dependence on *capitalist* patriarchy—particularly wage gaps, the types of work to which women are routinely assigned, and the frequent presence of male supervision of their labor—are among those conditions that still await redress, but they are conditioned by industrialization and the wage-based recognition of women's activity as labor.

V   Wage labor and race

Marx's discussion of the alienation inherent in wage labor is problematic not only in the case of women, but also in the case of subjects whose activity was administrated by familial patriarchy. I am thinking of the racial slavery of the antebellum Southern United States. Marx was familiar with the features of this slavery, because during the 1850s he worked as a European correspondent for Charles Anderson Dana's *New York Daily Tribune*, an abolitionist newspaper. The articles that Marx wrote for this newspaper were the source of his observations, sprinkled throughout *Capital*, about the nonpolitical state of enslaved peoples in the Southern United States. Marx's specific concern about this modern form of slavery is an underappreciated source of his rhetoric about the slavery of the wage worker. In addition to expressing a general set of concerns about slaveries, including the slaveries of antiquity, as modes of production, Marx's work is influenced by abolitionism and, through this movement, by the situation of the enslaved peoples of the Americas.

In *Capital*, Marx's tendency is to treat the condition of these peoples as similar to that of the wage laborers in the capitalist system. He argues that the difference between slavery and wage labor is simply a difference in the mode of extracting profit and that profit extraction is the key characteristic of both systems of domination. Marx (1887) writes, "The essential difference between the various economic forms of society, between, for instance, a society based on slave-labour and one based on wage-labour, lies only in the mode in which the surplus labour is in each case extracted from the actual producer, the labourer" (209).

Marx also takes some pains to show that the system of slavery in the South had moved away from those features that characterize patriarchal systems of production and toward those features that characterize capitalist production. He writes,

> As soon as people, whose production still moves in the lower forms of slave-labour, are drawn into the whirlpool of an international market dominated by the capitalistic mode of production, the sale of their products for export becoming their principal interest, the civilized horrors of overwork are grafted onto the barbaric horrors of slavery. Hence the negro labour in the Southern States of the American Union preserved something of a patriarchal character, so long as production was chiefly directed to immediate local consumption. But in proportion as the export of cotton became of vital interest to these states, the overworking of the negro and sometimes the using up of his life in 7 years of labour became a factor in a calculated and calculating system.
>
> (1887, 226)

Marx is right to emphasize the global economic pressures and their influence on slave labor; my point here is not to rebut those historical analyses that help us understand US slavery and its collapse as related to changes in economic life. But I question the reduction of slavery and its collapse to epiphenomena of the global economy.

In addition, in passages like that above, we must be wary of Marx's premature erasure of some key political distinctions. His assimilation of slave labor as one kind among many modern ways to extract surplus value erases a political distinction that Marx himself maintained earlier in *Capital*:

> In order that the possessor of labour may offer it for sale as a commodity, he must have it at his disposal, must be the untrammeled owner of his capacity for labour, i.e. of his person. He and the owner of money meet in the market, and deal with each other on the basis of equal rights, with this difference alone, that one is buyer, and the other seller.
>
> (1887, 126)

Though Marx will spend much of *Capital* showing how this relationship that appears to be based on equality is actually not so, the possession of one's labor as one's own is still a salient difference between a system of wage labor and a system of patriarchal, racially determined slavery, even when the latter has been influenced by the pressure of global economies.

As Steven Hahn (2005) claims in his book *A Nation Under Our Feet*, in the antebellum South, the recognition of a slave's economic entitlement in any form was controversial. Although a slave owner was in principle entitled to the full produce of slave labor, and to whatever monies might be earned by hiring out slave labor, by the mid-1850s there were a variety of exceptions to this principle. By the mid-1850s, Southern slaves had increasingly delineated a sphere of "free time" of their own, lasting all of Sunday and at least half of Saturday. If slaves worked during these periods, including any overtime for their owners, they were often paid. In the provisioning system that characterized slavery's later years, masters delegated to their slaves the work of feeding and clothing themselves. With this, slaves entered into what historians call an internal economy of laboring and exchanging the fruits of their labor on the market. This occurred alongside continuing slave labor. Economic activities of exchange both among slaves and between them and their owners thus actually began prior to the formal ending of slavery. Hahn documents political struggles between slaves and their owners to frame clear rules about free versus enslaved time. He also discusses the political struggles among slave owners, who accused one another of allowing their slaves too much economic freedom.

Hahn shows that this pre-Emancipation economic activity influenced the formation of a recognizably political consciousness among slaves. The symbolic political importance of this experience was fortified by John Locke's ideas about being entitled to the fruits of one's labor. These ideas were percolating in the century after the French Revolution, and they had a life of their own in slave communities, even during the highly conservative 1850s. Hahn (2005) claims that "slaves had become familiar with and could appropriate a powerful, if contested, national political discourse that exalted manual labor and associated freedom with economic independence" (135).

After Emancipation, appeals to the superior conditions of patriarchy were a staple of white Southern conservatism. These inevitably assimilated the labors performed after Emancipation for wages to those performed before Emancipation under the stewardship of a caring master. In doing so, they show the dangerous edge to Marx's identification of all forms of oppression as class oppression.

Both in the immediate aftermath of Emancipation and long after, the indictment of wage labor became a staple of backlash arguments that conditions for African-American peoples had been at least as good if not better during slavery. But we must recognize a political difference in the type of toil conditioned by a system of wage labor and that conditioned by slavery. The difference is significant even if the labors themselves are substantially unchanged. More provocatively, one might argue that the labors themselves are changed by the social condition of the person who performs them: a truth that emerges particularly clearly in the example of the wealthy tourist who pays to mine diamonds on the African continent!

Likewise, we must differentiate the types of alienation or estrangement from the self that are conditioned by wage labor from those enabled by slavery.[21] Against Marx's assimilation of all forms of class oppression into a single form, the systems of wage labor and slavery are not psychologically indifferent means of extracting profit.

The effects of the discourse of entitlement to the fruits of one's labor were significant enough that after Emancipation former slaves nearly universally expected land redistribution as a part of just compensation for past labors. They expected economic compensation for their former servitude and sought to refigure this servitude as a labor entitled to just such economic compensation. These expectations were almost universally unfulfilled. We hear their echoes in the debates that continue, or fail to continue, on the question of reparations for this period of US history. The unwillingness of our government even to consider this question shows the degree to which the economic entitlement of these African-American labors remains a racially fraught site of political contestation.

Thus, the economic recognition received when one participated in wage labor was an immense liberation for these subjects of patriarchy. The right to meet in the market and sell one's labor involved economic and political recognitions that had to be won at great expense. In this way, the conditions of the patriarchal system of slavery simply did not meet the conditions of freely sold labor that Marx lists as a requisite for participation in the capitalist world, however strongly he may wish to graft a story of economic exploitation onto the story of patriarchal exploitation. The relationship of Marx and subsequent Marxism to critical race theories has been correspondingly fraught, particularly insofar as Marx and Marxism offer only what Charles Mills (1998) calls a "class-reductivist" map of oppression (105). Such a map ignores or undermines the specificities of racism and its irreducibility to economic categories.

However, the restoration of Marx's connection to US abolitionist movements allows us to see Marx's work in another sense. I intimated above that abolitionism was a pivotal influence on Marx's work during the 1850s. In addition to his articles for Dana's abolitionist newspaper, Marx's notebooks from the 1850s indicate that he had made careful notes on abolitionist Thomas F. Buxton's books *The African Slave Trade* and its sequel *The Remedy*.[22] Marx studied African slavery in particular, and colonization in general, as bearing upon the broader field of political economy. For this reason, Marx's reliance on the vocabulary of slavery to characterize the plight of the wage worker resonates not only with slavery as a classical political category, but also with the more contemporary phenomenon of the slavery in the United States and the pressures to abolish it. Although Marx's work focused on the European world, worries over slavery in the Americas may have shaped Marx's concept of social class, particularly as this concept developed in the 1850s and 1860s.

Nevertheless, Marx's concept of economic alienation and subsequent abandonment of the project of liberal rights may not be appropriate for subjects who were not wage-laborers, but unpaid and unrecognized parts of patriarchal systems well into the modernity that Marx's philosophy attempts to explain. These subjects include both women and African-Americans. Thus, we must reconsider the critique of the liberal project and the critique of rights discourse that Marxism inaugurates from the perspective of such subjects. As Patricia Williams (1991) writes in her discussion of Marxist-influenced critical legal studies,

> Although rights may not be ends in themselves, rights rhetoric has and continues to be an effective form of discourse for blacks. The vocabulary of rights speaks to an establishment that values the guise of stability. The subtlety of rights' real instability thus does not render unusable their persona of stability.... What is needed, therefore, is not the abandonment of rights language for all purposes, but an attempt to become multilingual in the semantics of evaluating rights (149).

Although in this section I have conflated the position of African Americans and women with respect to Marx's notion of alienation, such a conflation has its limits. Following the work of bell hooks and others, we have come to understand that the historical subjection to a white, masculine patriarchy has meant different things for the white women and the racially marked subjects, including women, who live with the legacy of this patriarchy.[23] Racial and sexual oppression, although related, have different characteristics. However, Marxism's disproportionate emphasis on the plight of the white male wage laborer has been a target of feminist and critical race theorists alike, and on similar grounds. For this reason, my critique of regarding wage labor as exclusively alienating is similar for both women in general and racially marked subjects (including women).

VI   Wage labor and sexuality

Let me return to the topic of women and to the passage about rough, foul-mouthed, working-class women. For the nineteenth-century bourgeois Victorian, female wage labor was accompanied by the chilling specter of female sexuality. Sexuality was a favorite bourgeois obsession, associated with laboring women and women of color, and therefore forcibly and vocally expelled from the attributes of white, bourgeois women. But this displacement was hardly simple, as Michel Foucault reminds us. In fact, the bourgeoisie drew attention to its body and its sex, and asserted their importance via the prohibitions deliberately placed on the expression of white women's sexuality. Because of this, these prohibitions cannot be understood without reference to social class.

The critique of working-class girls in Marx's text is that they do not display these prohibitions: the young girls do not express decency or shame. But they are not supposed to do so, because working-class bodies and working-class sexuality are not important enough, in bourgeois society, to merit these forms of attention. Foucault (1990) cites Marx's *Capital* as evidence when he writes, in the first volume of his *History of Sexuality*, that

> the living conditions that were dealt to the proletariat, particularly in the first half of the nineteenth century, show there was anything but concern for its body and sex; it was of little importance whether *those* people lived or died, since their reproduction was something that took care of itself in any case (126).

Foucault rightly locates sexual repression in the norms of the bourgeois class. The bourgeois class used sexual repression as a way to draw attention to the bodies of its members and to highlight the importance of these bodies. Bourgeois bodies were valuable enough to warrant the extra social energies that sexual repression requires, including regimes of schooling, monitoring, and confessing oneself to a doctor. Sexual repression, at least in its stereotypical forms, is a product of the bourgeois class, and cannot be spoken of as a general phenomenon of human socialization. Foucault (1990) continues,

> Somewhat similar to the way in which, at the end of the eighteenth century, the bourgeoisie set its own body and its precious sexuality against the valorous blood of the nobles, at the end of the nineteenth century it sought to redefine the specific character of its sexuality relative to that of others.... It was here that the theory of repression... had its point of origin.... [The nineteenth century discourse of sexuality] said: "[Bourgeois] sexuality, unlike that of others, is subjected to a regime of repression so intense as to present a constant danger; not only is sex a formidable secret... not only must we search it out for the truth it conceals, but if it carries with it so many dangers, this is because—whether out of scrupulousness, an overly acute

sense of sin, or hypocrisy, no matter—we have too long reduced it to silence." Henceforth social differentiation would be affirmed, not by the "sexual" quality of the body, but by the intensity of its repression (128–129).

In this respect, a call for the extension of guilt and shame to the young working-class girls is actually an offer to make their bodies important enough for social consideration. It is an offer, on the part of stolid reformers, to extend the class markings of the bourgeoisie.

What this offer lacks is the insight, more readily available to us today or in any case at least less classically bourgeois, that sexual repression is not a necessary condition for highlighting a body's importance. Sexual repression and schooling in femininity are also a bizarre place to begin the reeducation of the working class. At the very least, proper nutrition and schooling in mathematics would seem more important. This shows us that even among its most progressive reformers, the bourgeoisie could not resist seeing sex, and emphasizing its preeminence, wherever it looked.

If, unlike these reformers, we interpret the laboring, actively sexual female body as a positive rather than a negative monstrosity, we might even conclude that industrialization has conditioned certain aspects of women's liberation. These include the freedom and independence from the patriarchal family that wage labor can offer, the freedom to own and express one's sexuality outside of the narrow bourgeois confines, and the freedom from the restrictive class- and race-specific strictures of gender performance mandated by bourgeois culture. Marx claims that particular means of production determine the social features of a historical era. New configurations of gender and sexuality are one such social feature of the new industrial environments, whether we read these configurations as liberating or monstrous. They are, in fact, both simultaneously liberating and alienating.

Marx's own attitude toward working-class and other female bodies is more difficult to discern. As with other passages in *Capital*, Marx's own view cannot be straightforwardly identified with those passages he cites, because he often cites passages critically. Still, we may safely say that Marx, always looking for revolution in a more traditional form, preferably with barricades, does not always spot the subtle liberations carried by capitalism itself, even though he knows that they will be there. Even if Marx did not realize this, the seemingly solid structures of sexual difference are among those things that capitalism melts into the air.

As for sexual difference, Marx claims, in *The German Ideology* (1846), that the division of labor that forms the genealogical template for all subsequent divisions, including class divisions, is the natural division of labor between men and women. But by the 1860s, Marx has still not seen one key consequence of his own analysis: thanks to industrial life's minimization of the importance of nature, this division is being undone. A girl at work is not, necessarily, a rough, foul-mouthed boy. She might simply be a rough, foul-mouthed girl, or, better still, a rough and foul-mouthed hybrid creature whose very existence challenges the rigid norms of Victorian gender.

Although I am wary of what seems to be Marx's uncritical rehearsal of some of these norms in his portrayal of women in *Capital*, other, earlier texts of Marx's on women's history suggest that he had some idea of the changes in systems of sex oppression that were consequent to industrialization. In July 1852, Marx began work on a set of excerpt notebooks on women and their status under patriarchal systems of rule. Marx never polished these excerpts into a text, although they form some of the background research that Engels developed in *The Origin of the Family, Private Property, and the State*. In these excerpts, Marx makes notes on historians that have charted the changes in women's conditions over time: from matriarchy, to primitive patriarchies, to courtly love, and finally, to the conditions for women laborers in industrializing England. Marx cannot have made such notes without reflecting on women's condition as essentially historical, and greatly variant, in different economic eras.[24]

This variance is why Marx's most substantive accounts of women in *Capital* are connected to his understanding of machine production and its effects on social life. When we look beneath the Victorianism of *Capital* and into Marx's corpus as a whole, we find that what Marx has actually accomplished is more radical than it first appears. He has begun to sketch the connection between machine labor and modifications in the importance of sexed divisions of labor common to previous eras. He has understood that what we today call "gender" is at work within a broad system of social meaning, corresponding only loosely to natural designations and influenced by social class in its deployment.

Marx explains the enhanced importance of gender to industrializing environments by claiming that gender responds to a need for principles of social variation in an environment where labor has ceased to supply these. Leveled and homogenous productive labor does not permit much distinction in role. Marx thinks both gender and, in other passages, race fill this gap in modern industrial production. A woman is no longer distinguished by her lack of guild-related skills; now she is distinguished by her gender alone. Paradoxically, industrialization does not elimi-nate characteristics of embodiment classified by the age as "natural," for example gender and race. Instead, it enhances their importance. As a result, virulent racism and misogyny are unleashed in capitalist human-ism, particularly as women and people of color head to the factories to "take" white, male jobs.

VII   Machinery and revolution

Marx concludes chapter XV of *Capital* with a negative assessment of technology's deployment in capitalism: "Capitalist production, there-fore, develops technology, and the combining together of various processes into a social whole, only by sapping the original sources of all wealth—the soil and the labourer" (I.IV.XV.10, 475). Following this statement, the burden is on Marx to show how the development of tech-nology might be differently conditioned in an alternative, communist modernity.

But in *Capital*, although the necessity of transition is continually asserted, it is poorly explained. How is technology to be liberated from its monstrous, capitalistic employment? (And the more monstrously Marx portrays this employment, the more difficult this question is for him to answer.) Will technology continue to develop in the communist mode of production, or is its potential for wealth already sufficiently developed such that no further development will be necessary? If the former, how will technology develop differently and will it still be rec-ognizable under the same concept? Finally, so long as the revolution has not been accomplished, what is the appropriate action when tech-nology is employed as a weapon to subdue the working class? And how exactly can this class bring about revolutionary change under condi-tions so alienating that it utterly lacks the key features of the human species, especially tool use, education, and political imagination?

Because *Capital* is Marx's last polished work, these questions of tran-sition are never satisfactorily resolved. We must instead speculatively construct, from the few pieces Marx does give us, some of what such an account might have contained.

Marx is critical of the effects of machine production in the alien-ated mode of capital. But machine production will continue after the proletarian revolution Marx forecasts in the *Communist Manifesto*, just no longer in the alienated mode. In fact, machines are the foundation for the surplus wealth that life under communism will require. The objectified forces of the human being, redistributed equitably, are the

foundation for wealth and free time. Therefore, Marx's critique of alienation cannot appeal for the historical return to more primitive modes
of production, nor is it critical of Enlightenment scientific progress and
its application in production, or the generalized work of science and
technology.

Marx cites the *Communist Manifesto* in chapter XV of *Capital* in
order to show how the constant revolutionizing of the means of production in the capitalist period not only marks a journey through
purgatory, but is also a positive accumulation of scientific resources.
Just as purgatory is a necessity for ascension to heaven, the season
in the capitalist inferno is a historical necessity because it lays the
foundation for the communist mode of production. Alienated labor
is the purgation. In its wake, it puts down a surplus objectification of human labor, heralding a new economic era. This surplus is
returned when the mode of production is changed from capitalism to
communism.

Marx cites his own *Communist Manifesto* at only two points in volume I of *Capital*, each time in a footnote.[25] The citation from chapter
XV is the first of these, found in Marx's discussion of the English Factory Acts. There Marx speaks generally about the "gradual alteration of
the instruments of labour" (I.IV.XV.9; MECW 1996, 35, 489; MEGA^2 II,
9, 425; MEGA^2 II, 8, 469). This alteration of the means of production operates as an historical principle for Marx, as I have illustrated
above.

Marx continues the passage by recalling how the work of analysis begun in the era of manufacture is continued and amplified
in Modern Industry. As we have seen, this forms the basis for his
definition of modern technology as the work of analyzing and replicating mechanically the motion of the human body in productive
labor:

> The principle which [Modern Industry] pursued, of resolving each
> process into its constituent movements, without any regard to their
> possible execution by the hand of man, created the new modern
> science of technology. The varied, apparently unconnected, and pet-
> rified forms of the industrial processes now resolved themselves into
> so many conscious and systematic applications of natural science to
> the attainment of given useful effect. Technology also discovered the
> few main fundamental forms of motion, which, despite the diversity
> of the instruments used, are necessarily taken by every productive
> action of the human body; just as the science of mechanics sees in

the most complicated machinery nothing but the continual repetition of the simple mechanical powers.

(I.IV.XV.9; MECW 1996, 35, 489; MEGA^2 II, 9, 425; MEGA^2 II, 8, 469)

Note that Marx is documenting the shift to a technological consciousness, applied to industrial production. At the end of the passage, the human body is discussed not in moral terms but in the thermodynamic vocabulary of productive mechanization.

For Marx in the *Grundrisse*, Modern Industry had both capitalist and communist components. Both periods had the same means of production as their foundation: machines. We might modify this account in light of the greater understanding of technological history that Marx displays in *Capital*. Capitalism was brought about by developments in the transmitting mechanism, or tool. These began during the Renaissance and reached their apex in seventeenth- and eighteenth-century technologies. In the steam engine, that peculiar invention of the nineteenth century, capitalism must have already spawned the instruments appropriate to a new, communist economic era and the material wealth this era requires. The keystone of this is the interchangeability of human and mechanical production of wealth. The transition to the communist era may mean additional changes in the means of production, but these will build on changes accomplished during capitalism and will hardly involve retrogression to hand tools or other, more primitive technologies. This also means that Marx has a stake in maintaining the specific difference of thermodynamic technology from the technology of all preceding eras. The steam engine is not simply a tool, for it can do what a tool cannot: make past living-labor act gratuitously.

With the invention of the steam engine, capitalism wears the economic structure that derives its profit from human labor alone as a fetter, or as a survival (in the technical sense of the term). Therefore, machines will be capital's undoing. The revolutionary character of machines is to bear its ultimate fruit in the overcoming of the very mode that produced these machines. In the communist era, machines are finally to live up to their promise of alleviating drudgery. They are to realize their surplus wealth in all of its vastness as free time (defined as time not spent performing labor for self-sustenance). In this, machines are unlike any of the preceding instruments of production.

Marx describes Modern Industry not only as productive of material wealth, but also as productive of a certain technological consciousness. This consciousness is continually dissatisfied with the current means of production. It "never looks upon and treats the existing form of a process as final. The technical basis of [Modern] Industry is therefore revolutionary, while all earlier modes of production were essentially conservative" (MECW 1996, 35, 489; MEGA^2 II, 9, 425; MEGA^2 II, 8, 470). The continual improvement of thermodynamic engines forms the historical backdrop to Marx's claims. Such machines are under constant revision and erasure; they are constantly changed and reconfigured with greater productivity of energy, and less heat loss, as their goal. Capitalism demonstrates its real greatness here. Against its own conservative tendencies, it has produced an essentially revolutionary technical structure and with this altered the way human consciousness regards the given, natural world and the possibilities of this world.

Marx cites his own *Communist Manifesto* to illustrate the point. The text he cites is the famous passage about life under bourgeois conditions of production as a life of constant revolution:

> The bourgeoisie cannot exist without continually revolutionizing the instruments of production, and thereby the relations of production and all the social relations. Conservation, in an unaltered form, of the old modes of production was on the contrary the first condition of existence for all earlier industrial classes. Constant revolution in production, uninterrupted disturbance of all social conditions, everlasting uncertainty and agitation, distinguish the bourgeois epoch from all earlier ones. All fixed, fast-frozen relations, with their train of ancient and venerable prejudices and opinions, are swept away, all new formed ones become antiquated before they can ossify. All that is solid melts into air, all that is holy is profaned, and man is at last compelled to face with sober sense the real conditions of life, and his relations with his kind.
>
> (I.IV.XV.9; MECW 1996, 35, 489; MEGA^2 II, 9, 425; MEGA^2 II, 8, 470; see *Manifesto* at MECW 1976, 6, 487; MEW 1959, 4, 465)

The bourgeoisie itself constantly revolutionizes the instruments of production. Subject to constant changes that will enhance productivity, machines emblematize this constant changeover in the means of production; this is why they are the means of production of capital *par excellence*.

Among the revolutionary shifts peculiar to technological consciousness is an understanding of mutual human involvement. This combats political fictions that would treat human beings as isolated units.

According to Marx, Modern Industry, defined by the change to machine production, has "rent the veil that concealed from men their own social process of production" (I.IV.XV.9; MECW 1996, 35, 489; MEGA^2 II, 9, 425; MEGA^2 II, 8, 470). Machines reveal the process of production in a way never before possible, because in working with them the social relations that always persist among humans are made visible and undeniable.

Machines resemble the human body, not as an individual body but as a class body. They reflect the general state of science as the sum of social knowledge. They reflect a surplus of abstracted wealth. They in turn reassemble the bodies of the human beings at work on and with them, changing the very notion of "human being," and the class, sex/gender, race, kinship, and class kinship implied by this term. Industrialization produces monsters with potential.

In their constant revolutionizing of the received division of labor, machines have the potential to revolutionize what for Marx is the most important division of labor: the polarizing division between the two classes.[26] Because of this, in Marx's *Communist Manifesto*, machines themselves are key elements of developing revolutionary consciousness as well as the material foundation for the communist mode of production. Habituation to industrial life may produce not only monstrosities, but also liberations from old patriarchal norms.

In an important passage near the end of chapter XV, Marx pulls together a number of these themes: the gradual self-overcoming of Modern Industry into its second, communistic form; the distinction implied therein between the means and the mode of production; and the still older distinction between objectification and alienation explored in Chapter 1 of this book. Marx's general philosophical point is that there are both positive and negative aspects to the employment of machinery in capital. The positives are the changes in social relations brought about when changes in the means of production transform social and political life, especially traditional class categories. The negatives are the monstrosities of working-class life, though these too may encompass positives that Marx cannot recognize, or at least cannot recognize within his portrayal of the logic of alienated life. Marx writes,

> By means of machinery, chemical processes and other methods, [the technical basis of Modern Industry] is continually causing changes not only in the technical basis of production, but also in the functions of the labourer, and in the social combinations of the labour process. At the same time, it thereby also revolutionizes the division

of labour within the society, and incessantly launches masses of capital and of workpeople from one branch of production to another. But if Modern Industry, by its very nature, therefore necessitates variation of labour, fluency of function, universal mobility of the labourer, on the other hand, *in its capitalistic form*, it reproduces the old division of labour with its ossified particularizations. We have seen how this absolute contradiction between the technical necessities of Modern Industry, and the social character inherent in its capitalistic form, dispels all fixity and security in the situation of the labourer; how it constantly threatens, by taking away the instruments of labour, to snatch from his hands his means of subsistence, and, by suppressing his detail function, to make him superfluous. We have seen, too, how this antagonism vents its rage in the creation of that *monstrosity*, an industrial reserve army, kept in misery in order to be always at the disposal of capital; in the incessant human sacrifices from among the working-class, in the most reckless squandering of labour-power, and in the devastation caused by a social anarchy which turns every economic progress into a social calamity. This is the negative side.
(MECW 1996, 35, 489–490; MEGA^2 II, 9, 425–426;
MEGA^2 II, 8, 470–471; emphases added)

In the account of capitalism's positive side, we see Marx at his least technophobic, with the full understanding that the human–machine hybrid symbiosis will produce new configurations of human activity and social life. In such passages, Marx's adoption of the thermodynamic paradigm, and his ability to spell out its positive consequences for social and political life, is most complete. Machinery, and, by extension, technology, take on enormous importance, whereas human labor diminishes or disappears. The elimination of scarcity accompanying technological change becomes a material catalyst for the political imagination. Machines, metaphors for and embodiments of the accumulated historical and scientific knowledge of the human species, are among the ultimate causal agents for a new form of political society.

5
Alienation Beyond Marx

Marx's critique of technological alienation is most fully expressed in his description of the role of machines in modern industrial life. But Marx's account of technological alienation, even at its most mature, is not without lines of tension. In fact, Marx's description of technology is vexed, and this vexation corresponds to an ambiguity in the social uses of science and technology in nineteenth-century capitalist society. On the one hand, Marx supports the scientific and technological revolution in the means of production that is expressed in machine usage. In this revolution, Marx sees the opportunity for machines to fulfill their promise to liberate human beings from drudgery, to shorten labor time and intensity, and to leave more time for self-cultivation, that is, to overcome or eliminate alienation. In this, he follows the utopian socialists of whom he is otherwise so critical, and he stays within the parameters of the Enlightenment attitude toward technology.

On the other hand, Marx has seen machines bring about the opposite effects. Machines intensify labor in its most horrifying forms because the mode of production in which they are employed has a single measure for calculating value: maximum production of surplus value. Capitalist production contains no category for understanding material wealth outside of this foreclosure, and capitalist society places no value on diminishing labor, only on increasing surplus value. Marx spells out the contradiction between the promise and the reality of machines when he writes that

> In the older countries, machinery, when employed in some branches of industry, creates such a redundancy of labour in other branches that in these latter the fall of wages below the value of labour-power impedes the use of machinery, and, from the standpoint of the

capitalist, whose profit comes, not from a diminution of the labour employed, but of the labour paid for, renders that use superfluous and often impossible.... In England women are still occasionally used instead of horses for hauling canal boats, because the labour required to produce horses and machines is an accurately known quantity, while that required to maintain the women of the surplus-population is below all calculation. Hence nowhere do we find a more shameful squandering of human labour power for the most despicable purposes than in England, the land of machinery

(I.IV.XV.2; MECW 1996, 35, 397; MEGA^2 II, 9, 343; MEGA^2 II, 8, 384–385).

Marx, witnessing the era of unregulated capitalism in England, saw how this mode of production did not value human beings as qualitatively different—superior kinds of energy—whose faculties are to be prioritized and preserved. Not only do machines turn into instruments of torture, exhaustion, and death, they become more valuable than humans themselves. Machines, supposedly the material instantiation of the Enlightenment narrative of progress, become the instruments of torture, death, and misery. The working-class human being is worth less than he or she was in the feudal period, less than animals, less than the slaves of antiquity, and far, far less than industrial machines themselves. Machines, far from overcoming and eliminating alienation, tend to exacerbate it.

I explored this contradiction in Chapters 3 and 4. In Chapter 3, I showed how Marx's conceptual inheritance from Justus Liebig explains his forecast of the role technology will play in a liberated social world. Marx claims that technological and economic changes form the basis for political and ideological changes. By eliminating scarcity, technologically enhanced production will create a society that need not replicate the struggle for scarce resources in its social and political functions. In his *Grundrisse* (1857–1858), Marx develops a theory of how machinery is really *already* the emblematic means of production of a liberated society, used to produce material wealth and decrease the time spent in alienating labor. To show this, Marx develops a contrast between material wealth and value. The former category includes all usable goods, the latter only those labor-based commodities that turn a profit in the capitalist system. In the *Grundrisse*, Marx envisions an elimination of value in favor of material wealth. In the *Grundrisse*, these positive aspects of machinery are still visible alongside Marx's development of the alienation brought on by the use of technology in the capitalist mode of production.

In Chapter 4, I explained Marx's account of machines in *Capital*. In contrast to the *Grundrisse*, *Capital* illustrates the ways technology operates in an alienated mode of production to make labor miserable and arduous. By depriving work of strength and skill, machines also deprive work of interest. Machines are not optimally employed under capitalism, where they are used to produce only value and not material wealth: to extort surplus value rather than produce useful goods.

In *Capital*, Marx also uses the effect of machinery on the concept of labor to explain changes in women's labor and social status in modernity, and, more broadly, to look at the changing composition of the working classes. His reasons for this become clearer when we turn to his notebooks from August 1852, where the historians he cites connect the themes of advancements in the arts directly with enhancement in women's social and political status.[1]

But this historical thesis creates a problem, because Marx also shows that the Industrial Revolution exploits women's labor and reduces their status: they are used to haul canal boats and perform other anachronistic tasks no one else will perform. He also shows how a virulent stripe of capitalist humanism, misogynous in character, appears as a backlash to the widespread entrance of women into waged factory labor. Marx "solves" this problem by positing alienated labor as a period of purgation, following which the communist revolution will restore the correct historical parallel between advancements in the arts and advancements in human society, which for Marx includes advancements in the status of women.

In this chapter, I will look at alienation, and the connection between alienation and science and technology, developed beyond Marx. I mean "beyond" in several senses. My discussion looks beyond Marx's own most famous texts into what was really an inquiry that occupied him for the rest of his life: the exact role of science and technology in political production. My discussion also looks beyond Marx into his contemporary context, both into those thinkers whose work influenced his and into the general attitudes about technology that dominated his age. Finally, I look beyond Marx to the twentieth- and twenty-first–century theories that have repeated, expanded upon, or fallen behind his insights about alienation. Let me expand upon these three senses in order to capture, to borrow a phrase from Negri, a Marx beyond Marx.

So far my discussion has been limited to Marx's well-known early and later texts, and has especially highlighted the *Grundrisse* and *Capital*. These texts are the most famous in the literatures about the problem of technology in Marx, though *Capital's* chapter XV continues to be under-theorized. In this chapter, I look beyond these texts—and therefore also beyond these literatures—into Marx's less parsed excerpt and manuscript materials. Though I have drawn on these materials in previous chapters, it has always been in the context of their meaning for one of the famous works. In this chapter I examine them directly.

The schema set out by Marx's major texts may in fact prevent us from viewing Marx's philosophy of science and technology comprehensively, because this philosophy is never definitively displayed in either the *Grundrisse* or *Capital*. In fact, each of the major texts brackets the role of science and technology in accord with a more comprehensive agenda. Because of this, I turn away from Marx's famous texts and to two less famous and far less parsed groups of texts: Marx's excerpt notebooks on science and technology from the 1850s onward and Marx's *Economic Manuscripts of 1861–63*. Particularly in dialogue with one another, these texts sketch some implications of Marx's philosophy of science and technology that anticipate later theoretical developments.

First, I sketch the range and the contents of Marx's excerpt notebooks on science and technology, the state of scholarship about them, and the chief sites in which these notebooks appear in the more polished texts. Second, I move to a particular case from the excerpt notebooks: the excerpts from Charles Babbage, particularly as these reappear in Marx's *Economic Manuscripts of 1861–63*. I use the comparison between Marx and Babbage as a starting point for showing some limitations in Marx's account of science and technology. In particular, a comparison of Marx and Babbage illustrates the breaking points at which Marx is unwilling or unable to move his thought into the new, energeticist paradigm that I described in Chapter 2.

The excerpts from Babbage, particularly in dialogue with the *Economic Manuscripts of 1861–63*, also show that Marx accepts the mechanical speed of machine production as a desirable consequence of industrialization. This leads me to an aspect of technologically mediated environments anticipated but not analyzed by Marx: the imposition of modern, machine-driven time, and the resultant alienation in embodied temporality. Following Postone, I suggest that forms of temporality can embody social domination (1993), and that this form of alienation is unaddressed in Marx's notion of a liberated society.

The chapter continues by offering a discussion of the technophobia characteristic of Marx's age, a technophobia that is one of the most salient signs and symptoms of capitalist humanism (see Chapter 4). I trace the political consequences of technophobic attitudes in

nineteenth-century thought and its etiology. This discussion contextu-
alizes the political import of nineteenth-century discussions of science
and technology, the environment in which Marx undertook his studies
and did his writing. Returning to Marx's major works, the discussion also
shows the degree to which Marx himself participated in the attitudes of
technophobia and technophilia.

Drawing on the suggestive genealogy I have given of the technophobia of the reactionary classes of the nineteenth century, a technophobia
that colludes with the worst excesses of capitalist humanism, the
chapter ends with some conclusions about some forms of technophobia present in twentieth-century theoretical accounts of technology. In
particular, I discuss the appearance of technophobia in Martin Heidegger's "The Question Concerning Technology" (1977) and in Carolyn
Merchant's *The Death of Nature* (1980). I suggest that Marx has already
given us the tools for diagnosing this technophobia as politically perni-
cious, and that we see the fruit of this in the critiques of Heidegger and
Merchant offered by Herbert Marcuse and Donna Haraway.

I also suggest that Marx's critiques of alienation and exchange-value
offer an earlier version of claims that will be made famous in Martin
Heidegger's twentieth-century indictment of technological modernity.
Marx's concepts are, however, more politically potent than those of
Heidegger, because they insist on the political shaping of conceptual
thought, including philosophical thought about science and technology and philosophical deployments of the concept of nature. They also
show, contra Heidegger, that technology has no essence apart from the
historical mode of production in which it is deployed.

From this perspective, the fractures that run through Marx's accounts
of science and technology do not appear as weaknesses. Rather, these
fractures are necessitated by Marx's attempt to hold together Enlightenment rationality, including its scientific and technological offspring,
with a critique of technological alienation. This attempt is as admirable
as it is atypical, being neither an unmediated Romanticism nor an
uncritical Rationalism. It is an attempt we see replicated in Marcuse and
Haraway, whose projects repeat much of the spirit of Marx's analysis,
including some of its key contradictions.

I   Science and technology in Marx's excerpt notebooks

Although Marx falls short of offering a developed philosophy of science
and technology, his texts from the 1850s onward contain evidence that
he was working on such a theory. In a letter to Engels near the end

of his life, Marx assigns an extremely significant role to technology in determining the economic basis of a society. He writes,

> What we understand by the economic conditions which we regard as the determining basis of the history of society are the methods by which human beings in a given society produce their means of subsistence and exchange the products among themselves (in so far as division of labour exists). Thus the *entire technique* of production and transport is here included. According to our conception this technique also determines the method of exchange and, further, the division of products, and with it, after the dissolution of tribal society, the division into classes also and hence the relations of lordship and servitude and with them the state, politics, law, etc.
>
> (25 January 1882, emphasis in original).

This reveals Marx's rising concern over the social and political productivity of technology and the form in which "the entire technique of production" casts the resultant society. Changes in scientific and technical life precede changes in economic life that ultimately affect political life. This also indicates that for Marx science and technology are thick, historically sedimented practices about which a story can be told. Science and technology have, moreover, anthropological and ontological consequences for human embodiment, class divisions, and exchange.

The need to demystify the technical basis of production as a part of his critique of capitalist society explains why, subsequent to the 1850s, Marx began studying the role of science and technology in production, a development we can see in both his published works and his unpublished excerpt notebooks. Between the works of the late 1840s and volume I of *Capital* (1867), Marx's account of the social productivity of science and technology undergoes considerable development, and, as we have seen, these developments affect his conceptions of labor, the interaction between the human being and nature, and the notion of revolution.

Marx's letters to Engels in 1853 show that he was at work determining which part of a machine is its most "revolutionary" element (Richta 1969, 25), that is, the element most likely to eliminate human labor in favor of production wholly by machines. In texts from volume III of *Capital*, which would be published by Engels only after Marx's death, Marx explored the theoretical problem most intimately connected with the social productivity of science and technology: the tendency of the rate of profit to fall, and the related inability of the capitalist system to sustain itself. And in the early 1880s, immediately prior to his death, Marx expressed a great deal of interest in the role electrification, as a decentralized power source, would play in transforming the communication and other systems of a liberated society, just as a liberated society would require and enable this use of electrification. We may conclude that Marx's concern over explaining the social and political productivity of science and technology remained one of the driving concerns of his mature work.

The material from Marx's excerpt notebooks of the 1850s and 1860s[2] shows the scientific sources from which Marx draws his vision of human beings, machines, and the labor produced by their dynamic interaction. These excerpt notebooks are not polished texts. Rather, they are the notes Marx made while reading and doing research. What they offer scholars is a record of his research and when it occurred, which is crucial for understanding the shaping of Marx's later work.

For the purposes of understanding Marx's view of science and technology as it developed in the 1850s and 1860s, the most important content in excerpts are the notes on Liebig's *Animal Chemistry*, Charles Babbage's *On the Economy of Machinery*, Robert Owen's utopian factory schemas, Eli Whitney, J. H. M. Poppe's *History of 18th Century Technology*, Andrew Ure's "Technological Dictionary," A. Quetelet's *Treatise on Man and the Development of his Faculties*, Knight's *History of Machinery*, plus notes on the development of railways in Germany and India (Marx 1850–1890; Müller 1982; Winkelmann 1982). The list is hardly exhaustive because it hits only the most important figures from Marx's reading catalogue. Marx synthesized some aspects of these texts in the "Fragment on Machines" in the *Grundrisse* and in the "Machinery and Modern Industry" chapter of *Capital* (see Chapters 3 and 4).[3]

The excerpts are also developed in Marx's *Economic Manuscripts of 1861–63*, which Marx wrote between the *Grundrisse* and *Capital*. In fact, the *Economic Manuscripts of 1861–63* contains details about Marx's philosophy of technology that were not yet developed in the *Grundrisse*, and that were subsequently eliminated from the account given in *Capital* because of its peculiar structure. In particular, Marx's most explicit vision of the form postrevolutionary labor will take is included in the intervening text, and I will explain this vision in more detail below. In addition, Marx has called a large portion of the *Economic Manuscripts of 1861–63*, " About *Science* and Capital" (emphasis added). The "Science" portion of the title was eliminated in *Capital*, which also eliminates some of the generalist discussions of science's social role that Marx had pursued in both the *Grundrisse* and the *Economic Manuscripts of 1861–63*.

Marx's excerpts on technology do not form a unified whole in his sketch notebooks. Rather, they are interspersed with his continued studies of the other themes of political economy and also with texts from the history of philosophy. In particular, Marx returns to reading and making notes on Hegel's *Logic*, Leibniz's *Hypothesis Physica Nova*, Descartes's *Opuscula Posthume*, texts from Hume and Locke, some of Montesquieu's *Esprit des Lois*, a history of women and paternalism, and notes on the division of labor as it was discussed in the classical texts of Xenophon, Plato, Aristotle, Tacitus, Aelian, and Thucydides as well as the modern texts of Smith, Ricardo, and Say.

The dispersion of the excerpts on science and technology among so many other types of text has made these excerpts difficult to identify, catalogue, and study. At the time of writing this book, some of these excerpts have not been published and remain in manuscript form. Despite the attempts on the part of Rainer Winkelmann and Hans-Peter Müller to publish Marx's excerpts on science and technology, their books remain limited. Müller and Winkelmann are primarily writing their histories as commentaries on twentieth-century technologies. Müller and Winkelmann also comment on the early twentieth-century debates within Marxism over Marx's view of technology, for example, Franz Borkenau's and Heinrich Grossman's debate over whether Marx expresses a technological determinism. Thus, Müller and Winkelmann approach the Marx excerpt archive with a selection principle that favors those excerpts that facilitate these goals (Schrader 2003, personal communication).

This limited treatment of the scientific and technological excerpts is also due to the state of the Marx excerpts as a whole. In the 1920s, the excerpts were eliminated from the collected works by Marx's first editor, David Rjazanov, as worthless scribblings. Then, in the 1930s, even Rjazanov's limited collected works project (Marx 1927–1935) was eliminated, along with Rjazanov himself, under pressure from Stalin. Scholarship on Marx's texts reemerged after Stalin's death in 1953, but then already under the ideological pressures of the Cold War. It is only in the 1990s, with the refounding of the international *Marx–Engels Gesamtausgabe*, that the excerpts have begun slowly to emerge. Even now, they are being included only in the German editions of the collected works, not in the English ones.

Among the excerpts that recently emerged from manuscript are
Marx's notes on Charles Babbage. Babbage was an English mathemati-
cian whose idea in 1842 for an "analytical engine," which anticipated
the computer of today, was rejected by the British Parliament for funding well into the 1860s (Day and McNeil 1996, 33). Marx's work on
Babbage in the excerpt notebooks is from the years 1845 and 1860. He
mentions Babbage by name in the definition of machines he sets out in
the *Grundrisse* (MECW 1987, 29, 80; MEGA^2 II, 1.2, 569). This definition
reappears in *Capital*'s account of machinery and Modern Industry in its
developed form, but without the explicit reference to Babbage. Turning
to the excerpt restores the debt Marx's account of machines owes to
Babbage, a lineage that otherwise progressively disappears between
Marx's excerpt notebooks and the account of machines he will give in
Capital. I discuss this lineage in the following section.

II   Karl Marx and Charles Babbage: the speed of production in the *Economic Manuscripts of 1861–1863*

As we have seen in Chapters 3 and 4, Marx suggests that the economic
basis of Modern Industry in machine production makes nineteenth-
century society ripe for social change: work with machines creates
material wealth that could support a liberated society, laying the foundation for the fast production of the material wealth that will be essential
under communism in order to insure free time. Work with machines
under capital also develops worker alienation and sharpens the impulse
to revolt, adding impetus to political revolution. In addition, Modern
Industry spawns a communications infrastructure that has the potential
to make this revolt speedy and well organized, aided in particular by the
printing press and the railroad.

Marx develops his most explicit picture of the form labor will take
after capitalism's demise in a text that he wrote in between the
Grundrisse and *Capital*, namely the *Economic Manuscripts of 1861–63*.[4]
Postrevolutionary labor is determined by speed and by the maximum appropriation and use of science and technology. Marx develops
this idea by selectively using material from Charles Babbage. In his
excerpt notebooks from 1845 and 1860, Marx has copied summaries of
Babbage's famous *Economy of Machinery and Manufacture*. In these notes,
Marx pays particular attention to Babbage's accounts of the division
of labor, the creation of large industrial operations, and the introduction of machinery into industries that had previously run on hand
labor.

In this section, I show that speedy labor with machines remains the foundation of the communist mode of production. But I also suggest that Marx's commitment to the revolutionary overcoming of alienation prevents him from seeing some concrete effects of machine labor on working-class agency and embodiment, and causes him to sacrifice contemporary interests to those of the future. For Marx, alienation must be sharpened before it can be eliminated. Because of this, Marx ignores the passages from Babbage's book where Babbage suggests that work with machines will not eliminate skill altogether but rather facilitate the development of new technological skills among the working class. Such a nuanced notion of skill never appeared in Marx's account in *Capital*. Moreover, for Marx, complicated machine labor will only be an aggregate of simple labors into which it could be analytically divided in units of time, not a positive transformative principle for the notion of labor itself. Babbage had already challenged this idea in his work, as I will illustrate below.[5]

Today, Charles Babbage's fame rests almost entirely on his development of analytical engines with the capacity for both complex, programmed calculation and memory. Though Babbage's engines were the forerunners of contemporary computers, the practical use for such devices was unclear during Babbage's own lifetime. His mania for developing them was derived from his sheer love for mechanizing calculation, a process through which human computational and transcriptional errors could be eliminated. Babbage's mania caused him to be eyed with some suspicion by his Romantic, humanist peers.

Machinery had become an object of interest for Babbage because without sufficient mechanical advances, he could not automate and embody the science of calculation. As we learned in Chapter 2, machinery became an object of interest for Marx because he needed to explain the contemporary changes in human productive labor in order to explain his prognostications for social and political life. Just as Babbage was led to agitate against class stratifications by his concerns about science, Marx was led to explore the social role of science because of his concerns over class stratification.

Unlike today, where technological know-how is the province of a certain educated class and ownership of technological objects a sign of relative wealth, the wealthier classes of Babbage's time tended to be nonusers of machine technology and ill-informed about its possibilities. At that time in England, an upper-class education was still largely theological. Babbage's mathematical genius was not enough to save him from failing his final exams at Trinity College in Cambridge when he chose to defend the thesis that God was a material agent (Swade 2001, 19). To put this in perspective using the terms of Marx's history, the upper classes of the nineteenth century were still steeped in survivals from the outdated ideologies of feudalism, and virulently so among the ruling classes who resisted science, democracy, and other markers of bourgeois life.

Conversely, the working classes were becoming habitual users of machines in production. This was a practical, materialist education. Gifted individuals from the working classes were gaining reputations as machine designers.[6] Babbage laments that "the workshops [of England]...contain within them a rich mine of knowledge, too generally neglected by the wealthier classes" (1989a, vi). In a telling remark, Babbage characterizes the future of science as a practice that "cannot fail to promote [intercourse] between the different classes of society" (263). Babbage wishes to hasten changes in ruling cultural ideas from old feudal to new scientific norms. He hoped that the metaphysical prejudices that fettered scientific advance among the upper classes would be removed, and suggested precipitous class mixing as a mechanism for bringing this about. Babbage himself enhanced his technical education by touring England's manufacturing workshops incognito (Babbage 1989a, 169–172). This explains how Babbage was able to publish his best-selling book *The Economy of Machinery and Manufacture* in 1835. Like Büchner's *Stoff und Kraft*, with which it was roughly contemporaneous, Babbage's book was immediately translated into all of the European languages.

While in exile in Paris in 1845, Marx began reading Babbage's book in French translation. In the 1845 excerpt notebooks on Babbage, Marx cites the advantages of machinery in amplifying human force and in saving the worker time. He also cites Babbage's division of machines into "1) Machines applied in order to produce force [*Kraft*] and 2) Machines with the simple purpose of transmitting force and executing work" (Winkelmann 1982, 51–72, my translation). For Marx, the productivity of force-producing machines lays the foundation for the post-revolutionary status machines will have in alleviating labor's unnecessary drudgery. We have also seen, in Chapter 4, how the division cited by Babbage here will be adopted by Marx, in *Capital*, as the technical distinction between the motor and the transmitting mechanism.

The nineteenth-century development of thermodynamic machines that produce force, and especially the development of the steam engine, was the age's specific technological addition to the transmitting mechanisms and tools that had begun to develop in the Renaissance.

Philosophers of technology beginning with Marx—or rather, with Babbage, from whom he takes the distinction—thus divide modernity into two Industrial Revolutions. The first revolution occurred in tools and techniques of dividing labor that blossomed in the seventeenth-century workshop; the second revolution transformed the power sources that conditioned production in the nineteenth century.

In his published works, Marx cites material from Babbage for the first time in *The Poverty of Philosophy* (1846), his critique of Pierre-Joseph Proudhon, whom he has accused of Hegelianism, and a bad Hegelianism at that (1963, 132–144). According to Marx, Proudhon misunderstood how a machine differs from the tools that precede it. Proudhon therefore believes that by uniting the detailed operations together, machinery cancels the division of labor that had been present in the manufacturing workshop and thus offers "a restoration and synthesis" for the worker.

Marx cites Babbage to show that machines, rather than restoring a laborer's lost functionality, in fact contribute to the intensification of the division of labor, which was just beginning to have the noticeable international features that economists today call the North–South split. Marx writes,

> The machine is a unification of the instruments of labour, and by no means a combination of different operations for the worker himself. "When, by the division of labour, each particular operation has been simplified to the use of a single instrument, the linking up of all of these instruments, set in motion by a single engine, constitutes a machine" (Babbage, *Traité sur l'Economie des Machines, etc. Paris, 1833*).... We need not recall the fact that in England the great progress of the division of labour began after the invention of machinery.... Thanks to the machine, the spinner can live in England while the weaver resides in the East Indies.... Thanks to the application of machinery and steam, the division of labour was able to assume such dimensions that large-scale industry, detached from the national soil, depends entirely on the world market, on international exchange, and on an international division of labour
>
> (1963, 138–140).

Marx continues by sketching the worker's alienation from labor divided in this way: labor is removed from its concrete attachments to embodied strength and skill. Labor no longer creates a particular complete object that the laborer goes on to use. Labor has turned into what Marx will in *Capital* call "abstract labor" but here calls "labour that has completely lost its specialized character" (Marx 1963, 144). In addition, this abstract labor must accommodate itself to "the unvarying movements of the automaton." The abstract labor is therefore socialized in symbiosis with other abstract labors and with the machine itself (141).

For Marx, these negative features do not inaugurate the positive technological education of the working classes claimed by Babbage. Instead, they produce a shift in consciousness, revealing the class kinship among workers, all of whom now participate in abstract labor. This leveling increases the likelihood that workers will come together in collective political action, because no hierarchical divisions among them remain. Marx writes that this is "the one revolutionary side of the automatic workshop": "the moment every special development stops, the need for universality, the tendency towards the development of the individual begins to be felt" (1963, 144).

The classes of the manufacturing era were divided amongst themselves by how they were ranked in specialized skills. According to Marx, the exacerbations of alienation from these old skills will eliminate the divisions among workers, consolidating the working class and humanity as a whole. This is why Marx must neglect the question of the development of new skills with machines that might again stratify the working class. He cannot view skill or facility with particular machines as a new "specialized character" of labor. If facility with one type of machines develops as a new, particularized skill, the consciousness of universal humanity will be disrupted by new, skill-driven class divisions.

Marx's account of the negative role of machine labor in developing a working-class consciousness of universality has not yet become his positive appraisal of the role of machine productivity after the revolution. For that we must turn to the *Economic Manuscripts of 1861–63*. For Marx, the intensified production of technologically optimized machine labor quickly creates a large number of use-values. Because of this Marx makes short stints of highly productive abstract labor with machines the foundation of the communist mode of production.

In 1860, exiled to London, Marx again took notes on Babbage's book, this time working from the English edition. These notes are shorter than those in the 1845 notebook. They begin where the others left off: by sketching Babbage's distinction between machines that transmit and those that produce force. Marx then wrote summaries of the portions of the second half of Babbage's book that were missing from his 1845 notes. These continue to emphasize the superiority of machines over natural operations, including human power and precision skill in wielding hand tools (Marx 1858–1862, 182–183; Winkelmann 1982, 101–103).

In the *Economic Manuscripts of 1861–63*, Marx uses this material to explain the superabundant productivity of labor that is mediated by machines. Here he uses Babbage's definition of machines as those "set in motion by a single motor, whatever this motor might be, whether the human hand and foot, animal power, elemental forces, or an automatic mechanism" (1991, 391). Marx concludes that "the moment when direct human participation in production was reduced to the provision of simple power, the principle of work by machinery was given. The mechanism was there; the motive force could later be replaced by water, steam, etc." (392). This marks the first part of the development of machinery.

Marx then turns to the second Industrial Revolution: the employment of the steam engine (MECW 1991, 392), a transition in which he is far more interested. The sheer force made available by steam is quantitatively and qualitatively different from the motive forces that sprang from human power and other sources, for example wind and water. With the steam engine, human beings make their accumulated past labor work for them, supplanting natural force with the human ingenuity embodied in machines.

The vast increase in force embodied in steam engines translates into both extensive and intensive development of labor's productive power. Running machines around the clock keeps profits high while the machine is still new. In the second half of his book Babbage writes, "[The owner of machines] quickly perceived that with the same expense of fixed capital and a small addition to his circulating capital, he could work the machine during the whole twenty-four hours" (1989, 152). Marx adopts Babbage's theories of machine obsolescence and extended working hours and will represent them without explicit attribution in *Capital*.[7]

On the whole, Marx offers us few concrete descriptions of the form labor will take after the communist revolution. But we learn in the *Economic Manuscripts of 1861–63* that the intensive increase of labor's productivity is essential to his conception of postrevolutionary labor. Marx writes,

> This tendency to replace extent by degree only emerges at a higher level of development of production. This is in a certain sense a condition for social progress. *Free time* is created in this way for the worker as well, and the intensity of a particular kind of labour therefore does

not remove the possibility of activity in another direction; this can, on the contrary, appear as a relaxation from it. Hence the extraordinarily beneficial consequences—statistically demonstrated—of [the development of production] for the physical, moral, and intellectual amelioration of the working-classes in England
(Marx 1991, 386, emphasis added).

With the intensification of labor's productivity, accomplished by the accumulation of past labor in steam-powered machinery, the technological foundation for communism is in place. Freedom for the worker will be in the form of free time. Only a short period of abstract labor will be required, because the high degree of productivity will mean necessities will be produced quickly, and this short stint will appear as a relaxing interval suspended in other forms of activity.

Marx does not envision a return from abstract labor to labor's concrete forms, only the minimization of time spent engaged in abstract labor. This is why Marx wrote in the *Grundrisse* that "machines will not cease to be agents of social production when they become e.g. property of the associated workers" (1991, 833). Alienation is overcome because workers own the machines instead of having little to no control over the means of production and the accumulation of past human labor it embodies; nonetheless, labor remains abstracted from skill, or at least from skill as it has been defined by Marx.

This leaves at least two problems for Marx. First, abstract, alienated labor as practical life activity is neither eliminated nor qualitatively transformed in this vision of speedy postrevolutionary production: it is merely made to occupy a minimal rather than a maximum part of practical life activity. Thus, abstract labor is only minimized, but does not cease to exist as a mode of human activity. Second, the dangers of operating machinery, already documented in Britain's Factory Acts, are not rectified in the communist future. Marx's concern over time, an older mode of calculating labor's extensive magnitude, obscures his worries about energy, a newer mode of calculating labor's intensive magnitude. The communist future, however, must offer us something more than free time against the backdrop of an unchanged notion of labor. The communist future must offer us qualitative changes in human practical life activity, not simply a reduction of abstract labor, and a continuation of the dangers that mechanical production poses to human beings.

In this future, Marx also empties the qualitative notion of freedom employed by Kant and Hegel to the empty bracket represented by free time. In the next section, we will see that such a way of conceptualizing time and freedom are contingent on the capitalist mode of production and its productivist metaphysic. Marx himself is not always able to get free of the capitalist mode of value that he criticizes so deeply in other parts of his analysis, nor is he always able to push this critique to its ultimate consequences.

At the end of Babbage's *Economy of Machinery and Manufactures*, in passages that Marx evidently read, even though he does not comment on them directly, Babbage agitates for absolute cooperation in manufacturing enterprises. In this proposal, the worker and the capitalist would shade into one another, because both would own the means of production and share in the profits of the operation: Babbage speaks of "partnership."

Babbage's concern is not persons but the optimization of technology, an optimization that he fears is undermined by the system of profit-extortion. He demands that

> a considerable part of the wages received by each person employed should depend on the profits made by the establishment... [and]... every person connected with it should derive more advantage from applying any [technological] improvement he might discover... than he could by any other course
>
> (1989, 177).

The passage is further evidence for Babbage's materialist, bottom-up view of the progress of science and technology. For Babbage, science and technology make far more progress via industrial application than by papers given at London's Royal Society. Babbage's sense of transformative working-class agency and knowledge about technology is also not among the material Marx draws from him in his excerpts. While Marx of course knows that pleasure and knowledge in working with machines might be a strong skill gained by the working class in the transition to technologically mediated labor, his discussions of alienation, deskilling, and political revolution can, at times, obscure this insight.

Developing this insight could have helped Marx explain how the technological basis of the capitalist mode of production had already laid the groundwork for changes in power relations among the classes. But because of the teleology Marx inherited from Hegel and Smith, the possibilities of real working-class knowledge and agency are excluded from any world prior to capitalism's revolutionary demise.[8] Babbage's suggestions of profit-sharing would be a simple, self-defeating reform of the labor market that might hold off the political revolution by making conditions for the working classes more bearable.

Marx's synchronic analysis of the mode of production known as capitalism emphasizes the practical effects of disenchanting and murderous labor on the worker. However, this increasing alienation of the worker from any interest or skill in the work drives the worker toward recognition of his or her universal status in a realm in which all participate in undifferentiated and abstract labor, and thus lays the foundation for revolutionary consciousness. John Elster will describe this structure, in *Explaining Technical Change*, as the Leibnizian inheritance of all functional explanation in the human and social sciences: "the argument that all apparent evils in the world have beneficial consequences for the larger pattern that justify and explain them" (Elster 1983, 56).

Although one might admire Marx's tenacity for an uncompromised vision of freedom from labor and alienation as the telos of industrial society, nonetheless one should hesitate before sacrificing the welfare of multiple generations to the logic of this telos. Under such a doctrine, any improvements in working conditions serve only to push back the date at which alienation will have become severe enough to bring about revolution. Paradoxically, the intensification of the very alienation Marx criticizes becomes one of the required intermediary steps of his project.

Babbage reasoned that low wages resulted in reduced social pressure for innovation, because in such a system human labor would always be cheaper than new machinery. Exploited workers also had no incentive to apply innovations of their own design to the production process, because they did not stand to gain from increases in its profitability. Babbage's solution was to raise wages.

Marx's refusal to accommodate bourgeois value leads him to scorn Babbage's strategy of profit-sharing as a means of improving working conditions and technological development. For the same reason, Marx also neglects Babbage's positive account of the developing technological agency among workers themselves. Only a total revolution, a parallel of the Nietzschean revaluation of all values that calls the good and bad into question on economic grounds, will suffice for Marx. Hence, he cannot consider schemes like agitating for better wages as anything other than counterrevolutionary: such schemes merely illustrate that the worker has adopted the bourgeois mode of valuation.

Moreover, although such schemes might raise the nominal wage to which the worker was entitled, Marx doubted that they would raise the amount of purchasing power above the bare minimum required for the sustenance of the working class. That said, it is clear from Marx's excerpt notebooks that he dislikes Babbage less than other political economists, probably because of Babbage's positive attitude toward the working class, his annoyance with the British Royal Society's fettering on scientific progress, his careful attention to machinery, and the quality of his work.

Marx's diagnosis of the alienating social effect of machine use in the capitalist mode of production is coupled with his admiration for the increased possibilities for producing wealth that will create free time in subsequent modes of production, for example, the communist mode. Thus, Marx's account of technology retains all of the characteristics of Enlightenment optimism as described by philosopher of technology Carl Mitcham: technology is the quintessential human activity that both socializes individuals and creates public wealth. A metaphysics that asserts that nature and artifice operate by the same mechanical principles accompanies this Enlightenment optimism (quoted in Scharff and Dusek 2003, 502).

At the same time, Marx's explanation of nature and artifice is not strictly mechanical. If it were, it would be accompanied by a metaphysics that has eliminated all final causation and reduced these transhistorical structures to contemporaneous efficient and material causations. Instead, Marx retains the teleology of the late Kant and Hegel in his explanations of social life. The contradictions of a particular era are resolved by an appeal to an overarching historical schema.

In *Capital*, Marx will even offer a variant of the Romantic skepticism about technology in his account of alienated labor that, as we shall see, relies on a notion of skilled labor conditioned and limited by the ideal of man wielding a tool: that is, conditioned and limited by the skills characteristic of feudal and manufacturing labors, not the new skills that might be developed in order to labor with machines. For Marx, only a repetition of the Enlightenment's foundational political gesture, or revolution, will be sufficient to restore the Enlightenment optimism of liberatory relations with technology, and with it the appropriate political expression of an already-accomplished economic and social reality. The dark period of technology-relations during capitalism will have served only to lay the technological foundation of production for life in the communist era. Thus, the Leibnizian theodicy invoked by Elster is manifested in Marx's thinking as a whole, and the French Revolution as a model for political change continues to cast its long shadow over the conceptualizations of late-modern political philosophy.

Marx's unwillingness to compromise the teleology of his history may have the disturbing political consequence that, Elster claims, "allows one to regard pre-communist individuals as so many sheep for the slaughter" (1985, 118), exhibiting all of the worst problems of eschatological reasoning. Viewed from this perspective, Marx's reasoning also replicates a structure that he already rejected in the *Grundrisse* (see Chapter 3). That is, the notion of generational sacrifice is closer to the Hegelian, Smithian, Darwinian, and Malthusian injunctions that forbid interference with the operation of nature than to Liebig's humanitarian demand that nature be interfered with, and its potential expanded, for immediate human use. It turns current generations of workers into an exchange-value for future generations. But by Marx's own criteria, such an instrumentalist view of humanity should be impossible.

III Machines and temporality: the treadmill effect and free time

Marx's continued hope for machine technology in postrevolutionary labor brings us to another blind spot in Marx's theory about science and technology. As I explained in Chapter 4, there are changes in the temporal world inaugurated by the presence of the scientific and technological lifeworld, and especially by the presence of the scientific and technological lifeworld peculiar to capitalism. In capitalism, time itself comes to be an instrument of social domination and social liberation. This temporality is reflected in Marx's extraordinary—and philosophically unprecedented—notion of freedom as "free" time.

Part of the monstrousness of machinery is its affront to pastoral time and pastoral timing. The speed at which machines operate—speeds sometimes beyond the capacity of the human perceptual apparatus—contribute to the demonic mythology of machines. As we saw in the example of the railway in Chapter 4, the habituation of human beings to the rhythms of modern industrial life was hardly without glitches. In fact, it took generations for it to be accomplished, and it may not yet have been fully accomplished. In a letter to his uncle, Marx reports of London:

> Politically and socially things are becalmed here.... The monotony is interrupted only by daily reports of frightful railway accidents. Capital here is not under as much police surveillance as on the Continent, and hence the railway directors do not care at all how many people are killed during an excursion, if only the balance looks to the comfortable side. All attempts to hold these railway kings responsible

for their homicidal neglect of all precautionary measures have hitherto been frustrated by the great influence which the railway interest
exercises in the House of Commons

(Letter of 17 August 1864; Marx 1979, 188).

The railway accident was a staple of Victorian culture, and it did not
take a sharp eye like Marx's to notice this. Nicholas Daly writes,

[W]hat I wish to emphasize is the typicality of this accident. The reit-
erations in the contemporary accounts of the instantaneous nature
of the crash, point to a popular perception of something qualitatively different in all industrial technology accidents: they occur
in "machine-time," not human time. Human agency cannot usually move rapidly enough to intervene, so rescues are few and far
between. In fact, such accidents are often too quick for the eye, perception taking place after the event: If you see it you are still alive....
We can understand the appeal of "railway rescue" plays in this light:
they envision scenarios in which a human agent can beat a mechanical agent; the human for a moment comes to enter and master the
temporal world of the machine

(2004, 23).

With the advent of the railway as a technical and theatrical social agent,
the human being must accommodate to the machine's temporal world.
Machines highlight, insist upon, and distribute a rhythm and temporality to the modern world. The most salient features of this rhythm and
this temporality are their beginnings in a speed beyond human perception. Constant small increases in the speed at which humans must add
their labor-power to production are also forced in the temporal world of
capitalist machines.

In order to function within this temporality, humans increasingly
come to rely on what Postone calls abstract time (1993, 201). By abstract
time, he means the conception of time that is "uniform, continuous,
homogenous... [and] empty of events" (202). He contrasts abstract time
with the concrete time of an event:

the time to cook rice or say one *paternoster*.... Concrete time is characterized less by its direction than by the fact that it is a dependent
variable. In the traditional Jewish and Christian notions of history,
for example, the events mentioned do not occur within time, but
structure and determine it (201).

We use abstract time when we describe the 5:35 P.M. at which the train is supposed to arrive. We use concrete time if we describe something as occurring after the arrival of the train. We use abstract time when we describe the Roman invasion of Carthage as occurring in 146 C.E. We use concrete time when we describe an event as "antediluvian." Our current dating system is an amalgamation of abstract and concrete time. It is abstract in the passage of years that can be analytically and evenly divided into still smaller abstract units, concrete in that it takes its point of origin from the *Anno Domini* or Common Era.

Abstract time is reckoned in years, months, and weeks, and in the minutes, hours, seconds, and nanoseconds of which these are composed. According to Joseph Needham, abstract time developed only in modern Western Europe, during the rise of capitalism (Postone 1993, 202). Abstract time was materially linked—and dependent upon—the development of the mechanical clock, an invention perfected in this same period (203). Over the course of capitalist development, the use of the clock became general, but it was only in the mid-nineteenth and early twentieth centuries that the clocks of various towns became synchronized, first within national environments and later internationally.[9] When this occurred, it also meant that abstract time became continuous with the abstract time in other environments. Today this feature is assumed as a matter of course in global capitalism, and has the practical consequence that I can fly to Asia, expect to land safely and according to schedule, reset my watch, and proceed in the same field of abstract time.

In order to conquer the capitalist machine's temporal world, humans become increasingly reliant on the device of abstract time. We have already seen one example of the usefulness of abstract time in the discussion of the railroad in Chapter 4. One of the first widespread set of social changes the railway brought with it, for the precise reason of avoiding the industrial accidents that human vision was too fallible to prevent, was the synchronization of times in English towns. This social change presupposes the seamless functioning of the mechanical clock. Prior to this synchronization, time in English towns moved to local, not very precise, rhythms that resembled concrete time more than abstract time.

Marx accounts for abstract time as the appropriate measure for abstract labor. That is, time is the only way to measure labor that has been stripped of all qualitative dimensions. For Marx, capitalist machines produce this form of temporality because, having adopted the historical skills of laborers, they produce the possibility of abstract labor. Because abstract labor has no qualitative features, it must be beholden to an external standard, a measure that holds indifferently for each type of labor, in order to determine its value. Abstract time is this standard. In *Capital*, Marx writes, "How, then, is the magnitude of this value to be measured? By means of the quantity of the 'value-forming substance,' the labour, which it contains. This quantity is measured by its duration, and the labour-time is itself measured on the particular scale of hours, days, etc." (quoted in Postone 1993, 189).

In factory labor, the labor of each individual cannot be measured in a product, because each individual does not make a whole product. Labor therefore cannot be measured by qualitative features of what is done, as when the craftsman finishes making a shoe. Instead the pure labor that occurs, in abstraction from any particular task, is measured in abstract time. I punch a clock and come home to report that I have labored 12 hours that day, not that I made three shoes, copy-edited two chapters, or took 22 photographs. Pauses from work are calculated in the same way: they fill the empty bracket of abstract time. Soon the whole of capitalist life, not just work, is determined in this fashion. The resultant empty brackets of time are the reification of the possibility of abstract human activity.

Once abstract time has been put into place as a social quantifier, it is subject to an additional modification. This is the introduction of a social average of production, the "socially necessary time" required to produce any given article. Once abstract temporality is in place as a means of calculating value, then, with reference to the society as a whole, a temporal norm for producing any given article can be calculated. Producers' time must conform to this norm, and any extraneous time in either direction must be eliminated if one's product is to approximate the norm. For example, in the American Philosophical Association's bulletin, the authors write, "It normally takes two months of relatively uninterrupted work to draft a good chapter, so it will take six months of very hard work to draft more than half of a dissertation" (May 2005). A social norm, quantified in abstract time, is thereby set up for a concrete amount of work.

When this happens, the average time of production is alienated from its source in human sociality. Instead, the socially necessary time of production becomes an objective temporal norm standing over producers. Postone (1993) writes,

> As a category of the totality, socially necessary labor time expresses a quasi-objective social necessity with which the producers are confronted. It is the temporal dimension of the abstract domination that

characterizes the structures of alienated social relations in capitalism. The social totality constituted by labor as an objective general mediation has a temporal character, wherein *time becomes necessity*
(191, emphasis in original).

There is one final twist. Because the means of production are constantly being transformed and machinery improved, articles are produced with constantly increasing rapidity. This leads to a dialectic between the labor accomplished in, say, one hour and the socially necessary labor time that determines this same hour. The effect of this dialectic is to constantly increase the intensive magnitudes of the abstract units. This year's hour is socially determined to be more labor-intensive than last year's, and this year's hour becomes the new baseline for determining what an hour means. Postone (1993) calls this "the treadmill effect" (298). In capitalism, this effect constantly ratchets up the intensity of labor that is socially expected to be performed in a given unit of abstract time. One must run for twenty minutes, just as before, but at a faster pace, because "twenty minutes" has come to be more intensively determined by social necessity.[10]

In capitalism, either the effects of abstract time are not limited to productive life, or productive life comes to permeate society as a whole. Whichever the case, abstract time permeates any environment where the commodity form mediates social relations (Postone 1993, 202). Indeed, all of the social forms characteristic of capitalism become characterized by their temporal dimension and abstract quantifiability (186). Activity itself becomes quantifiable and measurable according to a precise scale of minutes, hours, months, or days. As the notion of the time a particular task should occupy gains hold, activity becomes subject to the alienations of socially necessary time and the treadmill effect. As such, capitalist time becomes a new and embodied form of social domination: new, because abstract time is a historically recent mandate of consciousness, and embodied, because this mandate pervasively affects lived experience.

Capitalist time becomes a mandate not only of the factory floor or station platform but of society as a whole. The adoption of abstract temporality becomes, at first, a conscious mandate of capitalist life. But it later becomes a constitutive, even semiconscious, feature of modern human embodiment, particularly insofar as this embodiment is driven by capitalist norms. Ultimately, internal consciousness of both abstract time and the socially necessary time required by the tasks one regularly performs becomes a prerequisite for functioning in the capitalist world.

Our ability to quantify our activities in abstract units of time is a sign of the permeation of abstract temporality. In contemporary life we know the timing of most of our ritual activities with absolute precision. We know if a given activity has been accomplished with particular alacrity. We also know if it is taking too long: we know the socially necessary labor time. The trip to the store does not take the time it takes to make a trip to the store: it takes 15 minutes, 13 if traffic is light, and sometimes 20 if lines are long. The flight to Philadelphia takes an hour, slightly less if there is a tailwind, slightly more if you sit on the runway to wait for an open gate.

Often we need not even glance at our wristwatches in order to note even the slightest variations in these rhythms, and we might vary our schedules later in the day without these elements fully entering our consciousnesses. Indeed, we often emote our perception of socially necessary time, for example agitation in the case of a slowdown or elation in the case of unanticipated speed. We know what an hour, a minute, and ten seconds feels like; we adjust these abstract quantities within the historical context of the socially necessary. By doing this, we come to embody abstract temporality in the habituation of our perceptual and emotive life. In terms of alienated projections of the human being's activities and potentialities, time becomes the new god. We save it; we obey it; we do not question its existence or its history; and its sociality remains unseen.

Against this backdrop, we can understand the importance of Marx's unique attention to the portion of abstract time not absorbed by productive life. Marx appeals to "free time" for the worker as the end product of capitalist accumulation of wealth. In the *Grundrisse*'s "Fragment on Machines," he writes,

> *The creation of a large quantity of disposable time* apart from necessary labour time for the society generally and each of its members (i.e. room for the development of the individuals' full productive forces, hence those of society also), this creation of not-labour time appears in the stage of capital, as in all earlier ones, as not-labour time, free time, for a few. What capital adds is that it increases the surplus labour time of the mass by all of the means of art and science, because its value consists directly in the appropriation of surplus labour time; since *value directly its purpose*, not use-value. It is thus, despite itself, instrumental in creating the means of disposable time, in order to reduce labour time for the whole society to a diminishing minimum, and thus to free everyone's time for their

own development ... The measure of wealth is then not any longer, in any way, labour time, but rather disposable time

(1973, 708, emphases in original).

In *Capital*, Marx claims that this disposable abstract time is the material condition of freedom and political self-determination. Part of the worker's vulnerability is that he or she is not given the tools to distinguish when he or she is working to replace his or her own labor-power and when he or she is working to give up surplus value to capital. He or she is not the conscious master of these times, which together absorb nearly all of his or her life energies. Citing the British Factory Acts' limitation of the legal working day, Marx writes, "by making them masters of their own time [the Factory Acts] have given them a moral energy which is directing them to the eventual possession of political power" (I.III.X.7; 1887, 286, footnote). Marx recognizes the potential of the capitalist use of time to alienate and master the worker rather than being mastered by him or her. He also shows why time itself is an important political battleground.

Thus Marx's emphasis on free abstract time must be subject, in turn, to critique. Such a concept is defined dialectically against labor. But if, in accordance with the most radical strain of Marx's analysis, labor disappears, must free time not also disappear? Moreover, in his call for free disposable time, Marx shows his adoption of capitalist temporality, in which time is viewed as an abstract bracket to be filled or emptied, wasted or used. If Marx is not to capitulate to capitalist colonization of temporality, abstract time in its alienated form must not only be disposable, but disposed of altogether.

Only value, not wealth, can be measured in abstractions like time and money. Recall that by "wealth" Marx means objects of use and that by "value" he means objects of profitable exchange. Although value is an abstraction that requires an abstract measure, or is fungible, wealth is use, and use is not abstract. I can do nothing with abstract time itself, which is representational rather than directly useful. Like money, abstract time is more closely related to value than to wealth, and because of this it is tied to capitalism.

Hence, in the communist future, which is not subject to the calculus of value, time must diminish in importance. When we extrapolate Marx's visions of free time, therefore, we must not only envision the lengthening of the disposable hours the worker marks between short stints of productive labor. We must instead imagine a modern life freed from time, or at least modern life freed from time's abstract and alienating dominations. This modern life would understand time as a social product, useful for avoiding train accidents, but not a reified and absolute standard, conditioning all of human making, human embodiment, and human affect.

IV Technophobia and technophilia

Throughout my preceding chapters (but especially in Chapters 2 and 4), I have suggested that nineteenth-century attitudes to science and technology—and the corresponding reception of these attitudes—were highly politicized. I now wish to pick up on this and define the fault lines that, in the nineteenth century, distinguished the three central classes with respect to technology and, in particular, with respect to the mechanization of labor. These classes are the bourgeois, the proletariat, and the feudal aristocracy.[11]

Each class is marked by its relationship with, and its attitudes toward, the changes in the means of production consequent upon the application of thermodynamic science (especially the steam engine). Therefore, each class is also marked by the degree to which it accepts and integrates the account of human beings, nature, and labor offered by thermodynamic science. Some social classes are more willing to reduce human work to caloric exertion in accordance with thermodynamic law. Others are resistant to conceptualizing humans and machines in the same terminology. In the analysis below, I call the former "technophiles" and the latter "technophobes," and I stress how these identities are distributed by social class.

The bourgeois are technophiles, committed to the changes in scientific production to which their rising industrial success is tied. But historically, the most progressive political opposition to the bourgeois exploitation of labor is equally technophilic: physiologists who reconceptualize the laboring body on energeticist models, chart the demands of the fatigue curve, and begin to arbitrate labor questions on the basis of their discoveries. As I have shown in Chapter 2, even though Marx was careful to distinguish his social and political views from those of the scientific materialists, he nonetheless absorbs some of this energetic notion of labor.

In contrast to the bourgeois of both stripes, both the aristocratic and the proletarian classes demonstrate a marked technophobia: the former, in opposition to the bourgeois class's bids for power; the latter, in opposition to changes in labor that render their embodied habits of work superfluous. Although Marx's education in German idealism was marked by his criticism of certain aspects of idealism, this aristocratic education nonetheless armed Marx, in his formative years, with the concepts that can easily turn into a reactionary antitechnological romanticism, and certainly did so in other thinkers. Marx's understanding of the proletarian history of technological resistance is a later development in his thinking, acquired through his reading of Engels, Babbage, J. H. M. Poppe, and a critical reading of Andrew Ure.

Although Marx is wary of bourgeois technophilia, he also realizes that technophobia is a form of false consciousness. Marx is more concerned with the presence of technophobia in the working classes than with its lingering affects in the aristocracy. Fetishizing machines as the perpetrators of class inequalities results in a peculiar set of ideological relations between the workers and the means of production, that is, strife. In *Capital*, Marx illustrates this with the example of the burning of a ribbon loom at the stake in a public square in Hamburg in the seventeenth century.[12] Ribbon looms were technological predecessors of the mule and steam-powered looms of the Industrial Revolution. In a classic example of the misrecognition that alienation encompasses, the loom was accused of occult powers and burned to death (I.IV.XV.5; MECW 1996, 35, 431; MEGA^2 II, 9, 373; MEGA^2 II, 8, 418).

With nearly 400 years' hindsight, one is struck by the futility of burning a machine in a public square on the eve of the Industrial Revolution. But there is both a deeper absurdity and a deeper meaning to this execution. Here we see two historical eras of production, each with a different material substrate and mode of life, in conflict. We see the contradiction of a single people with itself and its own products.

Marx explains that revolts against the ribbon loom in particular were common among working people all over Europe. These revolts continued well into the nineteenth century as isolated workers' rebellions vented righteous anger on the fixed capital of the factories by smashing machines. (The Luddites are the most famous example of a group undertaking such rebellions.)

The passage from *Capital* ends thus: "It took both time and experience before the workpeople learned to distinguish between machinery and its employment by capital and to direct their attacks, not against the material instruments of production, but against the mode in which they are used" (I.IV.XV.5; MECW 1996, 35, 431; MEGA^2 II, 9, 373; MEGA^2 II, 8, 418). The burning of the machine is an example of the difficulty that those who operate within a given mode of production have in forming an adequate criticism of this mode as a totality, as opposed to the means (or instruments) by which the mode expresses itself. To use Marx's language, workers blame the gunpowder that might cauterize their wounds for hurting them.

The machine is burned in the square because handicrafts cannot compete with its productivity. Instead of diversifying their skills and abandoning their traditional modes of employment, workers attempt to retain the rights to do at great pains what machines can do quickly. The workers thereby attempt to preserve their traditional standards of life, and along with these are complicit in maintaining the regressive political forms by which these lives were regulated. Workers become complicit in the destruction of potential material wealth in favor of the preservation of the exchange-value of arduous, time-consuming labors.

In the *Communist Manifesto*, Marx writes critically of the nascent proletarians:

> [T]hey direct their attacks not against the bourgeois conditions of production, but against the instruments of production themselves; they destroy imported wares that compete with their labour, they smash to pieces machinery, they set factories ablaze, they seek to restore by force the vanished status of the workman of the middle ages
>
> (MECW 1976, 6, 492; MEW 1959, 4, 471).

The rebellion against the instruments or means of production (i.e. machines) is symptomatic of a form of false consciousness. The real target of proletarian ire should not be machinery but the conditions that give rise to inequalities in the distribution of the means of production, the conditions that conscript machinery into an exclusively capitalist usage.

Classes are separated by their relationship to the ownership of the means of production, that is, the ability to command the forces of science and technology. Thus, the inequalities of power between a machine and a tool are targeted by proletarians who have been excluded from mobilizing science and technology in their own interests. Instead of benefiting the society as a whole, access to technology becomes the marker of class differentiation and machines an instrument of class warfare. Likewise, genders are distributed by their access to technology, including the opportunity to receive a scientific and technological education. And because in the capitalist mode of production machines are employed only to increase value or profit, and not to increase the material wealth of the society as a whole, their potential advantages do not appear to workers/women.

This working-class technophobia has a counterpart in aristocratic ideology. Hatred and repudiation of technology was characteristic of displaced aristocrats interested in restoring their former privileges. Laurent Portes, curator of the *Bibliothèque Nationale*, shows that the distrust of technological advancement has a particular genealogy. First arising in aristocratic circles, hostility to technology quickly spreads to the rest of the society. Portes writes,

> Counterrevolutionary, reactionary, and aristocratic circles make up the first ranks of [those denouncing the practices of technology]; their disapproval has more than a little to do with the alleged egalitarianism of this so-called future ... [but i]t would not take long for the critique of a technological society—which at first had been associated with an elitist mentality—to sweep society as a whole
>
> (Schaer et al. 2000, 244).

Aristocrats hated technology as emblematic of the Enlightenment ideals and project that were causing them to die out as a class. Steam-driven engines, after all, were driven along burgeoning railway lines that carved up feudal estates. This hatred was accompanied by an anti-cosmopolitanism that, as we have seen in Chapter 4, joined the anti-Semitism and anti-industrialization of this form of capitalist humanism.

Technophobia was especially pronounced in German society, both as a reaction to the scientific materialists and because Germany retained its aristocracy longer than other European powers. Technophobia is also a staple of Romanticism. Neither technophobe nor technophile, Marx offers a critical challenge to both attitudes.

The reactionary technophobia among the aristocracy was accompanied by a spread of technophobia through social ranks to which the economic advantages of the attitude might not apply. This illustrates Marx's idea, from *The German Ideology*, of psychological alienation, a type of alienation I explored in Chapter 1. In psychological alienation, the upper classes infect the lower classes with their ideologies. For the lower classes, the idea that machines are evil joins forces with the appeal to and defense of labor itself, and thus the replication of the bourgeois subject's foundational moment, rather than the elimination of labor in favor of free time. There is no need to limit the access of the working classes to those instruments that might liberate them; they limit themselves by adopting technophobia as their own.

Conceptualizing workers as machines or machine-like may have been a means of protecting them from certain excesses, but it was also a disciplinary technique in which workers were reconceived as a kind of raw material educable through habituation into any possible form, so long as physical laws are respected. After a visit to one of Owen's factories in 1829, Robert Southey reported,

> [Owen's] humor, his vanity, his kindliness of nature (all these have their share) leads him to make these *human machines* as he calls them (and literally believes them to be) as happy as he can, and to make a display of their happiness. And he jumps to the monstrous conclusion that because he can do this with 2210 persons, who are totally dependent on him—all mankind might be governed with the same felicity
>
> (quoted in Jennings and Madge 1985, 157–158,
> emphasis in original).

Although Marx accepts the critique of metaphysics along with the critique of religion, espouses a materialism that has eliminated theological causation from natural explanation, and even introduces some energeticist language when describing human labor, he balks at the description of working-class human beings as merely or exclusively machine-like.

Instead, Marx gives a genealogy of machine labor that situates machines as a derivative of human industry, and emphasizes their historical evolution from this industry (and so from humanity). In this account, machines are the product of generations of human labor—both scientific and technological labor as well as the ordinary human labor that subtends its creation. Human creation, even its alien form of labor, remained the fundamental term for Marx, and nature's force remained divided into human and nonhuman types. Hence, human workers retain something machines cannot replace, though Marx's adoption of the energeticist vocabulary makes it increasingly hard to determine what this is.

At the same time, Marx gives a historical and genealogical account of machines, and of the rise of scientific and technological enterprise as a whole, and insists on their indebtedness to this historical, social, human labor. On economic grounds, Marx follows John Stuart Mill, who, contra the political economists, stressed the way that machinery makes labor more rather than less oppressive, lengthening the working day and rendering labor unbearably dull, tedious, repetitive, or otherwise alienating. Marx claims that "on the basis of capitalist production the purpose of machinery is by no means to lighten or shorten the day's toil of the worker,"[13] and he agitates for a mode of production in which machines' potential might be actualized. Marx tries to understand the contradiction by which machines, tools for the production of material wealth, result in impoverishment when employed to produce exchange-value, or he tries to reintroduce the problem of alienation at the heart of labor in capitalism (Chapters 3 and 4).

As we have seen, at its best Marx's demystification of technology critically indicts technological determinism, an attitude that misrecognizes changes in human labor and social life and attributes the properties of these changes to machines themselves rather than to the mode of production that shapes them. Marx thereby learned to read attitudes to technology as signs and symptoms of more profound political and economic attitudes, just as Feuerbach learned to read attitudes to theology as signs and symptoms that a particular human community had projected onto its gods. In this process, Marx revealed how machines are a repository for all manner of social attitudes. His account of the social productivity of science and technology is thus framed by his account of capital as a whole. He wants to demystify this mode of production so that it is not accepted and received in its alienated form: as a natural, ineluctable given, in which the historical properties of human labor are mistakenly perceived as belonging to machines themselves.

With respect to the technology question, Marx claimed that the economic and political means of production as they exist need not remain synonymous with the exploitative mode in which they were being employed. Alienation can end only with the continuing use of technology, but in a system of valuation in which the tyranny of exchange-value has been eliminated and use-value is once again in view. In fact, the use of technology in itself will increase the amount of material wealth and thus reduce the amount of labor necessary to sustain a society operating in a different mode.[14] Marx glimpsed the possibility of the production of material wealth that does not have the production of value as its ultimate aim, and with this the elimination of human labor both abstractly, as the standard of the system of production, and concretely, as a practice. New machines, not shaped by capitalism's norms of command and control, will also be a result (Feenberg 2002, 50).

Marx continued to insist that there was a distinction between machines and the society that supported them, that is, between the means and the mode of production. He could have developed this insight while still acknowledging that capitalism instantiates machines with politically negative features had he had access to an idea we find powerfully illustrated in Andrew Feenberg's work. This is the notion of levels in technological objects, levels with varying degrees of politicization. Feenberg writes,

> [The thesis that technology is politically neutral] reifies technology by abstracting from all contextual considerations. This approach is relatively persuasive because, as in other instances of formal bias, the decontextualized elements from which the biased system is built up *are* in fact neutral in their abstract form. The gears and levers of the assembly line, like the bricks and mortar of the Panopticon, possess no intrinsic valuative implication. The illusion that technology is neutral arises when actual machines and systems are understood on the model of the abstract technical elements they unite in value-laden combinations. Critical theory shatters this illusion by recovering the forgotten contexts and developing a historically concrete understanding of technology
>
> (2002, 82, emphasis in original).

Because Marx wanted to maintain the neutrality of technology as the substrate of a new noncapitalist society and yet sensed the political shaping of devices within the capitalist mode of production, he was often vulnerable to the very problem his analysis revealed. Marx sometimes used the term "machinery" as shorthand for "alienation," and "means of production" for the "capitalist mode." As we saw in Chapter 4, this is usually accompanied by a vocabulary of monstrosity through which Marx demonizes machinery. These rhetorical effects, more pronounced in *Capital* and the *Communist Manifesto* than in the *Grundrisse*, can make it easy to miss Marx's careful distinction between the means and the mode of production.

For Marx, science and technology represented not only the exacerbations of the old society, but also the foundations of the new society. The extension of material wealth wrought by human knowledge in the form of science and technology can then be used to enable the communist mode of production. Marx writes, "what else does growing productive power of labour mean than that less immediate labour is required to create a greater product and that therefore social wealth expresses itself more and more in the conditions of labour created by labour itself?" (1973, 831; MECW 1987, 29, 209; MEGA^2 II, 1.2, 607). These conditions could be good or bad, depending upon how the accumulated social wealth, or science and technology and access to it, is distributed. If human beings as a species are not radically divided in their access to this form of power and knowledge, it has the potential to put Promethean powers in everyone's hands.

The continued development of productive objectification will form the material foundation for the ensuing political changes Marx predicted, including revolution. The communist development of these means of production, or technological advance itself, will accompany their redistribution, or revolution. After this redistribution, the development of the means of production will continue, undivided by the competition that slows down capitalist science and technological advance.

In this sense, Marx offers us a critique of value, but not a critique of the guiding motivations of science and technology, nor a critique of the human being's position at the apex of the natural world. He never questions the use-value of production's amplification in increased material resources, only production's amplification of profit and exploitation. And though Marx recognizes the exploitation of the earth that capitalism enables, he does not generalize this peril to modernity as a whole. In Marx's view of machine use after the revolution, it is only wealth that accumulates, not the detritus, pollution, and environmental degradation that have been part of the lingering consequences of industrialization. This, too, is a mark of Marx's adoption of the Enlightenment view of technology.

As with Aristotelian exchange-value, technology must be limited by the proper bounds of human beneficence. However, within those bounds, technology's influence is wide-ranging and valuable. As Elaine Scarry (1985) writes, "So human is [historical] materialism in its premises that at no point does Marx ever imagine that the culture would be better served by a retraction of the impulse toward material making, even were such a retraction possible" (243). So long as progressive scientific and technological changes have human enjoyment and development as their goal, and are not used as instruments of class warfare, they are unquestioned goods.

V   Technophobia and twentieth-century theory

I have offered this suggestive political typology of technophobia, technophilia, and their criticism in Marx for historical reasons. This typology enhances our understanding of the nineteenth century, our understanding of the gap between its ruling ideas and its material composition, and our understanding of Marx. But I also have offered it for conceptual and genealogical reasons. For although Marx may have been among the first philosophers to pay attention to technology, his account was only the beginning of significant attention, lasting into the twenty-first century, to the category of "technology" itself[15] and the issues of living with technology.

This attention is distinguished by a singular feature. It does not move the account of technology far beyond the shape offered by Marx, a fact that we may attribute to the prescience of his account and its continuing significance. Thus, at its best, twentieth- and twenty-first–century philosophy of technology cycles among the poles of Marx's account, charting a relationship between the technical and the political and showing how this relationship is conditioned by capitalism; in this regard, the accounts of Donna Haraway and Herbert Marcuse are exemplary.

But before turning to the accounts of Haraway and Marcuse, we must also see how twentieth- and twenty-first–century philosophy of technology has not kept pace with Marx's major insights about technology. In particular, some critical indictments of technology have missed Marx's crucial insight that technophobia is an attitude that contains the reactive sensibility of capitalist humanism: neo-feudal, Romantic, and anti-democratic conservatism about nature and human life. Moreover, technophobic philosophies of technology portray the degraded deployment of technology characteristic of the capitalist mode as the essence of modern technology, which confuses the means of production with their deployment in an exploitive mode of production, and brackets their meaning in accordance with this deployment. Finally, technophobic philosophies of technology often use an uncritical concept of nature as a challenge to the technological world.

Below I look briefly at two important examples of technophobic indictments of modernity that, bidden or not, carry forward this treble conservatism: Martin Heidegger's "The Question Concerning Technology" and Carolyn Merchant's *The Death of Nature*. I pair my discussion of each text with what may be regarded as its Marxist corrective: Heidegger with Marcuse, and Merchant with Haraway. The ontological indictment of technology we find in Heidegger and Merchant is parried by the political diagnosis of technology in Marcuse and Haraway. The mistake made by both Heidegger and Merchant is to collapse Marx's distinction between the means and the mode of production, regarding the exploitative characteristics of technology as it is deployed in the capitalist mode of production to be the total essence of technology.

Heidegger's essay "The Question Concerning Technology" was published in German in the mid-1950s, and in English in the late 1970s.

The essay has had enormous influence on critical accounts of technology that seek to reveal technology as alienating. Heidegger argues that technology's real essence is to turn everything into a standing reserve or, to revisit Marx's use of a similar concept, to turn everything into an exchange-value for something else.[16] Technology thus pushes us in the direction of a fundamental philosophical inquiry into the notion of instrumentality. For Heidegger, technology itself is the mark of an alienated world that has lost the notion of noninstrumental value, or, as he puts it, "Technology is always itself directed from the beginning toward furthering something else, i.e. towards driving on to the maximum yield at the minimum expense" (quoted in Scharff and Dusek 2003, 256). Moreover, technology turns humans themselves into standing-reserves, that is, exchange-values.

Finally, technology's immersion in instrumentality is conditioned by a primary attitude toward nature. In indicting this attitude, Heidegger indicts not only modern technology but the modern scientific project altogether. He writes,

> When man, investigating, observing, pursues nature as an area of his own conceiving, he has already been claimed by a way of revealing that challenges him to approach nature as an object of research, until even the object disappears into the objectlessness of standing reserve. ... The modern physical theory of nature prepares the way not simply for technology but for the essence of modern technology (quoted in Scharff and Dusek 2003, 257, 259).

Heidegger's critique relies upon a concept of nature that somehow escapes human conceptuality, that is, a noncritical notion of the natural.

We have seen how, for Marx, nature became a fully critical concept: a concept not only marked by human observation and investigation, but, indeed, transformed by them. Against the modern thinkers who conceive of nature as independent of human shaping, Marx argues for the necessary dependence of this concept on the human world that forms it. This shaping can be for better or for worse: for example, the bourgeois conceive of nature as a battleground for scarce resources, and the human being as a miserly contestant for these resources. This concept of nature becomes ideological in that it allows humans to accept the relations of capitalist society as natural givens, and not to subject this givenness to political inquiry and transformation. For Marx, contra Heidegger, technology eliminates any scarce natural resources that could continue the myth of a miserly nature. But beyond this, Marx found it neither possible nor desirable to have a concept of nature independent of human shaping. Modern science, and the practical output of this science (e.g. technological devices), is as much the mark of a liberated world as it is the mark of an alienated world (see Chapter 3).

Heidegger's analysis is not therefore simply antitechnological, but ultimately antimodern. Heidegger argues not only against instrumentality but also against curiosity about the boundaries of the natural world and how these boundaries might be challenged, appealing to older, theological, prohibitions that warn against the manipulation of the received world. It is, however, unclear what Heidegger's analysis contributes to a politics that struggles within the modern world. Against this backdrop, such an analysis may even be harmful, because it shuts down the search for nonexploitive uses of science and technology that eliminate scarcity and equitably distribute material wealth; it might even lead thinkers away from political contestation altogether. Hence, Heidegger's analysis works symbiotically with the very forces it claims to combat, as a symptom of these forces.

Herbert Marcuse brings this out in texts that do not name Heidegger explicitly, but that clearly respond to his thought. In his 1941 essay "Some Social Implications of Modern Technology," Marcuse (1998) writes,

> Technics hampers individual development only insofar as they are tied to a social apparatus which perpetuates scarcity, and this same apparatus has realized forces which may shatter the specialized historical form in which technics is utilized. For this reason, all programs of an anti-technological character, all propaganda for an anti-industrial revolution, serve only those who regard human needs as a by-product of the [current] utilization of technics.... The philosophy of the simple life, the struggle against big cities and their culture frequently serves to teach men distrust of the potential instruments that could liberate them (63).

Marcuse's analysis follows Marx's distinction between good and bad uses of technology. The analysis also repeats Marx's prediction that the scarcity myth would not be perpetuated in the face of continued technological development. Marcuse then criticizes Heidegger's technophobia as a program of an antitechnological character that has failed to distinguish the means of production from its mode of employment. Applying Marx's insight about nineteenth-century technophobia to Heidegger's twentieth-century philosophy, Marcuse even argues that technophobia emerges as an ideology to reinforce the threatened scarcity of an alienated world, an ideology that works in tandem with the exploitive industrialization it claims to combat. In Marcuse's view, Heidegger's antimodernism is part of the lesson to distrust liberation, just as, in the nineteenth century, technophobia was a means of distancing the worker from the tools that could liberate him or her.

Although Marcuse's thought has traditionally been traced to the period he spent studying with Heidegger, more recent scholarship has suggested that Marcuse's Marxism was a more formative and lasting intellectual affiliation, which caused Marcuse to differ with Heidegger on crucial philosophical points, including the diagnosis of technology (Abromeit and Wolin 2005). The tensions in Marx's account are also alive in Marcuse's account, and, as with Marx, these tensions are expressed in different works.

In *Eros and Civilization*, Marcuse retains the postulate of material wealth and the utopian view of technology. He claims there that "the excuse of scarcity, which has justified institutionalized repression since its inception, weakens as man's knowledge and control over nature enhances the means for fulfilling human needs with a minimum of toil" (1966, 92). If anything, Marcuse is less utopian than Marx, because he postulates slight though tolerable decreases in the living standards of liberated societies, whereas Marx thinks these will continue to elevate. But Marcuse's account of technology in *One Dimensional Man* displays a vision in which technology is revealed in its alienating, capitalist usage.[17] Thus, Marcuse preserves a critical account of technology's use in capitalism alongside a continued belief in the ability of Enlightenment reason and science to better the human condition.

The residues of technophobia have also found their way into the feminist philosophical debates about science and technology that began in the 1980s. Citing Marx as an influence, Carolyn Merchant, in *The Death of Nature* (1980), criticized modern science and technology as the source of intensified subjugation of both nature and women. Her work was seminal, and touched off work in ecofeminism and cultural feminism that encourage the recapturing of a lost, natural, and "organic" worldview against a continuation of the modern technological domination of nature. In her concluding chapter, Merchant (1980) calls for a return to "the values and constraints historically associated with the organic worldview [as] essential for a viable future" (289). However, the values and constraints associated with the organic worldview to which Merchant appeals were feudal, and, as such, hardly liberatory in an unqualified sense for women or many other groups. Moreover, we see here the same error that we see in Heidegger, in which the means of production are confused with the exploitive mode in which they have historically been deployed.

Targeting the ideas of Merchant and Heidegger explicitly, Haraway criticizes their technophobia in a way Marx might have recognized:

> [T]here is a whole tradition of a kind of negativity in relation to science and technology—that it's the domain of the antihuman—that is part of the problem of trying to be accountable for these kinds of knowledge practices. That's what is exciting about science studies now as a body of pursuit ... All of these people understand scientific practice as this thick—semiotically and materially—rich historical practice, and none of them are very impressed by any of these negative philosophies and negative political theories about technological instrumentality
>
> (Haraway 2000, 23).

Like Marx, Haraway suggests that science and technology are not innocent, and even that particularly virulent forms of oppression are consequent to certain uses of technology. Technology can be complicit in prolonging alienation and in mystifying its origins. However, Haraway warns against the falsification of the scientific and technological tradition that occurs when one sees it only on its surface. This surface is often a mask of science's own self-mythologies about objectivity. In order to understand the work that science is really doing, this mask must be pulled away. Critiques of science and technology are especially problematic when they enable repudiation and ignorance of the practices of scientists and/or the inability to make factual claims. Likewise, critiques of politics are especially problematic when they enable the loss of political hope and action.[18] Like Marx and Feenberg, Haraway argues that greater attention to how technology works, and to what it is doing in particular instances, will bring greater clarity to discussions about its political import.

Haraway continues her Marxist feminist philosophy of science and technology[19] by arguing that women must do exactly what Marx suggested workers should do: seize and use machines as a way of what she calls "contesting for ... power and pleasure in technologically mediated societies" (1991, 154).[20] And Haraway diagnoses technophobia as what she calls an oppositional ideology, defined as an ideology that appears as the oppositional symptom of a fully technological reality.[21]

212   *Karl Marx on Technology and Alienation*

Let us recall Marx's diagnosis of the workers who burned a machine in a public square on the eve of the Industrial Revolution, and his analysis of the inauthentic forms of consciousness through which workers are duped into battling against their own liberation. Oppositional ideologies like those of Heidegger and Merchant are the machine burnings of twentieth- and twenty-first–century theory: recognitions and repudiations of an already accomplished set of changes—changes that lead only forward in time.

Nature itself as it is deployed in the texts of these thinkers must be such an ideology, for no concept of nature could come forth as self-consciously natural on undifferentiated ground. The idea of the "natural," as it is pursued in twentieth- and twenty-first–century theory, must therefore be a product of the technical, a product of the conceptual shaping that characterizes the modern world. And in their suspicion of noncritical and ahistorical deployments of the concept of nature, and of the ideological and political perils of these deployments, we may recognize the critical theories of Marcuse and Haraway as deeply and lastingly shaped by Marx.

Notes

Introduction

1. As we will see in my analysis of the importance of free time to Marx's system, it is hard to say if Marx himself survives this form of Marxist scrutiny, or if some of his own concepts, in turn, can be shown to be influenced by capitalist conceptuality.
2. For this reason, energetic science undermines what Bruno Latour calls the clean dichotomy between nature and humans, a dichotomy that characterizes earlier versions of the modern knowledge project (1993).
3. For an account of the genealogy of the concept of the "human" in late-mediaeval and early-modern anxieties about sex, race, and animality, anxieties that created those of the later colonial period, see Haraway (1989), West (2002), Gould (1993), Agamben (2004), Bataille (1991, 1992), Dyer (1997), Lévi-Strauss (1963, 1969), and Foucault (1970).
4. The language here is from *On the Jewish Question* (MECW 1975, 5, 155). I will revisit the citation in greater depth in Chapter 1. In the *Critique of the Gotha Program*, Marx also explicitly warned against alliances between socialists and feudal reactionaries.
5. See Sean Sayers' *Marxism and Human Nature* (1998) for a careful and compelling development of this argument.
6. The agonistic symbiosis of scientific and romantic literary cultures continued for some time after the nineteenth century. One of the more famous diagnoses of this is C. P. Snow's *The Two Cultures* (1998), a foundational text for science studies.
7. See Richard White's fine discussion of Greek friendship, especially the debate over whether this friendship, as it was characterized in the texts of Aristotle and others, was an expressive or an oppositional ideal of Greek culture (2001).
8. See Murray (1998).
9. The "Rubber Rooms" in Detroit, rooms in which mechanically displaced General Motors workers mark empty time until their pensions are fully vested, are a contemporary example of these contradictions. Most of these workers perceive this form of "free time" as an enormous burden and long to have their old jobs back. Tom Adams, however, enrolled in a doctoral program at the University of Michigan, and used the "empty" time in the rubber room to write a dissertation on labor history. See McCracken (2006).

1 Karl Marx's concept of alienation

An earlier version of chapter 1 was published as "The Dignity of Labor? A Marxist Challenge to Traditional Marxism," *International Studies in Philosophy* 38:2, October 2006, 181–196.

1. John Elster cites the passage in a different context as "definitive" evidence that "the creation of communism is not only the 'result' of capitalist alienation, but also 'the inherent purpose of the process'" (1985, 113), a theme to which I will return at the end of this section and again in Chapter 5.

2. In the *Economic and Philosophical Manuscripts of 1844*, the development of the latter two forms of alienation is foreshadowed when Marx writes that "the worker is robbed of the objects he needs most not only for life but also for work" (Section 5).

3. Unaware of the *Economic and Philosophical Manuscripts of 1844* and the *Grundrisse* at the time of publication of his work, Lukács mistakenly identifies objectification and alienation in *History and Class Consciousness* (Lukács 1971). The effect of conflating the distinction is a misreading of Marx that enables the category of labor historically peculiar to capitalism to operate ontologically: the very thing Marx wishes to call into question and combat.

4. Avineri belongs to the moderate strain of Marxism that, after the death of Stalin, revived the historical and theoretical study of Marx (Kolakowski 1978, Vol. III, 493–494). I have interwoven some of Avineri's observations from *The Social and Political Thought of Karl Marx* (1968) into my interpretation of Marx.

5. He will cite the passage only ten years later in the *Grundrisse*, and there only in a footnote (1973, 293).

6. The Hegelian *Hic Rhodus hic salta* formulation was a favorite of Marx's during his later years. See also the reappearance of this formula in *Capital*, at the end of the section on the transformation of money into capital, and immediately prior to Marx's section on the buying and selling of labor-power (I.II.VI; MECW 1996, 35, 177; MEGA^2 II, 8, 182; MEGA^2 II, 9, 144).

7. For the exploration of this theme, see Elster (1983, 1985). This is the chief merit of Elster's discussion, which otherwise confuses Marx's critique of the system of production as a whole with a critique of distribution. Kouvelakis locates the theodicy not in Marx but in Engels and in the subsequent codifications of "Marxism" (2003, 334).

8. For a fascinating account of the relationship between civil society and the political state, including an account of how both popular and intellectual prejudice came to favor civil society over the legitimate if violent exigencies of the political state, see Reinhart Koselleck (1998). Koselleck is influenced in his account by the Hobbesian notion of sovereignty.

9. Scholars attribute the extremely high level of abstraction in *Capital* to the influence of the *Logic*. Some of Marx's notes on the *Logic* are in the unpublished *Notizenheft* notebook from 1860 (IISG Marx Archive, Call Number B 96, 131–134). See also Schrader (1998), Uchida (1988), and Postone (1993, especially 139).

10. The import of the passage is disputed, depending upon whether one puts the emphasis on Marx's deep adoption of the dialectical method or on his superficial flirtation with Hegel's modes of expression, along with the degree to which one recognizes such a distinction between these two options as legitimate. The passage is thus cited both in texts that wish to stress the links between Marx and Hegel and in those which wish to distance Marx from Hegel. For an instance of the latter, see Hardt and Negri (2000).

11. My account of "alienation" in the history of philosophy is indebted to Oppolzer (1974). Unlike Oppolzer, I have omitted a treatment of Augustine and of the Roman Stoics Cicero and Seneca, although Stoicism especially was important to Marx. In general, the importance of the Stoics is seen in their repetition of the Platonic injunctions against philosophizing for money or comfort and in their praises of democracy. Augustine's theory of idolatry in *The City of God* illustrates the alienated worship of false gods, but, beyond this suggestive comparison, contains nothing of further structural importance to Marx's account of the commodity fetish. Marx himself gave up his original plan for turning his dissertation into a three-part larger work "which would treat 'in detail the cycle of Epicurean, Stoic, and Skeptic philosophy in their relation to the whole of Greek speculation'" (cited in Kouvelakis 2003, 237) in order to turn to the worldly matters of his day. So too, I am giving up a comprehensive account of Marx's relationship to the Stoic and Augustinian themes in order to treat more comprehensively how the themes of alienation and objectification developed, rather than originated, in his thought.

12. I have preferred to use a notation in addition to page numbering in all of my citations from the English editions of *Capital* that may assist readers in finding the passages in question in different editions. The first notation, prior to the page numbers of the various editions, reflects the following content: "Volume. Part. Chapter. Section." This schema applies only to the English editions, which follow the structural changes Marx added to the French edition. The original German editions are divided differently, so, when possible, at the end of the citation I have also supplied the MEGA^2 notation for the citation in question out of the third German edition from 1883.

13. The effect of Rousseau on the philosophy of Kant, Hegel, and Marx can scarcely be overestimated. Hegel's concept of civil society is designed to mediate the struggle that erupts between the Rousseauian general and particular wills. In Kant, Rousseau's influence can be seen not only in the political but also in the critical works. The divided Kantian subjectivity, struggling between the laws of reason and affect, echoes the gaps Rousseau introduced between the general and the particular wills in both morality and politics.

14. Grotius, an almost exact contemporary of Thomas Hobbes, wrote in Holland and Paris rather than England, but was also responding to the phenomenon of a gruesome civil war. Grotius espoused a conservative version of natural law.

15. The male gender is appropriate when speaking of contract theory. See Pateman (1988).

16. Despite this critique, which he makes of all of the social contract theorists, Marx often praises Rousseau's philosophy and even refers on one occasion to Rousseau's "habitual good sense" (*Grundrisse* 1973, Introduction). This is high praise from Marx, whose usual mode is to lambaste interlocutors whose theories and methods he does not adopt wholesale, and sometimes, as with Hegel, to lambaste those whose theories and methods he does!

17. See also Matteo Mandarini's explanation of the distinction (in Negri 2003, 266, fn 19).

18. See Chapter 1 in Gregory (1977) for a full account of Feuerbach's development in the intellectual climate that prevailed in Germany prior to Hegel's death.

19. "The philosophers have only interpreted the world, in various ways; the point is to change it." Retrieved July 30, 2007, from http://www.marxists.org/archive/marx/works/1845/theses/theses.htm.

20. In *The German Ideology*, Marx writes,

   > Man can be distinguished from animals by consciousness, by religion or anything else you like. They themselves begin to distinguish themselves from animals as soon as they begin to *produce* their means of subsistence, a step that is conditioned by their physical organization. By producing their means of subsistence, men are indirectly producing their actual material life
   >
   > (MECW 1976, 5, 31; MEW 1958, 3, 21).

   Note that production of the means of subsistence is what demarcates the human/animal boundary in this passage, and thus culture from nature, or again the cultivated from the given. The means of subsistence (or, later, the means of production) reflect surplus wealth that extends beyond immediate need. In *Capital*, Marx will claim that this same surplus conditions the development of all machinery, a development which requires the capacity for stored labor. Donna Haraway's *Primate Visions*, a history of the twentieth-century discipline of primatology, sketches the parallel debates that seek to demarcate the human being from his or her primate cousin in accordance with tool use, intellect, and the stored or surplus wealth they imply (Haraway 1989).

21. Some of the most interesting problems in Marx's theoretical apparatus occur when these two domains are unsynchronized. See Feenberg (2002) for an interesting discussion of Marx's overreliance on the political as a mode of social and economic transformation (54).

22. For a parallel passage directed at Rousseau that invokes the Terror still more specifically, see Hegel (1991, 277).

23. This is the subject of the text written by Marx immediately after the *Contribution to a Critique of Hegel's Philosophy of Right*, namely *On the Jewish Question*.

24. It is impossible for Marx to do this in his later political work, and the residual political influence of the aristocracy is a topic of *The Class Struggles in France* (1850), *The Eighteenth Brumaire of Louis Bonaparte* (1851), and *The Critique of the Gotha Program* (1875). But note the conspicuous lack of attention to the historical gap between the economic and the political in the *Communist Manifesto* (1848) and *Capital* (1867).

25. The "superstructural" is simultaneously distinguished from and related to the "substructural." The latter is determined by society's economic basis, and the former appears as a series of epiphenomena of this basis, including its political, theological, and intellectual expressions. The terms are already in use in the later Marx, but see Louis Althusser (1969, 1971) for the development and exposition of the terminology.

26. The gap between the political and the economic in Marx is usually characterized along these lines. Following Trotsky, Elster (1983) writes,

   > In the development of a society, there is a period during which it is politically ripe for communism, and a period during which it is economically

ripe, and these two periods do not seem to have any overlapping parts. At least this would seem to be a plausible argument for countries that cannot look to a successful instance to imitate, and if it is valid for these counties, there will be no instance to imitate. The argument can be broken only by showing that there are other roads to communism than an abrupt and wholesale change in economic relations, a task that cannot be undertaken here (227).

For a slightly different exploration of the gap, one which solves the problem by examining the relationship between communist and bourgeois revolutions, see my "Are All Revolutions Bourgeois? Revolutionary Temporality in Marx's *Eighteenth Brumaire of Louis Bonaparte*" (2003). For another road to communism that follows up on Elster's suggestion, see my "Sovereign Consumption as a Species of Communist Theory: Bataille's Marxism" (2006).

27. To be sure, feudal relations of domination were given by God. The political contest unfolded in debates over God's essence. The bourgeois relations of domination are given by nature, and the political contest unfolds in debates about the essence of nature.

28. We may recognize in deconstruction the strategy of Marxian demystification: as a movement, deconstruction retains this critical analysis of how what is viewed as natural is produced as such.

29. When Marx constructed his mature critique using the methodology of Hegel's *Logic*, he initially began not with the commodity as the foundational category, but with "production," which generated "consumption, distribution and exchange." See the introduction to the *Grundrisse*, where this is still the opening schema. This schema changed when Marx decided, in *Capital*, to address the historically specific and alienated forms of life in capitalism, not human objectification as an ahistorical whole. His schema then changed to one that begins not with ontological "production," but with the alienated historical form of this production: the "commodity." I will return to these features of Marx's method in Chapters 3 and 4. Also see Postone (1993, 139).

30. The other category Marx uses to describe this form of labor, "labor-power," is treated extensively in Chapter 2.

31. "[T]he different *components of the same use-value* are now produced as different commodities, independent of each other" (*Economic Manuscripts of 1861–63*; MECW 1988, 30, 267, emphasis in original).

32. Against this backdrop, we are in a position to make sense of Toni Negri's claim that in capitalist alienation, or the "real subsumption," "use-value cannot appear except under the guise of exchange-value" (Negri 2003, 25). He continues,

> There is no longer an external vantage point upon which use-value can depend. The overcoming of capitalism occurs on the basis of needs constructed by capitalism.... At first glance, *indifference* rules in real subsumption. Labour is quality, time is quantity; in real subsumption quality falls away, so all labour is reduced to mere quantity, to time. Before us we have only quantities of time. Use-value, which in *Capital* was still given as separate from, and irreducible to value *tout court*, is here absorbed by capital
>
> (25–27, emphasis in original).

I will explore the implications of the hegemony of abstract time in Chapter 5. The discussion will lead to reconceptualizing revolution from within alienated life or from within the real subsumption. See also Marilyn Strathern's work on the commodification of nature, what she calls nature "enterprised up" (MacCormack and Strathern 1980; Strathern 1992, 1999).

33. Marx's thinking does, of course, come very close to a labor theory of value. As we shall see in Chapter 2, this theory is complicated by the rising influence of thermodynamic science on Marx's notion of labor. Debates about the labor theory of value are a staple of the British analytical Marxism of the twentieth century, a logical positivist tradition that rejects what it calls "dialectics" or "bullshit" in favor of empirical economic modeling of Marx's theory. Its two main proponents, Elster and Cohen, often accept Marx's most general philosophical conclusions while rejecting the methods by which he derives them. There are also differences between them: Elster accepts, then explicates and defends, the Marxist philosophy of history that Cohen rejects. A rejection of the descriptive and analytic accuracy of the labor theory of value can be found in Elster (1985, 127–141). Elster calls particular attention to labor's continued heterogeneity, and thus the nonfungibility of the abstraction Marx invokes. He also criticizes the simplicity of Marx's economic modeling as inadequate to today's multisector economies. The labor theory of value is also treated throughout Cohen (1978). A lucid guide to Marx's theory of value by a Marxist of a prior generation is Isaak Il'ich Rubin's *Essays on Marx's Theory of Value*, originally published in 1928 (1972).

34. This is one of many ways Marx's later work is best understood against the backdrop of his earlier work. One disadvantage of attributing too much importance to the Althusserian "break" between the early and the late Marx is that these continuities become less visible. In the 1960s, Louis Althusser divided Marx's works into early and late blocks (1969, 227). Althusser characterizes the early texts as Marx's "humanistic" period, and the later block as his "scientific" period. Althusser dates the split from 1845–1846, the years in which *The German Ideology* was written. Althusser does not suggest that the philosophical study of Marx should be limited to either the early or the late texts; he went on to write a lengthy book on Marx's late work *Capital* (1971). But his characterization of Marx's late work as "scientific" rather than "humanist" requires qualification, because for Marx the terms would not have been mutually exclusive, nor would they have been controversial in the ways they became in the twentieth and early twenty-first centuries.

35. For a development of this reading, see Principe (1996).

36. Max Weber develops the Marxian strain of argument linking Protestant religious forms to bourgeois societies (1992). Although orthodox Marxists dispute Weberians over whether religion can play such a fundamental role in ordering the economic base and whether religion is part of the substructure or part of the superstructure, it is clear that neither Marx nor Weber was committed to posing the problem in such polarized terms. Even after Marx's "overcoming" of religion in his political and economic critique, in the doctrine on commodity fetishism, he still refers to religion as a structuring element of capitalism. So too Weber

ha[s] no intention whatever of maintaining such a foolish and doctrinaire thesis as that the spirit of capitalism...could only have arisen as the result of certain effects of the Reformation or even that capitalism as an economic system is a creation of the Reformation.... [but only wishes] to ascertain whether and to what extent religious forces have taken part in the qualitative formation and the quantitative expansion of that spirit over the world

(1992, 91).

37. See Feenberg (1999) for a parallel discussion of what he calls "technological fetishism" (210–216).
38. An excellent example of how machines become the locus for relations among persons can be found in Andrew Feenberg's discussions of machines designed to accommodate children's bodies. He writes,

When one looks at photos of child factory workers, one is struck by the adaptation of machines to their height (Newhall 1964: 140). The images disturb us, but were no doubt taken for granted until child labor became controversial. Design specifications simply incorporated the sociological fact of child labor into the structure of devices. The impress of social relations can be traced in the technology

(1999, 86–87).

A certain technological determinism, then, ignores this social imprint and, according to Feenberg, renders it possible to argue that machines require child labor because of their configuration.

39. Cf. Elster (1985) and Cohen (1978), both of whom argue for this reductive sense of alienation.
40. Retrieved 14 July 2006, from www.marxists.org/archive/marx/works/1865/value-price-profit/ch02.htm.
41. Hegel writes about manufacturing in the notes to the *Philosophy of Right* to illustrate the development of a class whose livelihood depends on the clever exploitation of development of raw materials, and who thereby attends to the universal in production (1952, §204; 1952, 132). Anticipating the problems of patent law, Hegel also compares the problems of maintaining rights to machine design with the problems of plagiarism of ideas from a literary text that has been made public (§68–69; 1952, 54–56). Here he seems to argue for the free appropriation of public ideas.
42. The passage in question from the *German Ideology* reads, "In the development of productive forces, there comes a stage when productive forces and means of intercourse are brought into being, which, under the existing relationships, only cause mischief, and are no longer productive, but destructive, forces (machinery and money)" (MECW 1976, 5, 52; MEW 1958, 3, 69).
43. For Marx, there is a temporal gap between the economic and the political. This gap makes it possible for certain anachronistic forms of social and political life to linger on in practice long after the economic relations that produced them are eclipsed. When Napoleon Bonaparte and, later, Louis Napoleon are crowned, they seize the anachronistic symbols of power of

a feudal order. As Marx shows repeatedly in his texts from the 1840s and 1850s, relations of production outstrip their political encapsulation. The economic and political are related by succession, not simultaneity. They are nonetheless related. See also Althusser's (1969) notion of "survivals" at the end of the essay "Contradiction and Overdetermination" for a subtle discussion of the slow manifestation of changed relations of production in social and political life (116).

2 Machines and the transformation of work

An earlier version of chapter 2 was published as "Capitalist Embodiment. Machines and the transformation of labour," *Beiträge zur Marx-Engels Forschung Neue Folge 2007*, October 2007, 197–211.

1. The gender-specific language is again intentional. Identified with matter rather than form and with nature rather than spirit, women were not conceptualized as participating in the form-giving capacity of labor. In Chapter 4, I will pick up on this strain of argument, its implications for women's transition to industrial wage labor, and the special relationship between women and alienation.
2. For a discussion of the division between spiritual/intellectual and physical labor and the enhanced significance of this division to the nineteenth and twentieth centuries, see Sohn-Rethel (1970, 1978).
3. These are the grounds on which Donna Haraway is critical of Marx (see the opening remarks to her lecture on the co-evolution of the human being and the dog, "Cyborgs to Companion Species," given at the University of Oregon's conference "Taking Nature Seriously: Citizens, Science, and the Environment" [February 2001]). A biologist critic of humanism, Haraway targets the "Marxist-humanist vision of man remaking nature." The other problem with Enlightenment humanism is that only some measure up to the bar as fit for consideration under the category "human."
4. The final section of the *Communist Manifesto* catalogues existing European socialisms, dividing them into reactionary, conservative/bourgeois, and critical utopian forms. In 1848, Marx still grouped communism with the latter, perhaps because of its radical vision of overthrowing the social order. Marx's criticism of the original utopian socialists Robert Owen in England and Charles Fourier in France is mild. According to Marx, Owen and Fourier lack not vision or imagination but scope, implementing their societies in marginal pockets alongside the dominant mode of production. Marx is much more critical of Owen's and Fourier's followers, whose works he accuses of conformity with existing productive orders. As a result, Marx regards their ideas as a species of impotent bourgeois socialism.
5. *The German Ideology* offers Marx's only sustained criticism of teleological thinking, a criticism he was able to formulate but not apply to his reasoning as a whole. Elster speculates that Engels may have tempered the teleological tendencies of Marx's thought, pointing out that Marx's teleological explanations are less frequent in pieces cowritten with Engels (Elster 1985, 109).
6. Political economy emerged as a discipline in the late seventeenth and early eighteenth centuries. The discipline of political economy may be defined,

following James Caporaso and David Levine, as "the express[ion of] the interrelationship between the political and the economic affairs of the state" against more traditional concepts that sharply delineate between the two spheres of affairs (1992, Summary). In Marx's time, the discipline encompassed the work of Adam Smith, Jean Sismondi, Thomas Malthus, J. B. Say, and David Ricardo. The discipline of political economy begins with Adam Smith's labor theory of value, which supplants the physiocratic assertion that all value derives from the land. Here we see a theory of value driven by energy and motion replace a theory of value driven by natural substance. Though critical of Smith's justifications of the bourgeois system, Marx will initially adopt aspects of the labor theory of value. Marx will then use the theory to develop the primacy of the laboring, or working, class as the transformative agent not only of the material world, but, with and through this, of the sociopolitical world.

7. See especially *Herr Vogt* and Marx's letters from the 1860s.
8. Although Marx's excerpt notebooks reflect a deep acquaintance with David Hume (Marx makes notes on parts III and IV of *On Human Nature* in German translation in 1841, and on a volume of collected essays in English throughout the 1850s and early 1860s), and although Engels and later Lenin attribute an empirical method to Marx's later work, Louis Althusser correctly argues that Marx is no empiricist, rightly emphasizing the Hegelian methodology that undergirds Marx's notion of "science" (Althusser and Balibar 1971). As for positivism, Marx's own comments on Auguste Comte are instructive. In 1866 he writes to Engels,

> I am now studying Comte as a sideline, because the English and French make such a fuss over the fellow. What they are attracted by is the encyclopedic, *la synthèse*, but this is lamentable compared to Hegel (although Comte, as a professional mathematician and physicist is superior to him, that is, superior in matters of detail, but even here Hegel is infinitely greater as a whole). And this shit-Positivism appeared in 1832!
>
> (1979, 213).

9. See Frederick Gregory's historical study *Scientific Materialism in 19th Century Germany* (1977). In addition to Gregory's artful treatment of the Vogt/Marx controversy, he emphasizes the differences among the materialists, highlighting ambiguities of position that I have necessarily passed over in my more summary account. I have drawn on Gregory's work exten- sively here.
10. The essay, originally published in 1959, formed part of the studies Kuhn did leading up to his famous work *The Structure of Scientific Revolutions*. This latter work argues that revolutions in science depend on cultural and historical contexts in linguistic communities that operate according to "paradigm shifts" (Kuhn 1996). The phenomenon of simultaneous discovery seems to imply that ideas take hold when the time is ripe, when the cultural and historical context is prepared to receive them.
11. According to Brush (1977), "Yehuda Elkana has argued that the gradual change in meaning of the word 'force' was itself an important part of the discovery of the conservation of 'energy'" (10).

12. The laboratory synthesis of urine bolstered the German chemical theory that organic and inorganic matters were composed of the same elements. Ostensibly, the synthesis proved that urine need not pass through the human body to acquire its distinctive properties, that vital human life added nothing to its composition that could not be added in the laboratory. In popularizations like Büchner's, it became the claim that nothing about human bodily synthesis was unique, including the operations of thought. Therefore, as Fredrick Gregory notes,

> Darwin did not create the sensation in Germany he had in England. The message communicated by the scientific materialists in Germany was already perceived, at least by their opponents, as a sensationalized degradation of man. Once Germans had been told that man's mind could be compared to urine, it came as no shock that man was now supposedly related to apes
>
> (1977, 175).

13. In the early twentieth century, not only human physical embodiment but also human psychic embodiment became modeled on the thermodynamic machine. An energeticist model can be discerned, for example, in Freud's model of the psyche. Jacques Lacan explicitly traces the dependence of Freud's model of the psyche to the steam engine in a 1955 lecture on "The Ego in Freud's Theory and in the Technique of Psychoanalysis" (1988, 74–76).

14. The general proximity of natural and social explanation in nineteenth-century thought helps to explain Marx's comparisons between natural development and the capitalist form, clarifying texts such as the following one from the *Grundrisse*:

> The conditions ... which express the becoming of capital, do not fall into the sphere of that mode of production for which capital serves as the presupposition; as the historic preludes of its becoming, they lie behind it; just as the processes by means of which the earth made the transition from a liquid sea of fire and vapour to its present form now lie beyond its life as finished earth
>
> (1973, 460).

15. See the *Grundrisse*, especially "Labor-power as capital" in section I of the chapter on capital. Marx writes,

> [The laborer] only sells a temporary disposition over his labouring capacity, hence he can always begin the exchange anew as soon as he has taken in the quantity of substances required in order to reproduce the externalization of his life [*Lebensäusserung*] .... What he exchanges for capital is his entire labouring capacity, which he spends, say in 20 years. Instead of paying him for it in a lump sum, capital pays him in small doses, as he places it at capital's disposal, say weekly. This ... gives no grounds for concluding that—because the worker has to sleep 10–12 hours before he becomes capable of repeating his labour and

his exchange with capital—labour forms his capital. What this argument in fact conceives as capital is the limit, the interruption of his labour, since he is not a perpetuum mobile... [Selling labour-power] brings [the worker] only subsistence, the satisfaction of individual needs, more or less—*never* the general form of wealth, never wealth

(1973, 293–294).

Marx's target here is Peter Gaskell's *Artisans and Machinery* (1836), in which Gaskell argues that labor is the capital of the worker. By reducing what the worker sells to labor-power, Marx takes issue with this formulation and with Gaskell's transformation of bodily exhaustion into a resource to be capitalized.

16. Retrieved 7 September 2006, from www.marxists.org/archive/marx/works/1865/value–price–profit/ch03.htm.
17. Retrieved 20 March 2008, from www.marxists.org/archive/marx/wprks/1865/value–price–profit/ch02.htm.
18. Barbara Ehrenreich defines "labor-power" with real precision when, in her contemporary ethnography of the working poor in the United States, she writes,

When I request permission to leave at about 3:30, another housekeeper warns me that so far no one has succeeded in combining housekeeping with serving at Jerry's.... With that helpful information in mind, I rush back to number 46, down four Advils (the brand name this time), shower, stooping to fit into the stall, and attempt to compose myself for the oncoming shift. So much for what Marx termed the "reproduction of labor power," meaning the things a worker has to do just so she'll be ready to labor again

(2001, 45).

19. This conceptualization of labor-power is from Marx's *Capital*, here cited in Rabinbach (1990, 75).
20. This is especially true if children can be made to work. It is also a condition of global capitalism.
21. See Henry Laycock's "Exploitation via Labour Power in Marx" for further exploration of the relationship of the concept of labor-power to Marx's theory of exploitation (1999).
22. See Stephen Brush's *The Temperature of History* (1977).
23. Marx is thus vulnerable to Hannah Arendt's critique that the constituting moment of the modern revolutionary traditions has been lost to the necessities and inevitabilities of the prior regime's collapse: the focus is too much on inevitability and tearing down, and too little on public political engagement except as a mode of tearing down. Arendt worries that this is the necessary consequence of all revolutions that get caught up with the social question of mass poverty (1965).

3 Machines in the communist future

1. Blumenberg's account of the reversal in the value of curiosity offers a general philosophical framework in which we might situate Carl Mitcham's

historical characterization of attitudes toward technology. According to Mitcham, technology is denigrated in the ancient texts and venerated in the modern. Nineteenth- and twentieth-century attitudes toward technology, taken as a whole, have vacillated uneasily between the two postures. See Scharff and Dusek (2003, especially 490–506).

2. Marx will explicitly target Malthus's vision of nature in his *Critique of the Gotha Program* (1875):

> It is well known that nothing of the "iron law of wages" is Lasalle's except the word "iron," borrowed from Goethe's "great eternal iron laws." The word *iron* is a label by which the true believers recognize one another. But if I take the law with Lasalle's stamp on it and, consequently, in his sense, then I must also take it with his substantiation for it. And what is that? As Lange already showed, shortly after Lasalle's death, it is the Malthusian theory of population (preached by Lange himself). But if this theory is correct, then again I *cannot* abolish the law even if I abolish wage labour a hundred times over, because the law then governs not only the system of wage labour, but *every* social system. Basing themselves directly on this, the economists have been proving for fifty years and more that socialism cannot abolish poverty, *which has its basis in nature*, but can only make it *general*, distribute it simultaneously over the whole surface of society! But this is not the main thing. *Quite apart* from the *false* Lasallean formulation of the law, the truly outrageous retrogression consists in [basing the law in nature]
>
> (quoted in Tucker 1978, 534–535, emphases in original).

3. Marx's notes are on Liebig's *Animal Chemistry, or Organic Chemistry in its Application to Physiology and Pathology* (1842) (IISG B 49).
4. See Chapter 1 for a discussion of the philosophical history of this term.
5. Two pivotal texts about machines appear in the *Grundrisse* in addition to the "Fragment on Machines" (1973, 776–778, and 818–833; MECW 1987, 29, 158–161, 198–211; MEGA^2 II, 1.2, 645–647 and 683–699). The first of these shows how labor's intensification can be derived—independently of competition—from the definition of fixed capital alone (see Section IV). There are many other pertinent texts that discuss not technology specifically, but science more generally. I have woven some of these into my explanation. For Marx, science and technology are more tightly connected than they are for us.
6. For an explanation of this technical term, see Chapter 1, Section II, "Other origins of 'alienation' and 'objectification'," of this book.
7. For an accurate account of Marx's concept of "need," see Heller (1976).
8. Feenberg (1999) worries that thinkers such as Habermas have lost this insight, leaving the realms of science and technology out of political consideration in order to favor more traditionally humanistic domains such as law and language. However, science and technology, as Marx already knew, are the site of some of the most important political mediations of the modern world. See Feenberg (1999, 151–180).

9. Marx's interest in railways in particular is pronounced in his notebooks from the 1850s, especially the railways of India (IISG B 63, 47–48) and Germany (IISG B 88, 29–31), as well as his comments about railways that entered the reports of the Royal Commission of London (IISG B 112, 105–129). In the *Grundrisse*, his philosophical analysis of a road develops these researches into a comment on the changing relationship of capitalist and state interests and investments with respect to such internal infrastructure (1973, 524–533).

10. For a refutation of the fall in the rate of profit, see Elster (1983, 178). The refutation is continued in Elster (1985).

11. Obviously, this is not true of machines that are sold as commodities. Marx notes this parenthetically: "Also included in the points listed above, so that it is not forgotten, is the circulation of fixed capital as circulating capital, i.e. transactions through which it changes owners" (MECW 1987, 29, 78; 1973, 687; MEGA^2 II, 1.2, 567). As for the wage, Marx never developed a full account of its workings, though he originally planned to do so in *Capital*. For a discussion of the incompleteness of Marx's account of the wage and the attendant problems, see Negri (1984, 72). Negri discusses Marx's inattention to topics that might interest the worker, for example the wage. These topics are cast aside in favor of those themes of interest to the capitalist, for example production. Negri calls this choice of topic the "bourgeoisification" of Marx's own writing.

12. For this reason, Foucault believes that the bourgeois class deploys sexual repression as a way of highlighting the bodies of its members and distinguishing these bodies from those of the working class. Capitalist sexuality takes a peculiar form as a consequence. See Chapter 4.

13. I have chosen a gender-specific pronoun to correspond to the predominant traditional guild regulations about gender.

14. Bataille's book on political economy, *The Accursed Share*, develops this point (1976, 1991). In his full corpus, Bataille also develops erotic expenditure, enjoyment, and destruction as nonproductive responses to the productivist metaphysic.

15. Foucault (1990) argues that this explanation is too simple. While I agree that it does not comprehensively explain capitalist sexuality, which has oppositional in addition to straightforward forms, I do think repression remains regulatory even, or perhaps especially, when sexuality explodes into discourse. The requirement to disclose is itself a way of highlighting the importance of the sexual domain of human experience and of bringing it under medical scrutiny.

16. Kolakowski writes that

> Fourier (1772–1837) enjoys the deserved reputation of a visionary and crank of the first order.... Nearly all his spare time was devoted to writing and only a small fraction of it to reading.... The extravagance of Fourier's description and the naivety with which he attributed his own tastes to others (sexual promiscuity, gluttony, love of flowers and cats, etc.) caused him to be regarded as a hopeless crank, with the result that some of his acuter observations were overlooked
>
> (Kolakowski 1978, Vol. I, 198–201).

17. The incomplete conquest of scarcity in countries where communism became firmly rooted in political life—that is, their nonindustrialization—was also a factor in this ideological twist.

18. Here I have borrowed Simone de Beauvoir's concept from *The Second Sex*. Of women, she writes, "They live dispersed among the males, attached through residence, housework, economic condition, and social standing to certain men—fathers or husbands—more firmly than they are to other women" (Beauvoir 1949, I, 19; Beauvoir 1989, xxv).

19. For the definition and analysis of the "symbolics of blood," see Foucault (1990, 124, and especially 147–150).

20. The vocabulary of survival is from Althusser, though both Kolakowski and Cohen use a different vocabulary to describe the same idea. Pierre Bourdieu's sociological notion of "hysteresis" follows a similar structure (1984). Survivals are regularly at issue in technological changes in the means of production and also in political life. Though he does not use the language of survival, perhaps no one writes more pointedly on the issue of technological survivals than Simondon. Comparing the automobile with the airplane, Simondon is astonished at the continued use of the former, which has become "weighed down with accessories" (1958, 24, my translation), its status as a concrete object obscuring its abstract purpose of swift travel. Simondon claims that technological objects go through two phases: a phase of implementation and a phase of ornamentation. The latter always belongs to technologies when they become survivals. An example of a technological survival in our own era is the contemporary computer keyboard, which may be ergonomically fitted to the hands, but that has retained the letter pattern mandated by the opposing arms of the mechanical typewriter.

21. Derrida also discusses this dependence of the fixed structures of the present on the past in terms of the metaphor of haunting (*Spectres of Marx* 1994). Survivals are ways the past haunts the present. Derridean hauntology is nothing less than a materialist account of spirit!

22. See especially the letter of November 1877 to the editor of the Petersburg literary-political journal *Otechestvennye Zapiski* (Marx 1979, 321).

4 Machines in the capitalist reality

An earlier version of chapter 4 was published as "Rough, Foul-Mouthed Boys: Women's Monstrous Laboring Bodies," *Radical Philosophy Today* 5, Fall 2007, 49–67.

1. Because of the complexities involved in interpreting *Capital*, Postone simply avoids it altogether, basing his interpretation of Marx's critical theory entirely on the *Grundrisse* (1993, 15, 21). Postone attributes what he calls "the crisis of traditional Marxism" to the difficulties of interpreting *Capital* properly.

2. The passage is cited in Chapter 1, Section I of this book, and I refer the reader there (MECW 1996, 35, 19; MEGA^2 II, 9, 24, 27; MEGA^2 II, 8, 55). Kolakowski relates that Lenin also discovered the importance of Hegel for Marx's later work: late in his life Lenin declared *Capital* to be incomprehensible to those

who had not first made a thorough study of Hegel's *Science of Logic* (1978, Vol. II, 462).

3. On these grounds, both Negri and Elster criticize Marx's vision of working-class agency in *Capital* (Elster 1985; Negri 1984).

4. "[M]ere social contact begets in most industries an emulation and stimulation of the animal spirits that heightens the efficiency of each individual workman" (I.IV.XIII; 1887, 309); "The combined working day...excites emulation between individuals and raises their animal spirits" (I.IV.XIII; 1887, 311).

5. For Marx, humans are not animals, or not exclusively animals. They are distinguished from animals, as we shall see in subsequent passages, by the faculty of the imagination.

6. Chapter XV in the English edition of the first volume of *Capital* has the title "Machinery and Modern Industry." The chapter corresponds to chapter XIII in the German editions of the work, where the title is "*Maschinerie und große Industrie.*" The English version of *Capital* follows the reorganization of the work that Marx performed when bringing out the French edition, where the chapter on machines is also chapter XV: "*Le machinisme et la grande Industrie.*" For a good French-language reader's edition of *Capital*, see Karl Marx, *Le Capital: Critique de l'Économie Politique, Livre Premier*, trans. Joseph Roy (Paris: Éditions Sociales, 1978).

7. Marx follows Hegel's philosophy of history in this category of the "prehistorical." Marx's concern is with capitalism, and he reverts to the prehistorical only in order to explain capitalism, how it came into being, and its revolutionary overcoming. In this, Marx falls prey to the teleological narrative of progress that has Western Europe as the site of its ultimate fulfillment. Perhaps Marx's doctrine of revolutionary internationalism surpasses Hegel's discussions of Spirit's more narrow borders. Perhaps it also surpasses the Enlightenment myths of noble savagery, when it recognizes worker subjectivity and does not see the worker simply as a natural force or antidote to corrupt civilization. And perhaps not. Socialism has proven extremely dangerous when it becomes a vehicle for a nationalized, imperialist, or primitivist appeal to the noble savage within.

8. The remainder of what Marx highlights in his partial transcription of Babbage's text is about the economies of scale that regulate the introduction of machinery into industry: "Whenever it is required to provide a great multitude of things, all of exactly the same kind, the proper time has arrived for the institution of tools or machines by which they may be manufactured. (216)" (Babbage in Marx, IISG B 91A, 183). I return to the relationship between Marx and Babbage in Chapter 5.

9. For a theory of the relationship between the periodization of the Industrial Revolution, the machine age in art, and the cultural logics of modernism and postmodernism, see Jameson (1991, 32–38).

10. For further connections between Marx and thermodynamic science and technology, see Rabinbach (1990), Cardwell (1971), and Foster and Burkett (2004, 2008).

11. The thinkers of the seventeenth, eighteenth, and nineteenth centuries were obsessed with the invention and implications of a perpetual motion machine. This can be explained by the symbolic function of machinery

as the overcoming and supplanting of the natural. A machine that, once set in motion, was capable of sustaining such motion indefinitely would have meant nothing less than human technological possession of the powers of creation, of self-causation (Dircks 1861; Scheerbart 1910). The dream continues through the mid-twentieth century. Cataloguing the achievements of Soviet pseudo-science, Kolakowski tells us that

> After Stalin's death, a still more sensational article appeared in *Pravda* to the effect that a machine had been constructed in a Saratov factory that gave off more energy than it consumed—thus finally disposing of the second law of thermodynamics and at the same time confirming Engels's statement that the energy dispersed in the universe must also be concentrated somewhere (in the Saratov factory, to be specific). Soon afterwards, however, *Pravda* had to publicize a shamefaced recantation—a sign that the intellectual atmosphere had already changed
>
> (1978, III, 150).

12. This extension is offered in Donna Haraway's famous figure of the cyborg (1985, 1991). Haraway's extensive familiarity with *Capital* and with Marx's ethnological notebooks suggests that her cyborg may have its origins in Marx's idea of bodily annexation; at the very least, the cyborg is prefigured in Marx. So too, Haraway's "Cyborg Manifesto" replaces "communist" with a term of identification that seeks to rectify humanist and vitalist residues.
13. The term is translated into English as "bureaucracy," and thereby loses the direct connections with the technological metaphor (1996).
14. For an overview of Ancient, Enlightenment, and Romantic commentaries on technology, see Carl Mitcham's "Three Ways of Being-With Technology" (Scharff and Dusek 2003, 490–506).
15. Neither popular text was solely authored by Marx. The *Communist Manifesto* of 1848 was penned conjointly by Marx and Engels. Engels's essay "Socialism: Utopian and Scientific" was written after Marx's death, and emerged in the 1880s and 1890s in France and England (Tucker 1978, 683).
16. See especially the first part of the "Chapter on the Working Day" in *Capital*, where these images of monstrosity are concentrated (I.III.X., 1–4; MECW 1996, 35, 239–282; MEGA^2 II, 9, 199–227; MEGA^2 II, 8, 237–280).
17. See Gilman (1990) and Haraway (1997, especially 215).
18. For a parallel insight that looks at arduous women's labor in the meatpacking industry in the United States at the turn of the century, see Horowitz (2003, 267–294, 279).
19. I will be unable to give proper attention here to the importance of class in the crafting of the concept "woman." As Pierre Bourdieu (1984) reminds us,

> Sexual properties are as inseparable from class properties as the yellowness of a lemon is from its acidity: a class is defined in an essential respect by the place and value it gives to the two sexes and to their socially constituted dispositions. This is why there are as many ways of realizing femininity as there are classes and class fractions, and the division of

labor between the sexes takes quite different forms, both in practices and in representations, in the different social classes

(1984, 107–108).

20. Along with Marx, we are justly skeptical about family values and other "bourgeois claptrap" that romanticizes family structures that are possible only for a privileged few. However, we can maintain, alongside this skepticism, the recognition that kinship structures have sometimes been a haven from the individualism of a capitalist economy, for example when sharing resources allows kinship groups to absorb vicissitudes of employment among their members. Witness also the appropriation of the term "family" by queer theorists and by gay, lesbian, bisexual, and transgendered persons to describe the self-selected kinship groups that try to replicate some of the features of the familial haven without replicating its oppressive, patriarchal structure.

21. See, for example, Orlando Patterson's (1982) discussion of "natal alienation" (5). According to Patterson, the natal alienation of the slave is expressed in his or her status as a socially dead person. This form of political exile may have been incompatible with the recognition implied by economic activity, leading to the tensions described by Hahn.

22. Karl Marx, *"Exzerpte aus Thomas Fowell Buxton: The African Slave Trade"* and *"Exzerpte aus Thomas Fowell Buxton: The remedy; being a sequel to the African Slave trade,"* in *Marx–Engels Gesamtausgabe* (MEGA²), *Vierte Abteilung, Exzerpte, Notizen, Marginalien, Band 9, Exzerpte und Notizen, Juli bis September 1851* (Berlin: Dietz, 1991), 494–501.

23. See hooks (1981).

24. Karl Marx, Excerpt from Heft XIX, Unpublished excerpt notebooks, London (Amsterdam: International Institute of Social History (IISG), Archival Collections, 1852), Call Numbers B 59, B 61. Marx drew the vision of women's history and character that he employs in *Capital* and other late texts from the figures contained in the excerpt notebooks: J. G. Eichhorn (1799), John Millard (1753), J. Jung (1850), J. A. de Leger (1803), Dr. William Wachsworth (1850), C. Meiners (1788–1800), Thomas de L'Ac (1773), W. Alexander (1782), and Druman (1847). Many of these figures belong to the *Querelle des Femmes* genre that characterized European letters from the fifteenth century onward. As Gary Kates argues in *Monsieur d'Eon is a Woman: A Tale of Political Intrigue and Sexual Masquerade* (1995), "Recent scholarship on the Querelle des Femmes literature has focused almost exclusively on the Renaissance and the seventeenth century. The eighteenth century participants have been overlooked by scholars . . . But . . . the Querelle des Femmes did not disappear after 1700; if anything, it became even bolder" (157). Feminist themes of the *Querelle des Femmes* genre seem remarkably contemporary, which argues like Simone de Beauvoir that women are not born, but made. The whole *Querelle des Femmes* genre may have been increasingly constrained by the bourgeois gender norms of the nineteenth century, the very norms under discussion in this chapter.

25. The second citation from the *Communist Manifesto* falls at the end of the book, in the chapters on the so-called "primitive accumulation" (MECW 1996, 35, 751; MEGA² II, 9, 662; MEGA² II, 8, 713; See the *Communist*

Manifesto at MECW 1976, 6, 494–496; MEW 1959, 4, 472–474). The passage refers to the proletariat as the "special and essential product" of Modern Industry. Among all its products, and surpassing them in importance, Modern Industry produces this class. Alienated, the class turns revolutionary and destroys the mode of production that brought it to life. Marx's revolution permutes the Oedipal drama: destroying the father's code, the mode of production, the proletariat keeps the mother, machines, the means of production, in order to spawn a new world. The new world is full of hope rather than degeneracy: it is utopian, not tragic.

26. For Marx, this division has its deep schematic origins in two differences he highlights from the *German Ideology*. The first is the difference between the sexes, or more technically, the active/passive division of labor in the sexual act. The second is the difference between intellectual and physical labor. Both distinctions relate to the classical distinction between the activity of form versus the passivity of matter. Spirit, form, and intellect are privileged over matter or involvement with it. This hierarchy recurs in the social divisions between male and female, upper and lower class, White and non-White, Christian and non-Christian, god and human, and the pure sciences versus their technological application. In thermodynamics, all of these metaphysical hierarchies are brought into question.

5 Alienation beyond Marx

An earlier version of chapter 5 was published as "Partial Liberations: The Machine, Gender, and High-Tech Culture," *International Studies in Philosophy* 34: 2, Spring 2002, 169–185.

1. See Chapter 4, fn 24, of this book.
2. In subsequent years, Marx's excerpt notebooks show that he remained interested in the theme of technology and even began to extend his definition of science and technology out of the bounds that typified the political economists, who focused on machines. Two examples are Marx's interest in his later years in the agricultural applications of chemistry and in Podolinsky's notion of energy (Kevin Anderson, personal communication). The excerpt notebooks that reveal this are currently being worked on by a team of translators connected with the newly refounded *Marx–Engels Gesamtausgabe* (MEGA^2) editions.
3. Also see Schrader (1980).
4. Scholars have neglected this text in favor of the other two. This neglect is part of a number of more general misunderstandings about the manuscripts of this period and their relationship to *Capital*. If we regard Marx's manuscripts from the 1850s and 1860s as draft outlines for *Capital*, we must take care not to misunderstand the role of a "draft." These "drafts" often contain much that does not make it into the final text, but which is instrumental in shaping the formulations given there. The differences between the manuscripts and *Capital* also provide clues about which materials were omitted because of *Capital*'s specialized method. Finally, sometimes questions that are neither answered nor raised in *Capital* were

resolved to Marx's satisfaction in earlier manuscript texts that he wrote for "self-clarification."

5. Negri also challenges it, claiming that it is one of those assumptions in Marx that must be corrected if we are to make his philosophy viable for today: "complex, productive, scientific labor is definitively irreducible to elementary temporal units" (Negri 2003, 27). This irreducibility affects the meaning "of the productive function of intellectual or scientific labor" (24).

6. For the construction of his difference engines, Babbage required the full-time collaboration of one such famous working-class machinist, Joseph Clement. Barely literate, Clement could charge any price he wished for his unique mechanical and drawing skills. His main contribution to Babbage's invention, and to the history of technology, was the standardization of machine parts (e.g. the threading of screws), so that these would be interchangeable (Swade 2001, 40–48).

7. K. Moene argues that this aspect of machinery gives workers power in an unanticipated way: "machinery *invites* strikes by making it more costly for the employer to have capital idling" (cited in Elster 1985, 145 fn).

8. For a description of the recurrence of this problem in Marx, see Negri and Fleming (1984). Also see Chapter 3 of this book. Finally, note the negative treatments of working-class agency in critical theory, and especially in Adorno (1984), Horkheimer (1975), Marcuse (1991), and Benjamin (1969). In Adorno, the threat of fascism as a working-class movement is sufficient to produce a wistful nostalgia for the bourgeois.

9. See Galison (2003) for a discussion of the effects of synchronization on Albert Einstein, who worked in a Viennese patent office documenting the inventions that helped accomplish this synchronization.

10. Changes in intensive magnitude are also why Marx is increasingly dissatisfied with using time as the measure of labor. Changes in intensive magnitude come with the new standard for measuring labor that I have described in Chapter 2: quanta of energy.

11. These class types are, of course, ideal-typical generalizations. For lack of space, I do not attend to what Pierre Bourdieu (1984) rightly calls class fractions, nor adequately to transitions in the class structure itself.

12. Witch burning, itself a product of the social, economic, and demographic pressures of early modernity's transition to capitalism, clearly furnished the precedent for this ritual. Brian Levack's history of early-modern European witch-hunts explains their connections with hatred and fear of the lower classes, misogyny, and social change. He writes,

> [I]f we wish to identify one factor that underlay both the formulation and the transmission of the cumulative concept of witchcraft, one that most solidly buttressed the belief that the devil was active in human affairs, then we should focus on the fear of rebellion, sedition, and disorder that beset members of the upper classes during these years. It is no coincidence that the earliest descriptions of the witches' Sabbath were written when Europe was experiencing a wave of social rebellion in the late fourteenth century. Nor is it any coincidence that the learned belief

> in organized witchcraft spread throughout Europe during a period of profound instability and chronic rebellion. The era of the great witch hunt was the great age of popular rebellion in European history
> (Levack 1987, 58).

13. *Economic Manuscripts of 1861–63*, MECW 1988, 30, 318.
14. In her criticism of Lenin for his formulation of liberation as "electrification plus soviets," Hannah Arendt demonstrates her own rather than Lenin's misunderstanding of Marx on the technology question. She criticizes Lenin's formula for placing too much emphasis on technical means, and not enough on socialization and socialism. But the communist mode of production does require technology (electrification) developed along with the possibility of an alternative social organization (soviets). Lenin was following the later Marx in emphasizing the dialectic of the relationship of the forces of production and the relations of production (Arendt 1965, 60). In general, Lenin's work has been misunderstood, in part due to bad translations of his Russian by those who may or may not have been familiar with his Marxist/Hegelian heritage. See forthcoming work, including new translations, by Michael Marder, currently of The New School for Social Research.
15. According to Schatzberg (2006), the 1887 English translation of *Capital* is one of the earliest instances in which the German word *Technik* was translated as "technology" (496–497).
16. See my analysis of the paradox of use- and exchange-value in Chapter 3. In this regard, we see that Heidegger was hardly the first philosopher to be concerned with an alienated world driven by instrumental use; the concern had already been expressed by Marx.
17. Marcuse's *One Dimensional Man* has even drawn fire from Haraway as recommending a politically disastrous primitivism rather than encouraging an ongoing engagement with a technologically mediated society (1991). Haraway's criticism is probably hasty.
18. See also Latour (2004).
19. Sandra Harding is another important founder of the tradition of scientific and technological feminism. Lack of space prevents me from discussing her work. Harding's study of the relationship between movements for social liberation and scientific objectivity (1986) led into her Marxian development of standpoint epistemology (1991).
20. This citation comes from Haraway's "A Cyborg Manifesto: Science, Technology, and Socialist Feminism in the Late 20th Century." The full title makes the now-famous essay's socialist intellectual heritage more visible. An early version of the essay was published in the journal *Socialist Review* (1985).
21. For more on Haraway's definition of an oppositional ideology, see the Introduction.

References

a. Works by Karl Marx and Friedrich Engels

Marx, Karl. 1850–1890. Excerpts from volumes III, VII, VIII, IX, XI, XII, and XX. Unpublished excerpt notebooks. Amsterdam: International Institute of Social History (IISG), Archival Collections. Call Nos B 45, B 48, B 49, B 54, B 55, B 58, B 59, B 61, and B 62.

——. 1857/58. Excerpts from the manuscript of *Zur Kritik der Politischen Ökonomie (Grundrisse), Volume VII*. Unpublished notebooks. Amsterdam: International Institute of Social History, Archival Collections. Call No. B 91/A.

——. 1861. "*Citatenheft.*" Unpublished notebooks. Amsterdam: International Institute of Social History, Archival Collections. Call No. A 52.

——. 1957–1990. *Marx-Engels Werke (MEW)*. 43 Vols Berlin: Institut für Marxismus-Leninismus, Dietz Verlag.

——. 1970. *A Contribution to the Critique of Political Economy*. London: Lawrence and Wishart (Orig. pub. 1859).

——. 1972. *The Ethnological Notebooks of Karl Marx*. Trans. Lawrence Krader. Assen, The Netherlands: Van Gorcum (Orig. pub. 1880).

——. 1973. *The Grundrisse: Foundations of the Critique of Political Economy (rough draft)*. Trans. Martin Nicolaus. London: Penguin (Orig. pub. 1857–1858).

——. 1975–2004. *Collected Works of Karl Marx and Friedrich Engels (MECW)*. 50 Vols. London: Lawrence and Wishart.

——. 1975, 1990-date. *Marx-Engels Gesamtausgabe (MEGA²)*, 2nd Edn 100 + Vols. Moscow, Berlin, Amsterdam: Institute of Marxism-Leninism, International Marx-Engels Foundation, Akademie, Dietz Verlag.

——. 1979. *The Letters of Karl Marx*. Ed. Saul Kussiel Padover. Englewood Cliffs, NJ: Prentice Hall.

——. 1981. *Die technologisch-historischen Exzerpte: Historische-kritische Ausgabe*. Ed. Hans-Peter Müller. Frankfurt-am-Main, Germany: Ullstein Materialien (Orig. pub. 1851).

——. 1996. The 18th *Brumaire* of Louis Bonaparte. In *Marx: Later Political Writings*. Ed. and Trans. Terrell Carver. Cambridge: Cambridge University Press, 31–127 (Orig. pub. 1852).

Marx, Marxists, and Marxisms. Retrieved July 8, 2008, from <www.Marxists.org>

b. References

Abromeit, John, and Richard Wolin, Eds 2005. *Heideggerian Marxism: Herbert Marcuse*. Lincoln: University of Nebraska Press.

Adorno, Theodor. 1984. *Minima Moralia: Reflections from Damaged Life*. New York: Verso.

Agamben, Giorgio. 2004. *The Open: Man and Animal*. Trans. Kevin Attell. Stanford, CA: Stanford University Press.

Althusser, Louis. 1969. *For Marx*. New York: Pantheon Books.

———. 1971. *Reading Capital*. With Etienne Balibar. New York: Pantheon Books.

Appardurai, Arjun. 1986. *The Social Life of Things: Commodities in Cultural Perspective*. Cambridge: Cambridge University Press.

Arendt, Hannah. 1965. *On Revolution*. New York: Viking Press.

Aristotle. 1984. *The Complete Works of Aristotle: The Revised Oxford Translation*. Trans. and Ed. Jonathan Barnes. Princeton, NJ: Princeton University Press.

Avineri, Shlomo. 1968. *The Social and Political Thought of Karl Marx*. Cambridge Studies in the History and Theory of Politics. Cambridge: Cambridge University Press.

Babbage, Charles. 1989a. *Economy of Machinery and Manufactures*. Ed. M. Campbell-Kelly. Vol. 2 of *The Works of Charles Babbage*. New York: New York University Press (Orig. pub. 1835).

———. 1989b. *Passages from the Life of a Philosopher*. Ed. M. Campbell-Kelly. Vol. 11 of *The Works of Charles Babbage*. New York: New York University Press (Orig. pub. 1864).

Bacon, Francis. 2000. *The New Organon*. Trans. Lisa Jardine and Michael Silverthorne. Cambridge Texts in the History of Philosophy. Cambridge: Cambridge University Press (Orig. pub. 1620).

Bataille, Georges. 1976. *Oeuvres Completes, Tome 8*. Paris: Gallimard (Orig. pub. 1949).

———. 1988. *The Accursed Share: An Essay on General Economy*. Vol. I. Trans. Robert Hurley. New York: Zone Books (Orig. pub. 1949).

———. 1991. *The Accursed Share*. Vol. II & III. Trans. Robert Hurley. New York: Zone Books (Orig. pub. 1949).

———. 1992. *Theory of Religion*. Trans. Robert Hurley. New York: Zone Books (Orig. pub. 1973).

Beauvoir, Simone de. 1949. *Le deuxième sexe*. Paris: Gallimard.

———. 1989. *The Second Sex*. Trans. H. M. Parshley. New York: Vintage Books (Orig. pub. 1949).

Benjamin, Walter. 1969. The work of art in the age of mechanical reproduction. In *Illuminations: Essays and Reflections*. New York: Schocken Books, 217–252.

Blumenberg, Hans. 1983. *The Legitimacy of the Modern Age*. Cambridge, MA: MIT Press.

Bourdieu, Pierre. 1984. *Distinction: A Social Critique of the Judgment of Taste*. Trans. Richard Nice. Cambridge, MA: Harvard University Press (Orig. pub. 1979).

Braidotti, Rosi. 1997. Mothers, monsters, and machines. In *Writing on the Body: Female Embodiment and Feminist Theory*. Ed. N. M. Kate Conboy and Sarah Stanbury. New York: Columbia University Press, 59–79.

Brush, Stephen G. 1977. *The Temperature of History: Phases of Science and Culture in the Nineteenth Century*. New York: B. Franklin.

Büchner, Ludwig. 1920. *Force and Matter or Principles of the Natural Order of the Universe: With a System of Morality Based Thereon*. Trans. J. Frederick Collingwood. New York: P. Eckler.

Caporaso, James A., and David P. Levine, Eds 1992. *Theories of Political Economy*. Cambridge: Cambridge University Press.

Cardwell, D. S. L. 1971. *From Watt to Clausius: The Rise of Thermodynamics in the Early Industrial Age*. Ithaca, NY: Cornell University Press.

Carver, Terrell. 1975. Marx's commodity fetishism. *Inquiry* 18: 39–63.

Cohen, G. A. 1978. *Karl Marx's Theory of History: A Defense*. Princeton, NJ: Princeton University Press.

Daly, Nicholas. 2004. *Literature, Technology, and Modernity, 1860–2000*. Cambridge: Cambridge University Press.

Day, Lance, and Ian McNeil, Eds 1996. *Biographical Dictionary of the History of Technology*. New York: Routledge.

Derrida, Jacques. 1994. *Specters of Marx: The State of the Debt, the Work of Mourning, and the New International*. Trans. Peggy Kamuf. New York: Routledge (Orig. pub. 1993).

Dyer, Richard. 1997. *White*. New York: Routledge.

Dircks, Henry. 1861. *Perpetuum Mobile, or, Search for Self-Motive Power during the 17th, 18th and 19th Centuries*. Austin, Texas: University of Texas Archival Libraries.

Echols, Alice. 1989. *Daring to be Bad: Radical Feminism in America, 1967–1975*. Minneapolis: University of Minnesota Press.

Ehrenreich, Barbara. 2001. *Nickel and Dimed: On (not) Getting by in Boom-Time America*. New York: Metropolitan Books.

Elster, Jon. 1983. *Explaining Technical Change: A Case study in the Philosophy of Science*. Cambridge: Cambridge University Press.

——. 1985. *Making Sense of Marx*. Cambridge: Cambridge University Press.

Feenberg, Andrew. 1999. *Questioning Technology*. New York: Routledge.

——. 2002. *Transforming Technology: A Critical Theory Revisited*. New York: Oxford.

Feuerbach, Ludwig. 1957. *The Essence of Christianity*. Trans. George Eliot. New York: Harper (Orig. pub. 1841).

Forest, Denis. 2001. Fatigue et normativité. *Revue Philosophique de la France et de l'Etranger* 1: 3–25.

Foster, John B., and Paul Burkett. 2004. Ecological economics and classical Marxism: The "Podolinsky Business" reconsidered. *Organization and Environment* 17 (1): 32–60.

——. 2008. Classical Marxism and the second law of thermodynamics. *Organization and Environment* 21 (3): 3–33.

Foucault, Michel. 1970. *The Order of Things: An Archaeology of the Human Sciences*. New York: Vintage Books.

——. 1990. *The History of Sexuality, Vol. 1*. New York: Vintage Books.

Galison, Peter Louis. 2003. *Einstein's Clocks, Poincaré's Maps: Empires of Time*. New York: Norton.

Gilman, Sander L. 1990. I'm down on whores: Race and gender in Victorian London. In *Anatomy of Racism*. Ed. David Theo Goldberg. Minneapolis: University of Minnesota Press, 146–170.

Godels, Greg. 1997. Marx, Engels, and the idea of exploitation. *Nature, Society, and Thought* 10 (4): 509–522.

Gould, Stephen Jay. 1993. American polygeny and craniometry before Darwin: Blacks and Indians as separate, inferior species. In *The Racial Economy of Science*. Ed. Sandra Harding. Indianapolis: Indiana University Press, 84–115.

Gregory, Frederick. 1977. *Scientific Materialism in Nineteenth Century Germany*. Dordrecht, Boston: D. Reidel.

Gunnarson, Ewa, and Lena Trojer, Eds 1994. *Feminist Voices on Gender, Technology, and Ethics*. Luleå, Sweden: Centre for Women's Studies, Luleå University of Technology.

Hahn, Steven. 2005. A *Nation Under our Feet: Black Political Struggles in the Rural South from Slavery to the Great Migration.* Cambridge, MA: Belknap.

Haraway, Donna Jeanne. 1985. A manifesto for cyborgs: Science, technology, and socialist feminism in the 1980s. *Socialist Review* 80: 65–108.

———. 1989. *Primate Visions: Gender, Race, and Nature in the World of Modern Science.* New York: Routledge.

———. 1991. *Simians, Cyborgs, and Women: The Reinvention of Nature.* New York: Routledge.

———. 1997. *Modest-Witness@Second-Millennium, FemaleMan-meets-OncoMouse: Feminism and Technoscience.* New York: Routledge.

———. 2000. *How Like a Leaf: An Interview with Thyrza Nichols Goodeve.* New York: Routledge.

———. February 2001. Cyborgs to companion species. Unpublished Essay. Presented at the University of Oregon's conference on "Taking nature seriously: Citizens, science, and the environment."

Harding, Sandra G. 1986. *The Science Question in Feminism.* Ithaca, NY: Cornell University Press.

———. 1991. *Whose Science? Whose Knowledge? Thinking from Women's Lives.* Ithaca, NY: Cornell University Press.

Hardt, Michael, and Antonio Negri. 2000. *Empire.* Cambridge, MA: Harvard University Press.

Hegel, Georg Wilhelm Friedrich. 1969. *Werke 3: Phänomenologie des Geistes.* Vol. 3, *Theorie-Werkausgabe.* Ed. Eva Moldenhauer and Karl Markus Michel. Frankfurt am Main, Germany: Suhrkamp (Orig. pub. 1807).

———. 1977. *Phenomenology of Spirit.* Trans. Arnold V. Miller and Ed. J. N. Findlay. Oxford: Clarendon Press (Orig. pub. 1807).

———. 1991. *Elements of the Philosophy of Right.* Cambridge Texts in the History of Political Thought. Ed. Allen W. Wood and Hugh Barr Nisbet. Cambridge: Cambridge University Press (Orig. pub. 1820).

———. 1995. *Lectures on the History of Philosophy.* 3 Vols Lincoln: University of Nebraska Press (Orig. pub. 1805–1806).

Heidegger, Martin. 1977. *Basic Writings.* Ed. David Krell. New York: Harper and Row.

Heller, Agnes. 1976. *The Theory of Need in Karl Marx.* Trans. Allison and Busby. New York: St. Martin's Press.

———. 1981. Paradigm of production: Paradigm of work. *Dialectical Anthropology* 6: 71–79.

hooks, bell. 1981. *Ain't I a Woman: Black Women and Feminism.* Boston: South End Press.

Horkheimer, Max. 1975. Materialism and metaphysics. In *Critical Theory: Selected Essays.* New York: The Seabury Press, 38–43.

Horowitz, Roger. 2003. Meatpacking. In *Gender and Technology,* Ed. Nina E. Lerman, Ruth Oldenziel, and Arwen P. Mohun. Baltimore, MD: Johns Hopkins University Press, 267–294.

Hyppolite, Jean. 1979. *Genesis and Structure of Hegel's Phenomenology of Spirit.* Chicago: Northwestern University Press.

Jameson, Frederic. 1991. *Postmodernism, or The Cultural Logic of Late Capitalism.* Durham, NC: Duke University Press.

Jennings, Humphrey, Mary-Lou Jennings, and Charles Madge. 1985. *Pandaemonium: The Coming of the Machine as seen by Contemporary Observers, 1660–1886.* New York: Free Press.

Kates, Gary. 1995. *Monsieur d'Eon is a Woman: A Tale of Political Intrigue and Sexual Masquerade.* Baltimore, MD: Johns Hopkins University Press.

Kolakowski, Leszek. 1978. *Main Currents of Marxism: Its Rise, Growth, and Dissolution.* 3 Vols. Oxford: Clarendon Press.

Koselleck, Reinhart. 1998. *Critique and Crisis: Enlightenment and the Pathogenesis of Modern Society.* Cambridge, MA: MIT Press.

Kouvelakis, Stathis. 2003. *Philosophy and Revolution: From Kant to Marx.* Trans. G. M. Goshgarian. New York: Verso.

Kuhn, Thomas S. 1977. *The Essential Tension: Selected Studies in Scientific Tradition and Change.* Chicago: University of Chicago Press.

——. 1996. *The Structure of Scientific Revolutions.* 3rd Edn Chicago: University of Chicago Press.

Lacan, Jacques. 1988. Freud, Hegel, and the machine. In *The Seminar of Jacques Lacan, Bk 2.* Ed. Jacques-Alain Miller and Trans. Sylvana Tomaselli. New York: Norton, 64–76.

Latour, Bruno. 1993. *We have Never been Modern.* Cambridge, MA: Harvard University Press.

——. 2004. Why has critique run out of steam? From matters of fact to matters of concern. *Critical Inquiry* 30 (2): 225–248.

Laycock, Henry. 1999. Exploitation "via" labour power in Marx. *Journal of Ethics* 3 (2): 121–131.

Locke, John. 1960. *Two Treatises of Government: A Critical Edition.* Ed. Peter Laslett. Cambridge: Cambridge University Press (Orig. pub. 1690).

Levack, Brian P. 1987. *The Witch-Hunt in Early Modern Europe.* New York: Longman.

Lévi-Strauss, Claude. 1963. *Totemism.* Trans. Rodney Needham. Boston: Beacon Press (Orig. pub. 1962).

——. 1969. *The Elementary Structures of Kinship.* Trans. James Harle Bell and John Richard von Sturmer. Boston: Beacon Press (Orig. pub. 1949).

Lukács, György. 1971. *History and Class Consciousness: Studies in Marxist Dialectics.* Cambridge, MA: MIT Press.

MacCormack, Carol P., and Marilyn Strathern. 1980. *Nature, Culture, and Gender.* Cambridge: Cambridge University Press.

Marcuse, Herbert. 1966. *Eros and Civilization: A Philosophical Inquiry into Freud.* Boston: Beacon Press.

——. 1991. *One Dimensional Man: Studies in the Ideology of Advanced Industrial Society.* Boston: Beacon Press.

——. 1998. *Technology, War, and Fascism, Collected Papers of Herbert Marcuse, Vol. 1.* Ed. Douglas Kellner. New York: Routledge.

McClintock, Anne. 1995. *Imperial Leather: Race, Gender, and Sexuality in the Colonial Conquest.* New York: Routledge.

McCracken, Jeffrey. 2006. Detroit's symbol of dysfunction: Paying employees not to work. *The Wall Street Journal*, CCL 1 March: A1, A12.

Mendelsohn, Everett. 1974. Revolution and reduction: The sociology of methodological and philosophical concerns in 19th century biology. In

The Interaction between Science and Philosophy, Ed. Y. Elkana. Atlantic Highlands, NJ: Humanities Press, 407–426.

Merchant, Carolyn. 1980. *The Death of Nature: Women, Ecology, and the Scientific Revolution*. San Francisco: Harper and Row.

Mills, Charles. 1998. *Blackness Visible: Essays on Philosophy and Race*. Ithaca, NY: Cornell University Press.

More, Thomas. 1989. *Utopia*. Cambridge Texts in the History of Political Thought. Cambridge: Cambridge University Press (Orig. pub. 1516).

Murray, Patrick. 1988. *Marx's Theory of Scientific Knowledge*. Atlantic Highlands, NJ: Humanities Press.

Negri, Antonio. 1984. *Marx beyond Marx: Lessons on the* Grundrisse. South Hadley, MA: Bergin and Garvey (Orig. pub. 1979).

———. 2003. *Time for Revolution*. New York: Continuum.

Oppolzer, Alfred. 1974. *Entfremdung und Industriearbeit*. Köln, Germany: Paul-Rugenstein Verlag.

Pateman, Carole. 1988. *The Sexual Contract*. Cambridge: Polity Press.

Patterson, Orlando. 1982. *Slavery and Social Death*. Cambridge, MA: Harvard University Press.

Pollack, David. 1988. The creation and repression of cybernetic man: Technological fear and the secrecy of narrative. *Clio* 18: 1–21.

Postone, Moishe. 1993. *Time, Labor, and Social Domination: A Reinterpretation of Marx's Critical Theory*. Cambridge: Cambridge University Press.

Principe, Michael A. 1996. Marx, natural religion, and capitalism. *Dialogos* 31 (67): 155–164.

Rabinbach, Anson. 1990. *The Human Motor: Energy, Fatigue, and the Rise of Modernity*. New York: Basic Books.

Rasmussen, David M. 1975. The symbolism of Marx: From alienation to fetishism. *Cultural Hermeneutics* 3: 41–55.

Richta, Radovan. 1969. *Civilization at the Crossroads: Social and Human Implications of the Scientific and Technological Revolution*. White Plains, NY: International Arts and Sciences Press.

Rousseau, Jean-Jacques. 2002. *The Social Contract and the First and Second Discourses*. Ed. Susan Dunn. Binghamton: Yale University Press (Orig. pub. 1762).

Rubin, Isaak Il'ich. 1972. *Essays on Marx's Theory of Value*. Detroit, MI: Black and Red.

Sayers, Sean. 1998. *Marxism and Human Nature*. New York: Routledge.

Scarry, Elaine. 1985. *The Body in Pain: The Making and Unmaking of the World*. New York: Oxford University Press.

Schaer, Roland, Gregory Claeys, and Lyman Tower Sargent, Eds 2000. *Utopia: The Search for the Ideal Society in the Western World*. New York: Oxford University Press.

Scharff, Robert C., and Val Dusek, Eds 2003. *Philosophy of Technology, the Technological Condition: An Anthology*. Blackwell Philosophy Anthologies, Vol. 18. Malden, MA: Blackwell.

Schatzberg, Eric. 2006. *Technik* comes to America: Changing meanings of *Technology* before 1930. *Technology and Culture* 47 (3): 486–512.

Scheerbart, Paul. 1910. *Das Perpetuum Mobile: Die Geschichte einer Erfindung*. Leipzig, Germany: E. Rowohlt.

———. 1980. *Restauration und Revolution: d. Vorarbeiten zum "Kapital" von Karl Marx in seinen Studienheften 1850–1858*. Hildesheim, Germany: Gerstenberg.

———. 1998. "Methode" und "Logik": Zur Integration von (Wert-)Substanz und Rechtssystem bei Hegel (1817–1830) and Marx (1857–1861). *MEGA-Studien* (2): 82–91.

Simondon, Gilbert. 1958. *Du mode d'existence des objets techniques*. Paris: Aubier.

Smith, Adam. 1976. *An Inquiry into the Nature and Causes of the Wealth of Nations*. Ed. R. H. Campbell and A. S. Skinner. Oxford: Clarendon Press.

Snow, C. P. 1998. *The Two Cultures*. Cambridge: Cambridge University Press.

Sohn-Rethel, Alfred. 1970. *Geistige und körperliche Arbeit: Zur Theorie d. gesellschaftlich Synthesis*. Frankfurt-am-Main. Germany: Suhrkamp.

———. 1978. *Intellectual and Manual Labour: A Critique of Epistemology*. Trans. Martin Sohn-Rethel. New York: Macmillan.

Strathern, Marilyn. 1992. *Reproducing the Future: Essays on Anthropology, Kinship and the New Reproductive Technologies*. Manchester, England: Manchester University Press.

———. 1999. *Property, Substance, and Effect: Anthropological Essays on Persons and Things*. New Brunswick, NJ: Athlone Press.

Swade, Doron. 2001. *The Difference Engine: Charles Babbage and the Quest to Build the First Computer*. New York: Viking.

Tucker, Robert C., Ed. 1978. *The Marx-Engels Reader, Second Edition*. New York: W. W. Norton & Company.

Uchida, Hiroshi. 1988. *Marx's Grundrisse and Hegel's* Logik. Ed. T. Carver. London: Routledge.

Wajcman, Judy. 1991. *Feminism Confronts Technology*. Cambridge: Polity Press.

———. 2004. *TechnoFeminism*. Cambridge: Polity Press.

Weber, Max. 1992. *The Protestant Ethic and the Spirit of Capitalism*. Trans. Talcott Parsons and Anthony Giddens. New York: Routledge (Orig. pub. 1904–1905).

West, Cornel. 2002. A genealogy of modern racism. In *Race: Critical Theories*. Ed. Philomena Essed and David Theo Goldberg. Malden, MA: Blackwell.

White, Richard. 2001. *Love's Philosophy*. New York: Rowman and Littlefield.

Williams, Patricia. 1991. *The Alchemy of Race and Rights: Diary of a Law Professor*. Cambridge, MA: Harvard University Press.

Winkelmann, Rainer. 1982. *Exzerpte über Arbeitsteilung, Maschinerie, und Industrie: Historisch kritische Ausgabe*. Frankfurt-am-Main, Germany: Ullstein Materialien.

Wright, Melissa. 1997. Crossing the factory frontier: Gender, place and power in a Mexican *maquilladora*. *Antipode: A Journal of Radical Geography* 29 (3): 278–302.

———. 1998. *Maquilladora Mestizas* and feminist border politics: Revisiting Anzaldúa. *Hypatia: A Journal of Feminist Philosophy* 13 (3): 114–131.

———. 2001. Desire and the prosthetics of supervision: A case of *maquilladora* flexibility. *Cultural Anthropology* 16 (3): 354–373.

Index

Postone, Moishe, 34, 60, 99, 121, 177, 193, 196
Potter, Edmund, 144
poverty, 70, 87, 115
Poverty of Philosophy (Marx), 66, 67–8, 185
private property, 29–31, 30–1, 32, 33, 40, 44, 56, 57, 113, 121, 127, *see also The Origin of the Family, Private Property, and the State* (Engels)
production
  and abstract time, 195–6
  and alienation, 13, 14, 16, 17, 38, 48, 52, 55, 59, 100, 195
  automation of, 57, 91
  collapse of system, 45
  collective, 96
  contradictions within, 91
  demise of, 5
  diminished need for, 64
  distinction between means and mode, 204–5, 207
  exploitation during, 33
  of food, 94, 95
  and historical injustice, 32–3
  instruments of, 56, 105–6, 109, 136, 137, 170, 171, 201
  introduction of machines, 2, 31, 62
  and labor, 107, 109, 120, 122, 187, 188
  mechanized system of, 57, 58, 64, 170, 177
  mental means of, 48
  and objectification, 56, 206
  ownership of means, 102, 201
  paradigm of, 64–5
  post-revolutionary labor, 187–8
  post-revolutionary speed, 177, 188
  and redistribution, 121, 122, 124
  and social change, 172–3, 182, 188
  temporality of, 195–6
  and use-value, 105, 106, 128
  and wealth creation, 32, 33, 57, 64, 68, 95, 96, 101, 102, 103, 114–15, 117, 118, 122, 149, 182
profit
  decrease of, 11, 21, 91, 99, 106–8, 112, 145, 180

  and enjoyment, 60
  and exchange-value, 52–3, 198
  exploitation for, 32, 160, 189, 206
  and human labor, 132, 136, 170, 175
  maximizing, 10, 12, 91, 127, 187, 190, 201
  motivation for, 33, 55
  and profit sharing, 189–90
  remaking nature for, 53
  sharing of, 189–90
proletariat, *see also* workers
  alienation of, 48–9
  and class kinship, 123
  destroy machines, 201, 212
  idleness of, 82
  lack of ownership, 43
  living conditions of, 165
  mental productions, 43, 48
  and revolution, 45
  and technophobia, 199, 202–3
Proudhon, Pierre-Joseph, 66–7, 68

"The Question Concerning Technology" (Heidegger), 178, 207–8, 209, 210
Quetelet, A., 180

Rabinbach, Anson, 69, 72, 76–7, 78–9, 82, 83, 90, 91, 114
The Railway Journey (Schivelbusch), 150
railways
  accidents, 149, 193, 199
  danger of, 192–3
  development of, 180
  lack of standardization, 149–50
  production systems, 105, 106
  and sensation drama, 150–1
  and social change, 194
Rasmussen, David, 50, 51
redistribution of the means of production, 121, 122, 124
religion, 36–7, 38
  and *acedia*, 82
  alienation, 54–5
  commodity fetish, 54–5
  and idleness, 78–9
The Remedy (Buxton), 163